PHILIP LAWRENCE HARRIMAN

THE NEW DICTIONARY OF PSYCHOLOGY

PHILOSOPHICAL LIBRARY

NEW YORK

PRINTED IN THE UNITED STATES OF AMERICA

FOREWORD

SINCE PSYCHOLOGY is a rapidly expanding field of knowledge, its vocabulary is constantly growing. A handbook or dictionary, therefore, cannot include all the terms and concepts of the science. Many terms, however, are sufficiently well-established in the literature to have a precise denotation, and an effort has been made to include them here. Wherever it was possible, the name of the person who first introduced the term, together with an important date, has been given. This information was obtained by consulting the standard reference books of psychology and cognate sciences. Many terms are used in a variety of connotations; hence the task of a lexicographer is difficult. Those terms which have been derived from the Greek seem to have the most precise denotations. Standard Greek dictionaries were consulted to ascertain the authoritative English equivalents for common roots, prefixes, and suffixes.

The author is indebted to his secretary, Miss Edithe Judith Miller, who typed the manuscript, looked up some of the information, and assisted in reading the proofs.

PHILIP LAWRENCE HARRIMAN
Bucknell University

A: Rorschach symbol for classifying responses in which the content refers to animals.

a-: Greek prefix for without, lacking, deprived of. (Before vowels and aspirate *h, an-* is used. In psychology and psychiatry the prefix is also used to denote a reduced amount of that which is designated by the root. From the standpoint of Greek, *hypo-* would be preferable in such instances.)

aasmus: asthma which is due to physiogenic causes.

abaca: Manila hemp, which is occasionally used for narcotic purposes, though cannabis indica is preferred by addicts.

Abadie, Jean Marie (1842–1932): French neurologist who contributed two important diagnostic signs: Abadie's sign, which is a spasm of the eyelid in exophthalmic goiter; and Abadie's symptom, which is a condition of analgia in the Achilles tendon when it is pinched and which occurs in locomotor ataxia.

abasia: incoördination in walking.

abaxial: out of the axis line.

abducens nerves: the sixth pair of cranial nerves.

abduct: to draw away from the midline.

Abelard (1079–1142): French theologian and educator who denied that the devil is the cause of mental disorders. His letters to Heloise are said to be examples of sublimation of the erotic impulse. He advanced the doctrine of conceptualism, which states that universals exist only in the mind, and yet they correspond to the relationships among things, since previously they existed in the mind of God.

aberrant behavior: that which deviates from the normal (average).

aberration: any mental abnormality.

abient drive: Holt's term (1931) to denote avoidant reflexive behavior in the animal when the stimulus is noxious. It is the opposite of adient (approach) behavior (Warren's term, 1919).

ability: proficiency in carrying out various skills, understandings, or adjustments. It is either general or specific. Spearman (1904) described general ability as a capacity defined by statistical analysis of test performance and as being a common or basic determinant of success. Specific abilities may be illustrated by the following: academic, arithmetical, athletic, mechanical, musical, reading, social, and the like. According to Spearman, the person may have a great number of diverse specific abilities, being relatively weak in some and strong in others.

abiotrophy: degeneration of tissues or a general deterioration of body.

abjection: depressed feeling-tone because of a loss of the sense of personal worth.

ablation experiments: animal experiments in which portions of the brain are excised after a habit such as maze-learning has been established. The experimenter notes the relationships between the amounts of destroyed tissues and their location on the one hand, and retention of the skill, on the other hand. Lashley (1929) is well-known for ablation experiments on rats.

ablutomania: incessant washing of body. It is said to symbolize an attempt to lessen tensions arising from guilt complexes, and it appears in the compulsive-obsessional type of psychoneurosis.

abmodality: condition of deviating from the mode (the measure which is of the greatest frequency in a distribution of scores).

abnormal: deviating from the norm. The term is used in three senses: (1) with the implication that the normal is the desirable condition (normative sense); (2) meaning that an all-or-none principle operates, and hence that *normal* and *abnormal* are dichotomous terms (pathological); and (3) the average (statistical). When the word is used to refer to the average or the mediocre, *normal* includes the group within the first standard deviation; and those at either end of the distribution are considered to be abnormal. In mental hygiene there is a growing tendency to separate the facts of pathology from those of the normal; in psychological measurement the statistical connotation is used.

abnormal psychology: an indefinite field which subsumes psychological facts and principles pertaining to psychopathology, occult phenomena, and the simpler types of unusual data. An experimental abnormal psychology is slowly being developed, and there is a gradually lessening emphasis upon divergent theories.

abortive jump: Maier's term (1939) for the manner in which rats avoided bumping their noses and falling into the net, by learning to strike the barrier with their paws and to turn their heads aside. Finally, even when the entrance to the reward was open, these rats persisted in abortive jumps.

aboulia (abulia): chronic indecision, with eventual loss of initiative. It is a pathology of conation.

Abraham, Karl (1877–1925): Austrian psychoanalyst who wrote upon the dynamics of repression.

abreaction: the expression of emotion connected with a mental conflict hitherto repressed, but, with the help of the psychoanalyst, now brought into the conscious mind of the patient. The patient is aware of many symptoms, but he is not fully aware of the nature of the conflict; hence emotional tensions are built up. The abreaction has been likened to the conversion experience of the religious convert, who feels that a great weight has been lifted from his shoulders. John Bunyan's allegory represents the analogue of what the Freudians mean by this term.

abrosia: a condition of fasting. In some types of hysteria (*anorexia*) and in catatonia, negative impulses may induce refusals to eat. The paranoid may prefer to abstain from eating rather than to risk being poisoned by imaginary enemies.

abscissa: the x-axis; more specifically, in representations of psychological data, the line of the graph which is at right-angles to the ordinate (or perpendicular axis).

absence: a brief lapse of consciousness, as in a fugue or attack of petit mal epilepsy.

absent-mindedness: inattention to those phases of a situation which other persons consider to be of major importance. Automatic behavior, misplacing articles, inattention to dangers, and forgetfulness are common forms of absent-mindedness.

absolute brilliance limen: the minimum intensity of brilliance (of any given wave-length) required to elicit a sensation of just noticeable difference from the other parts of the visual field. König (1891) is usually credited with being the first to discover this phenomenon.

absolute judgment: estimate of the intensity of a stimulus without referring it to other objective data as a standard.

absolute pitch: the ability to recognize the position of a given pitch on the scale, without requiring any other objective stimulation as a basis for making a comparative judgment. Once considered to be an inborn capacity, the sense of absolute pitch is now thought to be acquired through practice.

absolute refractory period: the condition of unexcitability in a nerve cell immediately after the impulse has been discharged. This phenomenon was first noted by Burch and Gotch (1899). The absolute refractory period is followed by a period of diminished excitability (refractory period), and then by a period of heightened excitability, before the protoplasm returns to normal.

abstinence symptoms: indications that the individual is beginning to experience physiological imbalances as a result of deprivation from drugs. Experimental studies of abstinence symptoms have been performed on monkeys with morphine addiction.

abstract behavior: the manipulation of symbols. It is distinguished (Goldstein, 1941) from concrete behavior, which involves the manipulation of things.

abstract ideas: mental states or activities lacking images. These are termed imageless thoughts, and they have been made a topic of study of the Würzburg psychologists. The doctrine is identified with Külpe (1862-1915), and R. S. Woodworth became its leading champion in America.

abstract intelligence: ability to use symbols and concepts in dealing with unfamiliar problems and difficulties. Verbal and mathematical symbols and abstract concepts are used in measurements of this type of intelligence.

abstract learning: that which does not involve concrete objects, but which occurs in situations comprised of symbols and abstract concepts.

abstraction: the process of generalizing from concrete experiences until universal principles have been derived. The process is emphasized both in the psychology of Thomas

Aquinas (1224–1274) and in the imageless-thought studies of Külpe and others (Würzburg School).

acalculia: inability to count, resulting from a cerebral lesion.

acatalepsia: dementia.

acatamesthesia: inability to respond normally to auditory or visual sensations because of mental disorders.

acataphasia: a form of aphasia which affects the manner in which words are arranged sequentially. It is attributed to a brain lesion, and not to psychogenic factors.

acathisia: inability to remain in a sitting position, as in certain forms of hysteria.

acceptance: allowing the client to have opportunity for complete expression of negative feelings without reproach on the part of the counselor. It is the antithesis of the moralistic approach in counseling, wherein the client's expressions of hostilities, misdeeds, or aggressions are either condemned or condoned.

accessory muscle: an auxiliary muscle which assists in the movements of the major muscle with which it is associated.

accident proneness: the tendency for certain persons to have a disproportionately large number of the accidents which occur within a given group of employees. Medical examinations, psychological analysis, or psychiatric studies may reveal the reasons why certain individuals have relatively more accidents than others; hence clinical investigations are made in many large industries to find the accident-prone employees and to assist them, if possible, to overcome their difficulties.

accommodation: the adjustment of the eye for vision at various distances. Thomas Young (1793) proved that accommodation is due to alterations in curvature of the crystalline lens. Monocular accommodation refers to the adjustment of the lens of one eye; binocular, to that of both eyes.

accomplishment quotient: the ratio of actual accomplishment to possibilities for achievement; hence a score for measured achievement over the mental age times 100. *Achievement quotient* is replacing this term.

accretionary growth: multiplication of tissues without qualitative change in the functions of an organ or an organism.

acculturation: the process of absorbing the folkways and mores of a culture which originally was alien to the immigrant.

accuracy compulsion: pathological zeal in accurate work, even with minute details and trivia. It is a form of perfectionism, and it is said to be a maladjustive habit whereby the individual seeks to escape from anxiety conflicts. Accuracy compulsives may perform detailed clerical work in a satisfactory manner, but a slight upset in routine causes them acute distress.

acedia: a type of melancholia.

acenesthesia: pathological feeling of having no material existence. It is the ultimate in a feeling of neurotic depersonalization, and, according to Janet, arises from a loss in psychic energy.

Ach, Narziss (1871–   ): member of the Würzburg School who made experimental investigations of volition and of determining tendencies. He also made introspective studies of reaction and found further evidence for the concept of imageless thought.

ache: an intense, throbbing pain.

acheiria: lacking hands.

achievement: status in a given skill or body of knowledge. Objective tests and essay examinations are employed to measure achievement. By referring an individual's achievement score to a table of norms, it is possible to obtain an achievement age. Thus, if a score represents the achievement of the average individual at 7 years 3 months, the achievement age would be 7 years 3 months. Tests of the objective type are available for determining achievement ages in the entire curriculum as well as in separate subjects.

Achilles tendon reflex: contraction of the muscles of the calf when the tendon back of the heel is sharply tapped.

achloropsia: green-blindness, or deuteranopia.

achondroplasia: defects in the cartilage at the epiphyses of long bones; hence children with this disorder have difficulty in locomotion.

achromatic: the series of grays which, in the Titchener color pyramid (1910), are distributed from white at one extreme to black at the other. Both Helmholtz (1860) and Hering (1874) differentiated between achromatic and chromatic sensations. It refers to the light-dark, or brilliance, dimension of visual sensation. Titchener reported that it is possible to distinguish 600 to 700 differences in the achromatic series.

achromatic vision: according to the duplicity (duplex) theory of vision (J. von Kries, 1894), the response which is mediated by the rods.

achromatopsia: total color-blindness. Only rod vision exists in the achromatopsic individual; hence capacity to distinguish among the grays, from white to black, with insensitivity to hues.

acolasia: general intemperance, with special reference to sex indulgence. It reveals a character defect rather than a somatic pathology.

acomon: the incus, or anvil; one of the three small bones of the middle ear.

aconative: an act which lacks purpose, meaning, or drive.

acoria: condition of greediness.

acouasm: a subjective noise in the ears (*tinnitus aurium*). It may be due to impacted cerumen, changes of air pressure in the middle ear, blocked eustachian tubes, quinine, or inflammation of tympanum or middle ear. Over-stimulation at a given pitch (as in a factory) may be a cause for some acouasms. (*akoasm.*)

acoumeter: apparatus for determining auditory thresholds.

acousma (akousma): see *acouasm.*

acousmatamnesia: inability to learn, retain, and recall or recognize sounds.

acoustics: the science of sound.

acquired character: a trait acquired in the life-time of the organism. Lamarck (1809) advanced the view that adaptive behavior produced inheritable alterations in the bodies of animals. This view was controverted by Darwin (1859) and Weismann (1892); and it was chosen as a subject for experimental investigation by McDougall (1927), who accepted the basic principles of inheritance of acquired characters.

acro-: end or extremity.

acroagnosia: inability to make interpretations of stimuli applied to hands or feet.

acrocephalia: a condition in which the head is abnormally high (vertical plane).

acroesthesia: hypersensitivity in hands or feet.

acrokinesis: a feeling of extreme vigor in arms and legs; hence the hysterical individual with this symptom is hyperactive in swinging the limbs.

acromegaly: a hyperpituitary disorder in which toes, fingers, and facial bones are enlarged; the nose is thickened and the lower jaw becomes enlarged. This condition was described by Pierre Marie (1886). The dysfunction occurs after age twenty, and the physical changes take place gradually.

acroparesthesia: abnormal sensations, such as numbness or tinglings, in the hands or feet.

act psychology: the point of view which emphasizes activities, rather than contents, of consciousness. Brentano (1874) was the leader in a protest against the current practice, particularly that of Wundt (1883), of analyzing the structure of consciousness into elements. Out of this emphasis, American functionalism was derived. Brentano has been referred to as the leader of the "Austrian group" as opposed to the "German group" who followed Wundt, and at one time the controversy between proponents of act psychology and content psychology was a live issue. Investigations of form-qualities (Gestaltqüalitaten) and esthetics made by Brentano and his group have become a part of modern psychology.

acting-out: gratifying a repressed desire by social behavior which brings unhappiness and suffering (Freud).

action, accidental: behavior which is consciously unintended but which gratifies a repressed wish (Freud). It occurs suddenly, thoughtlessly, and by chance; and the actor does not try to cover it up by pleas of awkwardness.

action current: the electrical phenomena which accompany the nerve impulse. Apparatus in electro-neurophysiology is used to amplify and measure action currents. Berger (1924) was the first to make clinical use of the fact that action currents in the brain may be recorded, though their existence was known as early as 1874.

actual neuroses: disturbances caused by toxemia resulting from such impairments of sex function as masturbation, coitus interruptus, and abstinence (Freud). The actual neuroses are differentiated from anxiety hysteria in that they do not refer to a specific situation (such as morbid fear of darkness), but are vague and general, though none-the-less painful and distressing.

acuity: keenness of sensation.

acute delirium: sudden onset of a fever of short duration with accompanying symptoms of mental confusion, hallucinations, and excitement.

acyanopsia: type of color-blindness in which blue is confused.

adaptability: the trait of being able to adjust to changing situations in a manner which is intelligent and which promotes morale.

adaptation: the gradual change which takes place in the acuity of a sense organ after prolonged stimulation. Aubert (1865) introduced the concept to refer to the adjustment of the eye to light intensity. He noted that, as one remains in a dark room for a long time, the intensity of the darkness seems to lessen. Hering (1872–1874) broadened the concept to include adaptation to light and to hue. The term now subsumes other forms of adaptation than visual alone. Zwaardemaker (1887), for instance, stated that he found olfactory adaptation to occur swiftly; and Johannes Müller (1838) had previously used the term with reference to gustation.

addiction habituation: the condition of a raised level of physiological tolerance for a drug, with a necessity to increase the dosage in an attempt to gain the psychological effects from its use. The dosage taken by Thomas de Quincey, the English essayist, is said to have been, at one period in his life, nearly a pint of laudanum preparation daily.

Addison's disease: an adrenal dysfunction in which the principal symptoms are a wasting away of tissues and great weakness. Restlessness, anxiety, apathy, headaches, lassitude, and vertigo are often mentioned as symptoms. The disease was defined (1855) by Thomas Addison (1793–1860), an English physician.

adenoma: a tumor.

adequate stimulus: the stimulus which normally elicits a given response, as contrasted with the conditioned (or associated) stimulus. The conditioned stimulus becomes potent to elicit the response originally attached to the adequate stimulus by the Pavlov technique (1890).

adiadokokinesis: inability to make coördinated successive movements, such as arm or finger movements. This condition occurs in cases of cerebellar lesions.

adiposis dolorosa: a disease occurring in middle life in which obesity is the outstanding characteristic. The patients complain of intense pains and of inability to remember; they usually deteriorate in intelligence and emotional control. The disorder was first described by Francis X. Dercum (1856–1931), an American physician. It occurs much more frequently in women than in men.

Adler, Alfred (1870–1937): a follower of Sigmund Freud who broke away (1912) and founded Individual Psychology, a point of view which emphasizes the ego rather than the libido. He taught that the basic feature of a neurosis is an attitude of inferiority resulting from frustration of the urge for superiority, and he emphasized goals rather than infantile determinants. According to Adler, the great problems of life are social adjustments, occupation, and love; and the life-style of the individual is developed by the ways in which these goals are sought. By the mechanism of compensation, an individual may acquire peculiar goals of superiority.

adolescence: the time of life from the onset of puberty to the

achievement of full adulthood. It is the period during
which social pressures of complex civilization complicate
the achievement of emancipation from family ties, of
finding a place in the vocational life of the community,
and of making sex adjustments; hence social psychologists regard adolescence as a by-product of social pressures, not as a unique period of biological strain and
stress.

adrenal glands: endocrine glands adjacent to the kidneys.
The adrenal medulla secretes adrenalin (epinephrin) in
states of intense emotion; the adrenal cortex supplies a
hormone known as cortin. Hyperfunctioning of the
adrenal cortex in childhood causes precocious puberty
in males, and a condition of masculinity in females. In
adult women, hyperfunctioning of the cortex results in a
condition known as virilism, in which excess hair appears
on the face and sex functions are inhibited. Deficiency of
cortin may result in Addison's disease (1855).

Adrian, Edgar Douglas (1889–   ): the physiologist who
established the all-or-none law of the nervous impulse
(1912). Bowditch (1871) had established the principle
for the action of the heart muscles. The all-or-none law
is the principle that the nervous impulse does not vary in
strength in a neuron (or nerve fiber), but that if the
tissues are excited at all, there is a constant amount of
discharge. An intense stimulus, therefore, excites a number of nervous impulses simultaneously or causes repeated
discharges in single neurons; but the intensity of nervous
impulse in a single cell is a constant.

adult: a fully matured organism. In a legal sense, the adult
is a person 21 years of age or older. In the sense of the
mental hygienist, an adult is a person who is able to
adjust to the environment in a realistic manner.

adx: a Rorschach symbol for responses the content of which indicated to Rorschach (1922) the condition of oligophrenia (mental deficiency) and to subsequent users of the Rorschach Inkblot Test the existence of neurotic traits (Beck, 1937).

aelurophobia (ailurophobia): morbid fear of cats.

acrophagia: the habit of swallowing air by hysterics.

aeschrolalia: a stream of filthy talk by certain types of psychotic patients.

advice therapy: the use of direct advice regarding possibilities for altering the life-style of the maladjusted person. It is an outmoded practice in modern psychotherapy, but it is one of the most common types of counseling by untrained persons. Since adjustment problems involve emotional factors, intellectualized advice does not deal with the basic causes of maladjustment; hence nondirective therapy is the recommended approach (Rogers, 1942).

affect: a broad term subsuming emotion, feeling, mood, and (usually) temperamental characteristics. Affects are more pervasive and enduring than momentary emotional states, and they are identified with drives and propensities. Their ideational contents are vague and generalized. Labile affects are subject to fluctuations; the condition of hypothymia refers to shallow affects; parathymia denotes the incongruous affects of the schizophrenic, who may jest about tragic events or weep when others are happy. Complaints of affective disturbances (hyperthymia or affective loss) are common at the period when a psychosis begins to develop.

affective psychosis: mental disorders which are characterized by marked disturbances in feelings, emotions, moods, and emotionalized drives. Abnormal excitement (mania) and depression (melancholia) are examples.

affect displacement: Freud's term to denote an affect which becomes attached to a totally different idea from that to which it originally belonged. He taught that affects are "free-floating" and may become attached to ideational content for which they have inappropriate reference.

affect hunger: Levy's term (1937) to denote the basic affective striving of the rejected child. The adult whose childhood was characterized by affect hunger may be an emotionally frigid person or make an over-response to expressions of affection.

afferent fibers: nerve fibers which lead from the receptor to the cord and the brain. They are also called sensory nerve fibers. The functional difference between afferent and efferent (motor) fibers was discovered by Bell (1807) and confirmed by Magendie (1822).

after-image: the continuance or the revival of a sensory experience after the removal of the stimulus. A few psychologists differentiate after-images from after-sensations, the former being considered to relate to central processes and the latter to physiological activities in the receptor; others would differentiate the terminal lag of a sensation (brief persistence of sensation after cessation of stimulus). Boyle (1663) described visual after-images, and Newton (1681) conducted experimental studies in the field. Goethe (1810) summarized the earlier studies of the phenomena, and thus gave impetus to research. Negative after-images are those in which brightness and hue are reversed; positive after-images those in which the sensation persists without change after removal of the stimulus.

after-sensation: the persistence of a sensation after the stimulus has ceased to excite the receptor directly. It is also called the terminal-lag of a sensation, and it is attributed to the continuance of the physiological activities in the receptor. Kottenkamp and Ullrich (1870), working on the problem of persistence of sensation in the tactual field, established the difference between terminal lag and after-image, though the terms are still used ambiguously.

age, anatomical: the degree of skeletal development of an individual as compared to that of other individuals at varying levels of chronological age. It is usually measured by X-rays of the cartilaginous tissues of the wrist, which slowly turn into bone; or by the closing of the fontanelle (the membranous space in the skull of the infant).

age, basal: the age level at which a person passes all the items on the Stanford-Binet or the Terman-Merrill.

age, mental: the level of mental development as measured by a test of intelligence. Binet (1908) introduced the technique of comparing the test performance of an individual child with the achievements of a cross-section of children of various chronological ages. The 1908 Scale includes items for measuring mental age (MA) from 3 to 12. Wechsler (1939) defines mental age as a score on an intelligence scale, which indicates how many items have been passed out of the total number of items. Doll (1919) stated that mental age does not increase beyond 13; Thorndike presented evidence (1923) to show that it may increase to 18. Thus, a controversy was introduced into the literature of intelligence measurement.

age, physiological: the relative degree of maturation of nervous tissues, muscles, and glands, particularly of the genitalia.

age, subject: the score on a measure of school achievement in a given subject of the curriculum, expressed in terms of the chronological age of a cross-section of pupils who make a similar score.

age, true: the actual chronological age of an individual from the time of conception to the present. Normally, the gestation period covers 280 days; hence the infant at birth is really 280 days old, unless delivered prematurely.

agenesis: defective maturation as a result of hereditary or adventitious factors.

agenitalism: lack of testes or ovaries; hence the absence of the secondary sex characteristics differentiating males and females.

ageusia: absence of taste sensitivity or a marked reduction of power of taste discrimination.

aggression-frustration hypothesis: view introduced by Dollard and others (1939) that aggressive behavior is compensatory for continued frustrations. Aggression is defined as behavior intended to harm some one or to injure that for which one stands; and the strength of aggression is inversely proportional to the intensity of frustrations. Aggression may be expressed in a generalized hostility towards society as a whole (psychopathic behavior) or towards a scape-goat (minority groups) as well as towards the person or persons actually responsible for the frustrations. The technique of catharsis of aggression provides for outlets for pent-up hostilities (release of negative feelings).

agitated depression: hyperactivity on the part of a manic-depressive, depressed type, without the flight of ideas which usually accompanies the manic type of the psychosis.

agitation: restlessness, as in a fever delirium or a psychosis.

agitophasia: excessive rapidity of speech, as in hyperkinetic hysteria or manic excitement.

agnosia: loss of ability to recognize persons, objects, places hitherto familiar to the patient. It denotes psychological concomitants of cerebral lesions, and usually takes one of the following manifestations: auditory agnosia (lesion in Wernicke area), which is loss of ability to comprehend spoken language; finger agnosia, which is a loss of awareness of fingers and their uses; musical agnosia, or inability to recognize melodies; and visual agnosia, or inability to recognize objects which are presented to the patient's view.

agonia: the extremity of grief. In the agitated melancholic, all the signs of anguish may be present except tears, and they do not fall because the lachrymal glands have been fatigued. Delusions of having committed the original sin are reported in the older literature as occurring among involution melancholiacs and agitated depressed patients.

agoraphobia: morbid fear of crossing open fields, parks, squares, or other areas in which the psychoneurotic has no shelter.

agrammatism: a type of aphasia in which the ability to speak or write grammatically has been lost or seriously impaired. The disorder was named and defined by Friedel Pick (1867-1926) as having an organic (cerebral) basis.

agraphia: absence of ability to express thoughts in writing. It is caused by lesions in the occipital lobe.

agriothymia: psychotic frenzy or rage.

Agrippa, Heinrich Cornelius (1486-1535): German physician who was among the first to combat the theory of demonological possession. For his liberal views he suffered calumny and persecution.

"ah-ah" experience: the sudden achievement of insight. In creative thinking (according to Wallas, 1926), the illumination (after preparation and incubation) comes as a sudden flash of insight. The catch-phrase to designate this characteristic of thought, comes, of course, from the tale about Archimedes.

ahypnia: insomnia. (Also called *agrypnia*.)

aichmaphobia: morbid fear of sharp instruments.

aim: a symbolically represented mode of achieving a goal whereby activity is motivated and sustained until the end has been attained.

akatamesthesia: a general inability to comprehend as a result of cerebral lesion.

akinesis: a condition of defective muscular coördination as a result either of organic pathology or neurasthenia, self-consciousness, and the like.

akoasm: subjective noise in the ear due to changes in air pressure in the middle ear, blocked eustachian tube, impacted cerumen, pathology of the organ of Corti, changes in the liquid in the inner ear, or similar causes. It is also termed tinnitus aurium.

alalia: inability to speak because of paralysis of the muscles used in speech.

albedo perception: discrimination among various surfaces because of varying amounts of light-waves reflected. The quality of illumination as well as the surface of the object itself influences the discrimination.

Albertus Magnus (1193-1280): teacher of Thomas Aquinas and an interested student of biology and psychology.

Alcmaeon: Greek physician of the 6th century B.C. who was the first to dissect a human body and who taught that the brain is the organ of the mind.

alcoholism: a condition arising from excessive use of alcohol and necessitating medical treatment. The slogan, "Alcoholics and sick people," refers not only to the grave possibility of organic pathology, but also to the likelihood of psychiatric difficulties which led the individual into the condition (Seliger, 1942).

alcoholomania: irresistible craving for alcoholic drinks.

alertness test: a speed test of general intelligence in which the score is determined by the amount and the accuracy of tasks completed. Such types of tests are differentiated from power tests, which determine the level of difficulty an individual can reach in a graded series of tasks. Freeman (1926) has reported evidence for differentiating alertness tests from power tests.

Alexander of Tralles (7th century A.D.) : eminent Byzantine physician who proposed to treat hallucinations by outwitting the patient.

alexia: inability to read as a result of brain pathology. The condition was defined by Wernicke (1874).

alganesthesia: absence of the sense of pain.

algesia: heightened sensitivity to pain.

algesimeter (algometer): apparatus for determining the threshold for response to pain. The most common form consists of a piston with a pointed end, the pain limen being determined by the amount of pressure against the skin required to elicit awareness of pain.

algolagnia: the desire to include pain as a component of the sex act. An individual who must inflict pain on his sex-partner is said to have active algolagnia; one who must receive pain, passive algolagnia. The terms were introduced by von Schrenk-Notzing.

algophilia: pathological pleasure (chiefly sexual in nature) upon enduring pain.

alienation: Falret's term (1837) to denote mental disorder. Thus, an alienist is a physician who is competent to diagnose and treat patients with mental disorders. Falret prevailed upon the French authorities to revise the legal terminology and to employ simpler and more appropriate phrases.

alienation, coefficient of (k): a ratio indicating the lack of relationship between two sets of variables.

all-or-none law: Adrian's principle (1912) regarding the discovery that the stimulus elicits the greatest discharge of which the neuron is capable at the time. In other words, stimulus intensity does not affect the intensity of the nervous impulse, which is either excited or not excited.

allo-eroticism: sensory pleasure (principally sexual) stimulated by other people. It refers to heterosexual adjustments as contrasted with auto-eroticism, or concentration of libidinal interests upon the self.

allophasia: incoherence of speech in a fever delirium.

allopsychic delusion: Wernicke's term for false, unshakable beliefs which are projected upon factors outside the patient and which are usually attributed to malign forces or hostile intentions of others.

allotriogeusia: perversion of the sense of taste.

alogia: inability to speak. Some writers restrict the term to denote conditions arising from organic lesions; others use it to refer to hysterical conditions as well.

alpha rhythm (Berger rhythm): the spontaneous electrical rhythm of the brain discovered in 1924 by Hans Berger. It is the 10 per second rhythm, the amplitude of which is between 10 and 75 mv. and which appears in a developed form at about age 9 or 10.

alternating insanity: Falret's term (1854) for a condition now termed manic-depressive psychosis, circular type.

Alzheimer's psychosis: a rare, precocious form of senile dementia which appears as early as the third or fourth decade of life and in which the rate of deterioration is rapid. It was defined by Alzheimer in 1906.

amytal interview: the technique of eliciting free and uninhibited expressions from the patient while the psychiatrist has placed him under narcosynthesis by the method of sodium amytal injection. The patient thus achieves full catharsis for recent experiences which, if left unexpressed, might precipitate a psychoneurotic condition.

amaurosis: total blindness or a marked diminution in vision because of a lesion in the nervous system.

amaurotic family idiocy: a familial, hereditary type of mental deficiency with blindness. It was defined by Tay (1881) and Sachs (1887); hence it is often called Tay-Sachs disease.

ambiguous figure: an illusion which was defined and analyzed by E. Rubin (1915).

ambidexterity: proficiency in the use of either the left or the right hand.

ambilateral: affecting both sides.

ambivalence: Bleuler's term (1930) to describe contradictory feelings and motives which are simultaneously directed towards the same person or situation.

ambivert: one who is neither an extravert nor an introvert.

amblyopia: dimness of vision arising from toxic conditions or from hysteria.

amentia: mental deficiency.

ametropia: a general term for all conditions of imperfect retinal images due to refractive defects in the eye.

amnesia: loss of memory. Inability to recall or recognize data occurring directly after the trauma or the emotional shock is called anterograde amnesia; when the reference is to events immediately before, retrograde amnesia.

amplitude of light wave: the vertical distance from base to crest, which determines the intensity of the visual sensation (Titchener, 1896).

ampulla: the enlargement at the end of a canal, as at one end of each of the semi-circular canals or at the end of the tear duct.

amusia: inability to recognize or to reproduce hitherto familiar melodies as a result of a cerebral lesion. Inability to comprehend tunes is called sensory amusia; if the ability to hum, sing, or play has been lost, motor amusia.

anabolism: the constructive phase of metabolism, as contrasted with katabolism (catabolism).

anacamptometer: apparatus for measurement of the strength of reflexes.

anaclitic object-choice: libidinal cathexis pertaining to an object which hitherto met self-preservative needs.

anacroasia: a type of aphasia in which spoken language is not comprehended, but the same words, when read by the patient, are understood. It is the result of a cerebral lesion.

anaglyphoscope: apparatus invented by Oppel (1855) for reversing light and shade whereby the relief is altered in the picture before the person's view.

anadipsia: intense thirst.

anagnosasthenia: a type of psychoneurotic reaction in which great discomfort is incurred by reading. When congenial types of work demanding greater use of the eyes are found, the sense of eye-strain disappears.

anal erotic: the stage of libidinal organization in which sphincter responses bring erotic gratification (Freud). At first, the libido has diffuse outlets (polymorphous perverse); then come the three somatic localizations: oral, anal, and genital. In the anal stage, pleasure is first discovered in expulsion; next, in retention.

anal reflex: contraction of the anal sphincter when the mucosa is touched.

analgesia (analgia): absence of pain sensitivity.

analogies test: measure of ability to reason in which a fourth term is to be chosen, the clue to the choice having been supplied by a relationship among three terms which are given. C. Burt, who introduced the tests (1911), stated that they involve perceptions of relationships; hence give a basis for inferring the level of general intelligence.

analyst: one who is qualified to use the technique of psychoanalysis. In Europe, laymen were permitted by Freud to practice analysis, but in America a doctorate in medicine is required. Anna Freud is the most famous lay analyst.

Analytical Psychology: the systematic formulation of psychological principles which Jung started to work out in 1910, following his break with the Viennese Psychoanalytic Society. He discarded Freud's emphasis upon the primacy of the sex drive, broadened the concept of the unconscious, emphasized the exciting causes for neuroses, and introduced a different procedure for dream interpretation.

anamnesis: the history of the patient's life up to the time of the onset of the mental disorder. *Catamnesis* is the history of the patient during the period of the mental disorder.

ananastasia: psychoneurotic lack of energy to rise from a recumbent to a sitting position. It occurs principally in hysteria.

anaphia: loss of the sense of pressure (touch).

anarithmia: inability to count as a result of cerebral lesion.

anarthria: loss of ability to articulate words as a result of a cerebral lesion.

anatomical age: the age measured by maturation of the skeletal system as compared to the anatomical maturity of typical individuals at various chronological ages.

androgyna: a female with genitalia resembling those of a
   male.

anemia: a deficiency of blood or a lack of red corpuscles or
   hemoglobin. In school children it may be indicated by
   difficulties with the curriculum or with classroom routine.
   In adults it may occur in cases mistakenly diagnosed as
   psychoneurotic. At one time physiologists conjectured
   that sleep is the result of cerebral anemia, but subsequently both cerebral anemia and cerebral congestion
   were found in sleep (Cameron, 1935).

anesthesia: absence of sensation, especially of pain. It may be
   general or local, psychogenic or organic. In hysteria many
   incongruous types of anesthesia have been reported, particularly by Janet (1920). Cases of "glove" and "stocking" anesthesia are believed by some to occur as a result
   of unintentional suggestions given by the psychiatrist who
   questioned the hysteric. The term is used to subsume any
   marked reduction or absence of a given sensory function,
   such as anosmia (lack of smell), ageusia (lack of taste),
   and the like.

Angell, James Rowland (1869-   ): a leading American
   functionalist. He defined mental activities as the means
   whereby the individual adapts himself to the environment; functionalism (1907), as a study of the responses
   of the whole individual; and psychology, as the study of
   responses which cannot be explained in the mechanistic
   terms of physiology. He opposed the analysis of states of
   consciousness (*Titchenerism*), and emphasized the functional aspects of consciousness.

anima: Jung's term for the personality.

animal magnetism: a mysterious fluid or force which F. A.
   Mesmer alleged that he possessed and by means of which
   he professed to effect miraculous cures. He chose the term

because it suggested the counterpart of natural magnetism (electricity), which was then attracting wide attention.

animal psychology: the study of the behavior of animals under controlled laboratory conditions, as opposed to armchair theories about their mental processes and anecdotal stories regarding their behavior. E. L. Thorndike (1898) was among the first to conduct experimental studies of animal behavior. He used escape problems which allowed him to keep quantitative records of successes-errors and times. Yerkes began his long series of experimental studies about a year or two later.

animism: the belief that inanimate objects have mental processes analogous to those of human beings. E. B. Tylor (1881) stated that primitive people believed that all objects in nature have minds or souls, and that natural forces are the work of maleficent or beneficent gods.

aniseikonia: disparity in the size of retinal images.

ankle clonus: alternate rigidity and release of tension in calf muscles when the foot is suddenly dorsiflexed. The condition is indicative of lesion in the spinal cord.

annoyer: a situation which is avoided or changed if possible (Thorndike, 1913). Examples of original annoyers are the following: hunger, bitter substance in the mouth, putrid smells, and the like. In the learning process (Thorndike's explanation), annoyers tend to weaken the bonds between situations and responses.

anismetropia: inequality in the refractive mechanisms of the eyes.

ankylosis: immobility in a joint because of ossification of cartilage.

anodimia: absence of the sense of smell.

anoetic: hazy; on the periphery of consciousness.

anoesia: lack of common sense or understanding.

anoia: mental deficiency of the lowest grade; idiocy.

anomaloscope: apparatus devised by Nagel (1896) for measuring various forms of color-vision anomalies.

anomaly: any obvious deviation from type.

anomia: loss of ability to name objects. It is said to occur in cases of lesions in the temporal lobe (Grinker, 1944).

anomie: individual or group norms of behavior.

anopia: blindness because of pathology in the eyes (not because of lesions in the nervous system).

anorexia: lack of appetite.

anorthoscope: a stroboscope devised about 1830 by Plateau in which a distorted drawing is made to appear regular in outline if viewed through slits in a revolving collar, the drawing being revolved at a different speed. These devices were once known as visual whirlers, and they were used in studies of perceived movement about eighty years before Wertheimer's classic investigation (1912).

anosmia: absence of sense of smell.

anosphrasia: anosmia, or loss of sense of smell.

anoxemia: deficiency in the oxygen content of the blood, with accompanying symptoms of disturbance in mental functions.

antagonism of muscles: the opposition of action in two sets of muscles, the one being relaxed while the other is tensed. Thus, in the iris the sphincter contracts to narrow the pupil, while the radials relax; conversely, when the pupil dilates, the radials contract and sphincter relaxes. Muscular tonus results from the fact that neither muscle in the pair is ever entirely relaxed even when there is no exertion.

anterograde amnesia: inability to remember events which happened after the shock or the trauma. Essentially, it is the lack of ability to remember what was never learned; hence it is paradoxical to call this defect amnesia.

anthropology: the study of man as a unit in the animal kingdom (Tylor); the science was founded by Prichard (1843), and it has become a broad field with ambiguous limits. Physical anthropology deals with similarities and differences in morphology among men and animals as well as among human races; cultural anthropology, with the development of racial traits and cultures, primitive societies, psychological characteristics, languages, and allied topics.

anthropometry: Bertillon's method (1883) of identifying each separate individual by a system of physical measurements. The system includes the following basic measurements: length and breadth of head; length of middle finger and of left foot; and length of forearm from elbow to end of middle finger. For purposes of criminal identification, the method of finger prints supplanted anthropometry. The search for a relationship between morphological characteristics and racial or psychological traits has been of recurrent interest, however, and has occasioned some controversy.

anthropomorphism: in the theological sense, the attribution of human-like traits or form to the deity. Psychologists, since the rise of scientific studies of animal behavior, have used the term to refer to the popular tendency to interpret the behavior of lower animals in terms of human psychology.

anticipatory response: the preliminary adjustment which facilitates the reaction to an expected stimulus. It is observed in the set of a sprinter, who establishes the necessary adjustments preparatory to getting off the mark when the starter's pistol is fired. In reaction-time experi-

ments, the subject may be instructed to take a mental and
postural set. McDougall (1923) sought to identify an
activity termed pre-perception as a characteristic of the
conative process and as an influential factor in anticipatory responses.

antimetropia: refractive disparities in the eyes. Astigmatism
might affect one eye, and near-sightedness the other.

anuresis: retention of urine, as in certain types of fever. Unlike retention of feces, anuresis is not considered by psychoanalysts to afford erotic gratification.

anxiety: according to Freud's later theories, the basic cause
for repression, the principal anxiety being the dread of
becoming helpless and alone in a hostile, unfriendly universe. The anxiety may be "free-floating" or diffuse; it
may be related to specific objects or situations (*e.g.*,
phobias). Previously, Freud had upheld the view that
anxiety results from repressions (conversion of affect); in
1923 he modified the theory to include a primary anxiety.

anxiety hysteria: the conscious manifestations of the anxiety
ascribed to a specific object or situation, the repressed
libidinal element being converted into a physiological
symbol or a generalized state of anxiety. Many of the
concepts underlying this condition are being altered by
contemporary psychoanalysts, and a new terminology is
being evolved (W. Menninger, 1946).

apathy: morbid indifference; a condition in which zest for
life has been lost.

aphanisis: a condition of psychic impotence said by E. Jones
(1929) to be the basis of many conditions of anxiety reactions.

aphasia: a broad term subsuming the loss of various speech
functions as a result of cerebral lesions. Broca (1861) discovered the site of a cerebral lesion in the brain of a man

who had lost the ability to speak more than a few words for about three decades. He preferred the term *aphemia* to denote the condition. Head (1920, 1926) described the psychological, anatomical, and physiological aspects of the disorder. Though he did not believe in "centers," he did say that lesions in various areas destroy various abilities in the speech function.

aphemia: Broca's term for loss of ability to speak as a result of cerebral lesion (1861).

aphia: the sense of touch (pressure).

aphonia: inability to utter words or sounds as a result of hysteria or intense emotion. Some writers restrict the term to denote a pathological condition in the larynx; others use it to designate psychogenic types of speechlessness.

aphrenia: a class term for mental disorders.

aphronesia: lack of common sense, as in states of intoxication or certain types of psychoses (*e.g.*, schizophrenic reaction, hebephrenic type).

aphthongia: a speech disorder resulting from muscular spasms of the tongue.

aplasia: failure of an organ to develop as a result of congenital factors (primary aplasia), or diseases in infancy (secondary aplasia).

apopathetic behavior: that which meets the individual's needs in a social situation but which does not indicate adequate socialization. The young child who "shows off" before company exhibits a more or less normal pattern of apopathetic behavior; the exhibitionistic adult displays the psychoneurotic form.

apoplexy: a stroke.

apparatus: any instrument which facilitates the observation of a mental function or psychological state under rigorously controlled conditions.

apperception: a term introduced by Leibnitz (1695) to denote attention, and adopted by Herbart (1816) to refer to the totality of conscious activities which are involved in the choice and the interpretation of a given sensory element. In a broader sense (*Herbartian*), it is the sum of all former experiences—either sensory or reflective—which is involved in the attribution of meaning to any datum. This totality Herbart referred to as the *apperceptive mass*.

appersonation: a term used by some psychoanalysts (*e.g.*, Sperling, 1937) to denote the tendency to introject various objects as a means of ego-enhancement.

appetite: a drive which originates in and is sustained by tissue lacks, such as hunger and thirst (Hobbes, 1651).

applied psychology: the practical application of psychological facts and principles to the problems of everyday life. Hugo Münsterberg (1863–1916) is generally credited with being the "father of applied psychology" when (*c.* 1900) he commenced to investigate the psychology of the witness.

Appunn, Antoine: a Parisian instrument maker who devised apparatus for measuring auditory sensitivity for low frequencies (*c.* 1880). This device is known as *Appunn's lamella.*

apraxia: loss of specific habits as a result of brain lesions. It is displayed by an inability to carry out purposeful movements, to execute acts hitherto more or less automatic (tying shoelaces, etc.), or handling objects.

aptitude: a capacity in any given skill or field of knowledge, on the basis of which a prediction may be made regarding the amount of improvement which further training might effect. Tests of linguistic intelligence such as are employed in schools, for instance, are measures of academic aptitude. Specific measures of various aptitudes have been developed; measures of talent in music (Seashore, 1919); art (McAdory, 1929); science (Zyve, 1929); and the like.

aqueous humor: the liquid in the anterior chamber of the eyeball (the space between the cornea and the lens).

arachnoid membrane: the membrane lying between the dura mater and the pia mater, all of which cover the brain and the spinal cord.

areflexia: absence of reflexes or suppression of certain reflexes as a result of lesions.

Aretaeus of Cappadocia: a great physician of antiquity (first century A.D.) who taught that mental disorders are not the result of possession by demons, but that they ensue from organic pathologies. He observed that elation and melancholia are related; hence he is credited with having recognized the manic-depressive disorder.

argumentativeness: emotionalized rationalizations to defend positions which are unconsciously admitted to be untenable. Argumentativeness pertains to beliefs, not to objective judgments.

Argyll-Robertson, Douglass (1837–1909): Scotch physician who defined a pathology of the pupil in which there is reflex accommodation but a failure to respond by contraction when a light is flashed into the eye. It occurs in tabes dorsalis, alcoholic avitaminosis, encephalitis, and the like.

Aristotle (384–322 B.C.): Greek philosopher who wrote the first textbook on psychology (*De Anima*) and developed the basic doctrines of association. The term "traditional psychology" is often used to refer to the point of view expounded by Aristotle and developed by subsequent philosophers, especially by Thomas Aquinas (1224–1274) and other Scholastics. He paved the way for the development of empirical science, and he is often called the "father of psychology."

Aristotle's illusion: the illusion of two-ness produced by crossing the index and the middle fingers, between the tips of which a thin rod is placed. This is the first tactual illusion to be described in the literature of psychology.

arithmetic mean: the sum of the scores divided by the number of cases.

arithmomania: obsessive counting or thinking in terms of mathematical symbols. Samuel Johnson is said by Macaulay to have counted fence posts by touching them.

armchair psychology: a term of derision used by Scripture (1895) to denote psychological theories and speculations which are not based upon empirical investigations.

Army Alpha and Beta tests: the measures used (1917–1918) to appraise the intelligence of recruits in the Army of the United States. The Alpha was devised for English-speaking literates; the Beta, for non-English-speaking soldiers and illiterates. The data from the use of these tests furnished a storehouse of material for developing a body of facts and theories regarding the psychology of the young male adult.

Arnauld of Villanova: a psychiatrist of the thirteenth century who, while believing in the organic etiology of mental disorders, accepted the theory of demoniacal possession. Although a disciple of Galen, he firmly believed in astrology and alchemy.

arteriosclerosis, cerebral: chronic inflammation of the muscular wall (*intima*) of arteries of the brain (*hypertensive encephalopathy*). Patients are said to require both medical attention and psychotherapy, since emotional crises aggravate the disease.

Asclepiades: Greek physician of the second century B.C. He distinguished between transient or acute and chronic diseases, and he developed the method of continuous baths and swinging chairs whereby to sooth delirious patients. He is said to have been the "father of music therapy" in the treatment of mental disorders.

aspiration, level of: Hoppe's term (1930) for the reciprocal relationship between the goals which an individual sets for himself and his experiences with successes and failures. The term is an inadequate translation of *Anspruchsniveau*. In general, experiments confirm the view that successes tend to maintain or heighten the level of aspiration; failures, to lower it.

assets-liabilities technique: a counseling procedure in which all the assets-liabilities of the client are tabulated, and then, by a directive approach, the client is shown how to convert liabilities into assets and to become reconciled to the persisting liabilities about which nothing can be done.

associated movements: those muscular activities which accompany the principal execution at any given time. The term also refers to the reciprocal innervation among pairs of muscles, whereby, for example, contraction of biceps is accompanied by relaxation of triceps.

association: the manner in which (according to Aristotle's *De Memoria*) ideas tend to cluster together, the laws being: contrast, similarity, and contiguity in space or time. Thus, the recurrence of the one tends to evoke (redintegrate) the other by association.

association, clang: the tendency of the mentally disturbed person to respond to a stimulus word by a neologism which resembles the sound of the first. According to some theorists, language originated in the tendency of primitive man to make clang associations with various phenomena of nature (imitative sounds).

associationism: the revival of the Aristotelian theory of learning, with a systematic formulation of underlying philosophical principles, by British and Scotch philosophers of the mid-nineteenth century. John Stuart Mill introduced the concept of "mental chemistry" to account for the fusion of ideas (1869). Alexander Bain (1818–1903) and Herbert Spencer (1820–1903) are regarded as the last of the associationists. James Mill (1773–1836) is mentioned as the most vigorous proponent of the doctrine of associationism.

association-test: the method devised by Jung (1910) in which the subject responds to each of one hundred discrete words, thereby revealing abnormal associations. Kent and Rosanoff (1910–1911) developed frequency tables for words in a revised list. Tests of association are classed as either free (Jung-type tests) or controlled (restrictions being placed upon the response, such as opposites, whole-part, genus-species, and the like).

associative illusion: any geometrical illusion based upon the device of associated lines which, being familiar to the subject, cause an over- or under-estimation of size, relationship, or shape.

associative memory: the process of recall in which the subject engages in free association until he revives the recollection desired. If he is trying to recall an author's name, he suppresses affective disquietude and engages in free association until the name occurs.

associative shifting: Thorndike's term (1914) to denote the transfer by identical elements from a task containing elements ABCDE to one with B C E or with A E F G, etc.

assonance: similarity of sound, as among vowels: tendency to use alliteration.

astasia-abasia: hysterical reaction in which the patient can neither walk nor stand, though retaining coördination while lying in bed.

astereognosis: inability to recognize objects by feeling them. It indicates a cerebral lesion (parietal lobe) and is usually unilateral.

asthenia: general weakness as a result of either psychogenic or somatogenic factors.

asthenopia: weakness of vision as a result of refractive defects, weakness of eye muscles, general ill health, and the like.

astigmatism: a refractive disorder due to defects in curvature of cornea, lens, or eyeball.

astigmatometer (astigmascope): apparatus for measuring the degree of astigmatism.

asymbolia: inability to comprehend symbols, whether words or signs, as a result of cerebral lesion.

asymmetry: difference in size and/or function of organs which lie in different sides of the midline of the body and which are normally similar in structure and/or function.

asynergia: condition of incoördination among muscles which normally function in unison.

atavism: the recurrence in an individual of a peculiarity of structure or behavior which did not appear in immediate ancestry but which occurred in primitive man. The term is misleading and confusing.

ataxia: muscular incoördination caused by lesions in the nervous system. It usually indicates pathology in the extrapyramidal motor system.

ataxiameter: apparatus for recording postural sway. It is often used in experimental studies of suggestibility (Hull, 1933).

athetoid movements: slow tentacle-like writhings of arms, trunk, head, fingers, toes. They may be caused by the following: lesions in basal ganglia, defective development of the corpus striatum, infantile cerebral diplegia, involvement of pyramidal tract or ritualisms.

athletic build: the Kretschmer somatotype (1925) associated with the normal personality.

athymia: (1) absence of the thymus gland; (2) depressed affect.

athyria: absence of thyroid or cessation of thyroid activity.

atomism: the materialistic doctrine, expounded by Democritus (400 B.C.), that man is nothing more than a group of atoms. Various types of atoms account for the varieties of mental activity.

atonicity: reduction of the contraction of muscles; flaccidity of posture.

atrophy: degeneration of tissues.

attention: vividness of experience at any given moment. Wolff (1754) defined it as a "mental faculty"; Ribot (1889) emphasized the anticipatory behavior or the postural set for the stimulus; and Titchener (1896) described it in terms of a focus and a margin in consciousness. The following characteristics or types of attention are sometimes differentiated; primary, or unlearned; forced, secondary, or voluntary; and derived primary, or learned.

attention span: the number of objects which can be attended to in a brief interval of time. Locke (1690) makes passing reference to experiments on this topic.

attitude: a mental set to respond to a situation with a prepared reaction. Whereas sets may be temporary matters, attitudes are more or less stable. Techniques for measurements of attitudes were devised by Thurstone and Chave (1928). Attitudes denote bias, preconceptions, convictions, feelings and emotions, hopes and fears; opinions are the verbal formulations of attitudes. The attitude scales measure the manner in which a person responds to a standardized list of opinions on any given subject.

attitudinal reflexes: the bodily adjustments of animals which follow head movements (Magnus, 1925). Neck and labyrinthine reflexes are involved in the maintenance of these postures, which are retained as long as the head is kept in a given position.

attributes of sensation: Titchener's list (1896) of the characteristics of a sensation: quality (that which distinguishes one sensation from another); intensity; clearness; and duration.

Aubert, Hermann (1826–1892): German physiologist (and psychologist) who worked on vision.

audition: the sense of hearing. The apparatus for measuring auditory acuity is called an audiometer.

Aufgabe: the mental set which the individual brings to bear upon (or is directed to assume towards) a task. Watt (1905) established the concept, and Ach (1905) brought it into wide attention.

Augustine (354–430): theologian who was the first to employ the method of introspection in the study of psychology and who defined the individual Ego and the Will. For more than five centuries his system of psychology was taught without modification.

aura: the forewarning which some patients have before the onset of a grand mal convulsion.

auricle: the outer portion of the ear.

Aussage test: a measure of ability to report accurately upon what has been observed (Stern, 1907).

autacoid: secretions of endocrine glands (Sharpey and Schafer, 1913). Excitants are called hormones; inhibitors, chalones.

authoritarianism: a method for control of group behavior in which a leader sets the tasks, defines the methods, and judges the results, meanwhile remaining aloof and impersonal (Lewin, 1939).

autism: morbid pre-occupation with oneself, together with indifference to other people and with a tendency to retreat into pathological fantasies.

autistic thinking: vicarious gratification for deprivations and frustrations by wishful fantasies (Bleuler, 1911).

autochthonous delusion: morbid belief which is considered to be foreign to the normal personality of the patient and which is interpreted by the patient as coming from factors in the environment. Whereas autopsychic delusions arise from within personality, autochthonous delusions represent projections.

auto-criticism: the ability to formulate plans for action and to weigh and consider the possible outcomes before actually trying them out. According to Binet (1909), this ability is one of the four basic aspects of intelligence, the others being comprehension, invention, and direction or set.

auto-eroticism: achievement of sexual pleasure by manipulation of one's own erogenous zones.

auto-hypnosis: self-induction of a trance-like state by suggestions or by setting up a train of thinking. Coué (1857–1926) popularized a technique of auto-hypnosis. Behanan (1937) has given a psychological account of the methods of self-hypnosis used by practitioners of Yogi.

automatic behavior: activity which is not initiated or sustained by the usual methods of voluntary control. Solomon and Gertrude Stein (1896) made an objective investigation of this type of behavior; Freud (1898) and Prince (1914) developed influential theories to account for it.

automatic writing: composition done while the writer is unaware of what is being done, the attention being directed elsewhere or the writer being in a trance-like condition. Janet (1889) became particularly interested in the phenomenon because it furnishes support for his theory of dissociation.

autonomic nervous system: the nervous system which innervates the smooth musculature, thus maintaining the vital functions of the organism. The thoracico-lumbar portion (*orthosympathetic*) outflow of impulses maintains (in general) the normal functioning of blood-vessel walls, heart, bladder, and so on; the para-sympathetic (*mesencephalic-bulbo-sacral*) outflow speeds up processes. These contradictory functions, however, are not antagonistic but synergic. Autonomic imbalances create tensions (Kempf, 1918), and they cause the somatic disturbances in pathologies of affect. Cannon (1929) reported the classical research on the autonomic functions in emotional conditions. Grinker (1944) prefers the old term "vegetative nervous system," since it is not completely autonomic and since it cannot be separated from somatic activities.

auto-psychic delusion: a pathological belief which arises within the personality of the patient and is not attributed to situational factors.

avalanche concept: Cajal's theory that the sensory impulse is redistributed to an ever-increasing number of motor fibers. Jelliffe and White (1923) state that in certain forms of epilepsy there may be a sudden discharge of nervous impulses through a relatively narrow system of fibers.

Avenarius, Richard (1843-1896) : German philosopher who developed a theory of science that was accepted by Külpe and Titchener. He believed that conscious activities (or states) can be scientifically observed just as readily as any other data of science can.

aversion: unpleasant attitude towards a person or a situation, with a tendency to withdraw (Hobbes, 1651).

avitaminosis: the condition of malnutrition, as in the alcoholic who refrains from eating during the attack of dipsomania. Many of the symptoms hitherto attributed to the effects of the alcohol are now thought to be due to the condition of malnutrition.

avoidance reaction: withdrawal from an unpleasant or dangerous situation. Once thought to be an example of "instinctive wisdom," it was analyzed by Holt (1915) as a conditioned response in the animal. A reflex removes the animal from the situation, and by repetition this situation evokes the conditioned response which effects withdrawal.

awareness: consciousness of stimulation.

axiological proposition: one which interprets or evaluates an observed datum. Hence it is contrasted with an existential proposition, which merely describes the datum. Many of the propositions of "armchair" psychologists are said to be axiological; hence there are differences of opinion. The propositions of scientific psychology are existential; hence there cannot be disagreement if the observations have been accurately made and the statements are valid descriptions.

axon(e): the process of the neuron which transmits the

nervous impulse from the cell body to the next dendrite. Cajal developed a method of staining (1889) whereby he was able to observe the functional relationship between the axon and the dendrite of the next cell in the chain. Golgi (1873) had previously observed the axon process.

Azam, E.: French physician who published an account of a multiple personality (1876), and who expounded Braid's theories of hypnotism in France. He considered that hypnotic behavior and hysteria are similar phenomena; and Broca called this theory to the attention of Charcot, who developed it into an influential doctrine.

B: Rorschach's symbol (1922) for responses determined by perception of human beings in motion in the Inkblot Test.

babble stage: period of simple vocalizations which the normal infant uses in play at about two months of age (P. Cattell, 1940).

Babinski, Joseph (1857–1932): French neurologist who defined hysteria as heightened suggestibility and who advocated the use of persuasion ("pithiatism") to effect cures (1908). He believed that the symptoms reported by Charcot's patients were the result of suggestions unintentionally given by the physician's questions.

Babinski reflex: extension of the toes when a blunt object is drawn across the sole of the foot. In the infant, it is a normal reflex; in the adult, it indicates a lesion of the pyramidal tract of the cord.

babyhood: the stage of life which precedes walking. The upper limits are variously set at one year, fourteen months, and eighteen months.

bacillophobia: morbid fear of infection by microbes.

backward child: euphemism for a child of subnormal intelligence. Backwardness, however, may be caused by adventitious factors, such as timidity, malnutrition, illnesses, uncorrected sensory defects, cultural impoverishment of the environment, and the like.

backward conditioning: the establishment of conditioned reflex when the adequate stimulus precedes the conditioned stimulus in the training sequence. Pavlov (1927) reported that the conditioned stimulus must precede or overlap the adequate stimulus; but there now seems to be evidence that backward conditioning may be established (Hilgard and Marquis, 1940), though with great difficulty.

Bacon, Francis (1561-1626): English philosopher who advocated the use of the inductive method. He advocated a mathematical appraisal of human abilities; and he shifted the emphasis in psychology from theological and metaphysical concepts to an objective, empirical standpoint.

Baillarger, Jules (1809-1890): French neurologist and psychiatrist who studied hallucinations and the effects of alcoholism.

Bain, Alexander (1818-1893): Scotch philosopher and psychologist who founded the first journal devoted to psychology (*Mind*, 1874), expounded a trial-and-error theory of learning, incorporated the doctrine of psychophysical parallelism into psychology, and suggested to William James much which was incorporated into the *Principles of Psychology* (1890).

Baird, John Wallace (1873-1919): American psychologist who developed the method of complete introspection. In studies of higher mental functions, he advocated a thorough description of every phase of consciousness; hence for momentary events, he would have many pages filled with introspective data.

balance, sense of: vestibular equilibration, which was first investigated by Purkinje (1820-1827). He and Flourens (1824) reported on the functions of the semicircular canals; James (1882) performed some classical experiments on the effects of rotation.

Baldwin, James Mark (1861-1934): American psychologist who deplored the tendency to refrain from advancing theories in psychology and to concentrate upon laboratory research exclusively.

ballistic movements: sweeping motions of the entire arm. In studies of efficiency in industry, output can sometimes be increased when workers are trained to use ballistic movements rather than jerky motions.

Bárány chair: apparatus for rotating a person in a test of vestibular sensitivity. Purkinje, in his studies of dizziness (1820–1827), established the basis of this method for exploring the functions of the semicircular canals.

baresthesia: sensation of pressure. Meissner (1856) established the fact that deformation of the skin is the adequate stimulus for baresthesia. He introduced the classical experiment of hand immersion, in which pressure is felt only at the water line.

baresthesiometer: apparatus for measuring sensitivity to pressure. It usually consists of a small piston with graduated scale, so that the amount of pressure to reach the threshold of consciousness may be measured when the stimulus is applied.

barognosis: the ability to estimate weight. Weber (1834) found that the ability to sense difference between two weights depends upon a constant ratio between them. The size of an object affects the estimate of weight, large objects being overestimated and small ones underestimated (*size-weight illusion*).

baryecoia: partial loss of hearing.

baryencephalia: stupidity.

baryglossia: thick speech, as in states of intoxication or extreme weakness.

barylalia: thick speech as a result of pathology in the vocal apparatus.

baryphonia: deep, heavy voice.

barythmia: melancholia or depressed mood.

basal ganglia: a broad term usually applied to the various bodies of gray matter at the base of the brain.

Basedow, Johann Bernard (1732-1790): German educator who founded a school (1774) in which children were treated like children. Elsewhere at this time they were regarded, and dressed, as if they were miniature adults.

Basedow, Karl Adolphus von (1799-1854): German physician who defined a condition known as exophthalmic goiter. In this affliction the eyeballs are protuberant, and normal convergence is lost.

basal anxiety: the fear of being helpless in a potentially hostile universe (Horney, 1937). Freud (1936) reversed his early theories about the relationship between repression and anxiety, and stated that persons repress because they are anxious and insecure

basilar membrane: the lower side of the membranous cochlea upon which lies the organ of Corti. This membrane separates the scala vestibuli from the scala tympani in the cochlea of the inner ear. Its upper aspect is called the membrane of Reissner. Corti and Reissner published their findings in 1851.

basophobia: hysterical fear of standing up or of attempting to walk. The patient insists that he cannot keep from falling.

bath therapy: immersion of the patient in a tub kept about 95 degrees F. in order to reduce excitement. This is one of the oldest of the humane treatments used with manics.

bathyesthesia: the muscle sense. Kinesthesia is the more common term.

battery of tests: a group of measures designed to appraise various abilities of a person in order to determine fitness for employment or to assist in counseling.

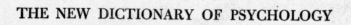

THE NEW DICTIONARY OF PSYCHOLOGY

Bayle, Armand L. J. (1799-1858): French physician who established the fact that general paralysis has a unique pattern of symptoms unlike those in other forms of mental disease, and who made a thorough study of one hundred cases, upon the basis of which he differentiated three stages: monomania, mania, and dementia.

Bayle, François (1622-1709): French physician who categorically denied that witches or demons were responsible for the behavior of deranged persons.

Beard, George Miller (1839-1883): American physician who defined neurasthenia, or Beard's disease. Symptoms include the following: fatigability, insomnia, vague aches and pains, loss of interest, irritability, pessimism, and epigastric disturbance.

beat effect: awareness of slight differences in the periodicity of two tones close together in frequency (Jean Sauveur, 1701).

Beauchamp case: Morton Prince's account (1905) of a patient who had, in addition to her normal self and a hypnotic personality, three distinct "selves." Owing to the eminence of the psychiatrist and to the literary quality of the report, this is one of the most famous records of a multiple personality in the literature.

Beaunis, Henri (1830-1921): French psychologist who, with Alfred Binet, established a psychological laboratory at the Sorbonne (1889) and founded the first psychological journal of France (1895).

Bechterev, Vladimir Mikhailovich (1857-1927): Russian neurologist who, with Pavlov, worked out the details of the conditioned reflex, and who called the science of human behavior "reflexology."

Bedlam: the priory of St. Mary of Bethlehem (London), which was opened in 1402 as a "lunatic asylum." Bethlehem Hospital is the oldest European institution that has been in continuous use. At one time, attendants charged a fee for visitors who wished to be amused by the behavior of the patients.

Beers, Clifford Whittingham (1876–1943) : author of an important autobiography (1908) relating his experience with a major psychosis and founder (1909) of the National Committee for Mental Hygiene.

behavior: anything whatsoever that is done by a living organism. Human behavior includes mental activities, consciousness, muscular functions, and the like. Strict objectivists would limit the term to denote neuromuscular activity, and they would account for consciousness in terms of a motor theory.

Behaviorism: a frame of reference in psychology (founded by J. B. Watson) which lays stress upon observations of overt behavior, derides the method of introspection, rules out consciousness, and emphasizes the theory of a machine-like quality in animal and human activity.

bel: a unit of intensity differences in sound.

belief: a proposition which is largely based upon the wish-to-believe rather than upon critical evaluation or scientific experimentation.

Bell, Charles (1774–1842) : Scotch physiologist who established the fact (1811) that the anterior spinal nerve-roots are motor; the posterior, sensory; who discovered that when the flexor relaxes the extensor contracts (*reciprocal innervation*), and who described the muscle sense. He developed the doctrine of specific energies of nerves (though Johannes Müller is usually assigned the credit).

Bell, Luther (1806–1862) : American physician who defined acute mania and who labored to achieve hospital reforms.

Bell-Magendie law: the principle that the ventral spinal nerve-root is motor; the posterior, sensory. Bell announced the principle in 1811; Magendie, in 1822.

belongingness, law of: Thorndike's principle (1932); items integrated into a pattern are better remembered than those which merely occur in close proximity.

beneceptor: any receptor which is affected by stimuli contributing to the health and welfare of the organism; hence the antithesis of a nociceptor (though even pain may be said to have value as a danger signal).

Beneke, Frederich Eduard (1798–1854): German psychiatrist who emphasized the possibility of interaction between mind and body, and who was interested in developing psychobiology.

benign psychosis: a mental disorder in which a favorable prognosis is indicated if psychiatric treatment begins early, or in which there is likely to be a spontaneous remission.

benign stupor: August Hoch's designation for the condition of stuporous melancholia, which is to be differentiated from the more ominous stupor of the schizophrenic patient.

Benussi, Vitorio (1878–1927): Austrian psychologist. He defined *bow movement*, which is the apparent deflection caused by an intermediary obstruction between two successive stimuli of light. The apparent motion between the two stimuli seems to bow around the obstruction.

berdache: transvistism, or the desire to wear the apparel of members of the opposite sex.

Berger, Hans: contemporary Austrian neurologist who is credited with the discovery of the clinical use of the electrical activity generated in the brain (1924). The basic facts had been known since 1874, but Berger demonstrated the applicability of the principles to studies of brain diseases. Originally, he described the occipital rhythm (*Berger rhythm*); five others have been identified by subsequent research. Electroencephalography is now used for research purposes and as a part of the clinical examination of patients.

Berkeley, George (1685-1753): English philosopher who opposed the nativistic doctrine of visual space perception and laid the basis for empirical studies in this field. He also upheld the view that mind is the basic reality in the universe.

Bernard, Claude (1813-1878): French physiologist who worked with Magendie and who is best known for researches on the function of the liver.

Bernhardt, Martin (1844-1915): German neurologist who defined a form of paresthesia.

Bernheim, Hippolyte (1840-1909): French psychiatrist who, at Nancy, disagreed with Charcot's theory of hysteria. He upheld the position that hypnosis is merely a condition of suggestibility, and not the induction of a state of hysteria. The controversy between the Nancy and the Salpêtrière schools aroused a great deal of interest at the time.

Bessel, Friedrich Wilhelm (1784-1846): German astronomer who read of the dismissal of Kinnebrook at Greenwich (1796), and then undertook research on reaction times, thus discovering the personal equation in scientific observations. He published his famous report in 1822.

bestiality: sexual relations with an animal. Male perverts usually employ the method of intromission of the penis into the vagina of a female animal; female perverts often achieve the orgasm by the method of lingual stimulation by an animal.

beta hypothesis: Dunlap's suggestion (1932) regarding the technique of extinguishing a faulty habit by deliberately practicing the habit on a regular schedule. The classical example is the manner in which he overcame the habit of typing *h-t-e* by repeated typings of this faulty sequence of letters.

beta movement: type of apparent movement in which two visual stimuli presented at optimal distance and time seem to combine into a single movement. It was described in 1913 as a result of further investigations of the Wertheimer phenomenon (1912).

Bethe, Albrecht (1872–): German naturalist who explained the social behavior of ants and bees in terms of mechanistic principles.

bias: an intellectual pre-judgment of the validity of propositions. Prejudices involve a high degree of motivational-emotional factors; biases are less invested with these factors. Bacon's "idols" (1620) illustrate the difficulty in separating a bias from a prejudice.

Bianchi, Leonardo (1848–1927): Italian psychiatrist who wrote on suggestive therapy.

Bicêtre: French institution for demented persons where (1793) Pinel ordered the fetters to be removed. Chevigné, one of the patients whom he released from confinement, saved Pinel's life when a Parisian mob threatened the great psychiatrist with lynching.

Bichat, Marie François Xavier (1771–1802): French anatomist who described various tissues of the body and who distinguished between voluntary and involuntary muscles.

bi-dimensional eye-movement camera: apparatus designed by Brandt (1937) for making a record of fixations and excursions of eye movements.

bifurcation: division into two branches.

bilateral transfer: carry-over to the unpracticed hand (or foot) of a skill achieved by practice with the other. Weber (1844) observed that some children can do legible mirror-writing with the non-preferred hand, the preferred hand having been used in ordinary writing.

bimodal: a frequency distribution with two peaks. Landis (1940) reported some evidence supporting the hypothesis that certain traits (*e.g.*, adjustment habits) are not distributed on the normal curve (unimodal).

binaural: pertaining to both ears. Lord Rayleigh's work (1877) on localization of auditory stimuli introduced the concept of binaural ratio. He believed that the cue for locating a sound on the right or the left is the intensity difference of the sound wave as it affects the ears.

Binet, Alfred (1856–1911): French psychologist who founded the first psychological journal published in French (1894), conducted important experiments on higher mental functions, and is best known for his scales for the measurement of intelligence. The first scale was developed in 1905; the second, 1908; and the final revision, 1911. His collaborator was Th. Simon, a former student who had achieved a reputation for his studies of the behavior of mental defectives (1900).

binocular: pertaining to both eyes. Wheatstone (1833) investigated the problem of binocular parallax, and thus developed the empirical view of depth perception in vision. Owing to the lateral distance between the two eyes, the retinal images are disparate, a fact which is clearly brought out by the stereoscope and which was described, though not explored, by Harris in 1775. Radically disparate colors presented to each eye separately are rarely combined; but, after one is seen, the other comes into view (Breese, 1899), a phenomenon known as binocular (or retinal) rivalry. The principal differences between binocular and monocular vision were first described by Panum (1858).

biogenesis: the biological dictum that living organisms are produced only by the living, never by non-living, organisms (Schwann, 1837). At one time, there was strong opposition to the doctrine, particularly upon the part of theologians.

biological heredity: the tendency of the offspring to resemble the parents, because of the transmission of a genetic constitution to which each parent contributes half. Mendel (1866) described the mechanisms of inheritance in sweet peas; T. H. Morgan (1916) worked out the details about genes in Drosophila melanogaster. Studies of human heredity do not approximate these investigations in scientific exactitude; hence the topic is pre-empted by many controversialists and theorists. A persisting source of confusion is the failure to distinguish between biological and social heredity.

biology: the science which deals with living plants and animals.

bionomics: the study of the relationships between organisms and their environments.

biosocial relationships: those which depend upon biological factors and which primarily meet the interests of the dominant group. The doctrine of racial inferiority-superiority status "justified" white persons in keeping Negro slaves, and the Nazis in their program of conscripting "inferior" people for manual labor. The term also refers to the relationship which exists between a domesticated animal and its owner.

birth hemorrhage: referring to a rupture of blood vessels in the brain of an infant during the process of birth. It is mentioned as a possible cause for certain personality disorders and deficiencies.

birth trauma: Rank's theory (1923) that birth itself is a traumatic experience and that the anxiety of psychoneurotics recapitulates the psychological concomitants of birth. Freud stated that he found no empirical evidence for this theory, but for a few years Rank gained some adherents in America.

biserial coefficient of correlation: the ratio between two variables one of which is expressed in terms of only two categories.

bisexuality: condition of hermaphroditism, in which both male and female sex organs exist.

bitter: a taste sensation which appears in the earliest classification (Bravo's, 1592) and which has remained as one of the indisputable gustatory qualities. Alkaloids (*e.g.*, quinine) are the stimuli.

Bkl: symbol used by some Europeans to denote perception of movement in small areas of the Rorschach Inkblot Test figures.

black: in the Hering color theory (1874), a positive sensation that is the complement of white.

black and white series: the intensities of grays between black and white (Titchener, 1910); or the variations in either direction of intensities from a neutral gray (Dimmick, 1920).

blaming others: a familiar type of projection in which other persons are considered to be the cause for an individual's frustrations and conflicts. It is said to be the mechanism out of which paranoid beliefs may develop.

blast-injection technique: the induction of convulsive seizures in an animal by blasts of compressed air. Maier did not observe seizures when he subjected rats to the blasts alone

(1939); but Hall and Martin, working with rats inbred to accentuate, on the one hand, emotional traits, and, on the other, non-emotional traits, succeeded in inducing convulsions by the air blasts (1941). The emotional (timid) rats were the less affected by the stimulus. There is a tendency to refer to the effects of the air-blast technique as an audiogenic seizure.

blend: the fusion of sensory elements into a pattern experienced as a whole.

Bleuler, Eugen (1857–1939): Swiss psychiatrist who introduced the term "schizophrenia" (1911) to replace the Kraepelinian designation "dementia praecox." He stated that a weakening of associations is the essential feature in this disorder, and he defined autistic thinking as the essential feature of the cognitive functions of these patients. He grouped together a number of reaction types under this heading, and he opposed the Kraepelinian dictum that this form of dementia is incurable.

blind-alley job: one in which the worker has (or believes that he has) no opportunity for advancement, and hence loses morale. The American Youth Commission reported (1937) that 43% of employed youth regarded their jobs as blind alleys.

blind diagnosis: a term referring to the diagnoses given by experts in the Rorschach Inkblot Test whereby they can detect psychoneurotic and psychotic traits from the protocol alone, even though they have no other data pertaining to the patient.

blind spot: the area of the retina where the optic nerve enters. It was discovered by Mariotte in 1668.

Blix, Magnus: Swedish physiologist who (1882) discovered that cold, warmth, pain, and pressure are separate elements of cutaneous sensation.

blocking: a condition of interference with free action by the simultaneous arousal of contradictory motives. According to psychoanalysts, recall may be blocked by repressions.

blue: a visual sensation the stimulus for which is wave-length of about 478.

Bodin, Jean (1530–1596): French legalist who established the tradition of differentiating between a medical and a legal definition of a mental disorder.

body-mind problem: a controversial issue introduced into psychology by Descartes regarding the nature of mind and its relation to the body. Descartes (1650) wrote that animals are automata, but that human beings have minds as well as bodies. He believed that the pineal gland is the point of interaction. Spinoza (1665) presented the double-aspect theory, God being the universal principle. Leibnitz (1695) developed the theory of psychophysical parallelism, with a preëstablished harmony between the two. The doctrine of epiphenomenalism is very old (Democritus, 400 B.C.), and has been favored as a working hypothesis by many psychologists. Modern psychologists tend to refer the problem to metaphysicians.

Boerhaave, Hermann (1668–1738): Dutch physician who wrote an important textbook on the diagnosis and care of mental disorders (1728).

bone conduction: a method of stimulating the hearing mechanism of the inner ear through apparatus transmitting the vibrations to the cochlea. If the lesion is in the tympanum or the middle ear, the patient is able to hear by this technique.

Bonet, Théophile (1620–1689): French pathologist who performed autopsies on the bodies of some patients with psychoses.

Bonnet, Charles (1720-1790): French physiologist who anticipated act psychology (as opposed to content) and who also anticipated the doctrine of specific nerve energy (Bell, 1811; J. Müller, 1826).

borderline intelligence: the level of intelligence above that of the moron and below that of the dull normal. Terman (1916) set the intelligence quotient between 70 and 80.

Bosquillon, Edouard (1744-1816): French physician who advocated the liberal use of the technique of bleeding for the treatment of mental disorders.

brachycephaly: having a skull the width of which is more than 9/10 the length.

brachymetropia: nearsightedness.

bradyesthesia: blunted sensations.

bradylalia: abnormal slowness in speech, a pronounced hiatus occurring between words or phrases.

bradylexia: abnormal slowness in reading, usually as a result of faulty methods of instruction which established the habit of lip movements in silent reading.

bradyphrasia: extreme slowness in talk as a result of a brain lesion.

Braid, James (1795-1861): English physician who identified mesmerism with sleep, and hence introduced the term *hypnotism* (Greek for "sleep"). He attributed the trance, not to mysterious "animal magnetism," but to the results of staring, relaxation, and shallow breathing.

brain: encephalon. The following parts are frequently mentioned: (1) epencephalon, which includes the pons, medulla, and cerebellum, (2) mesencephalon, or the midbrain (*corpora quadrigemina, crura cerebri,* and *Sylvian aqueduct*); (3) metencephalon, or afterbrain (*post-oblongata*); (4) prosencephalon, or forebrain (*anterior commisure, anterior preforated space, corpus callosum,* *corpus striatum, fornix, hemispheres, olfactory lobes,* and *septum lucidum*) ; and (5) telencephalon, or end brain (forepart of the *prosencephalon*). Its external aspect is mapped by reference to gyri (convolutions) and sulci (fissures).

Bramwell, J. Milne: English physician who visited Liébeault at Nancy (1889) to observe his use of hypnosis in therapy and who wrote an important book on hypnosis (1903).

Brentano, Franz (1838–1917): leader of the Würzburg school (act psychology). He opposed Wundt's emphasis upon content and stressed the importance of experiencing.

Breuer, Josef (1842–1925): Austrian physician who collaborated with Freud (1895) in an important book on hysteria and with whom Freud commenced his medical practice upon the return from France to Vienna. Breuer used the method of therapeutic hypnosis (*mental catharsis*) as early as 1875.

Bridgman, Laura (1829–1889): American woman who, at age two, lost sight and hearing. Her dreams (*kinesthetic*) were investigated by Jastrow, Hall, and others; and many reports were published on the manner in which she was educated. Donaldson (1890) reported that parts of her brain were undeveloped.

brightness: intensity of a visual sensation. It is dependent upon the degree of saturation and upon the intensity of the illumination.

brilliance: the attribute of a visual sensation on the basis of which it may be arranged on the scale of grays (from white to black). *Brightness* is usually employed to refer to stimulus; *brilliance,* to the sensation.

Broca, Paul (1824–1880): French physician who located the brain area which mediates speech (Broca's area, 1861),

introduced the technique for determining the ratio between the skull and brain sizes, and initiated modern
methods of brain surgery.

Brown, John (1735-1788): Scotch physician who developed
the theory that the energy-level of the nervous system
may rise or fall. His concept of neuro-asthenia was used
by Beard (1875) in defining a condition known as neurasthenia and by P. Janet (1925) in his account of psychasthenia.

Brown-Séquard, Charles Edouard (1817-1897): French
neurologist who described a condition in which hyperesthesia and paralysis affect one side and anesthesia the
other side of the body.

Bruecke, Ernst Wilhelm (1819-1892): Austrian physiologist
with whom Freud studied from 1876-1892 and under
whose direction he worked on the histology of the nervous
system.

bulb: medulla oblongata.

bulimia: pathological craving for food, as by deranged
patients or mental defectives.

burnt: one of the six fundamental odors in the Henning
olfactory prism (1915). It is also called *empyreumatic*.

Burton, Robert (1577-1640): English author who wrote the
Anatomy of Melancholy (1621), a collection of items
bearing upon mental disorders as well as upon a multi-
plicity of other topics.

C

C: response to Rorschach Inkblot figures (**II, III, VIII, IX,** and **X**) which is determined by the colors alone.

CA: chronological age.

CAVD test: Thorndike's battery of tests (1926) which measure academic intelligence, the following specific abilities being appraised: completion, arithmetic, vocabulary, and directions.

c-factor: Spearman's designation (1927) for a factor, defined statistically, which is identified as zest, alertness, energy as displayed in psychological tests.

cacergasia: mental deficiency.

cacesthesia: unpleasant sensations, as those associated with certain physical and mental disorders.

cachexia: condition of malnutrition and general weakness as a result of drug addiction. The four stages in addiction are sometimes differentiated as follows: (1) experimentation, (2) hesitation, (3) definite habituation, and (4) cachexia.

cachinnation: senseless laughter, as in manic-depressive psychosis, manic type, or in the hebephrenic form of schizophrenia.

cacodemonomania: the delusion that one is under the spell of evil spirits, witches, or demons. Sprenger and Kraemer's *Malleus Maleficarium* (1487) is said to have established this mass delusion, which persisted into the early part of the 18th century.

cacogenics: the study of the ill-effects of bad heredity.

cacopathia: the most serious mental disorders. The term is attributed to Hippocrates.

cacophonia: harsh, unpleasant voice, as in laryngitis or other pathologies of the vocal mechanisms.

cacosmia: disgusting or unpleasant odors, as in mental disorders when the patient complains about vile odors not sensed by normal persons.

cacothymia: Hack Tuke's term (1892) for a mental disorder which is accompanied by lewd behavior or profanity.

caecitas: total blindness.

cafeteria feeding: the method of allowing recently weaned infants to select their own diet from among as many as twenty different foods (C. M. Davis, 1928), the infants choosing the foods upon which they thrived.

caffeinism: toxic condition resulting from excessive drinking of strong coffee, the symptoms including irritability and insomnia.

Cajal, Santiago Ramon y (1852-1934): Spanish histologist who found evidence to declare that neurons are functionally, not anatomically, related. The juncture between them is called the synapse. Waldeyer (1891) gave credit to Cajal (1889) when he called this the neuron theory.

Calkins, Mary Whiton (1863-1930): American psychologist who opposed the materialistic emphasis and who cited evidence for the primacy of consciousness of self as the basic datum in psychology.

callback: a second interview in a market survey or public-opinion sampling to check upon the consistency of the informant's opinions or upon the honesty of the interviewer.

Calmeil, Jean (1798-1895): French psychiatrist who investigated the problem of general paralysis among patients with mental disorders. He came to the conclusion that gross pathologies of the brain were the basic causes of the mental symptoms.

campimeter (perimeter): apparatus for mapping color zones of the retina. Aubert (1857) first reported on the differential sensitivity of various parts of the retina, and Landolt (1872) described more completely the differential sensing of various hues on the parts of the retina.

canal-boat children: a group of English children who, measured by intelligence tests, compared favorably with town children at an early age but most disadvantageously at older age levels (Gordon, 1923). The study is often cited to illustrate the ill-effects of impoverished environment upon intelligence development.

cannabis: hemp. The leaves are dried, mixed (sometimes) with various substances, and smoked ("reefers"). The effects are variously reported—distortion of the sense of time, euphoria, heightening of sex desires.

Cannon, Walter Bradford (1871-1945): American physiologist who investigated the physiology of emotions and developed the concept of homeostasis. He reported (1915) that the physiological aspect may occur without awareness of the existence of an emotion, and that various emotions may have similar physiological patterns. *Homeostasis* (1932) denotes the tendency of the body to maintain constant states of equilibrium.

capacity: the potentiality for improvement of a given function (skill, understanding, and the like) under optimal conditions of training. Capacity is inferred from measures of abilities; the individuals whose scores are used in a judgment of capacity must have had equal amounts of training or opportunity, thereby comparisons may be established.

carcinomaphobia: obsessive, unfounded fear that the individual has a cancer.

cardiac: pertaining to the heart.

cardiograph: apparatus for recording heart beat.

caries: cavities in the teeth. Pressey (1933), emphasizing the statistical concept of normality, states that the normal sixth-grade pupil has, among other deficits, one or more caries.

Carpenter, William Benjamin (1813-1885): English physiologist who doubted the applicability of the doctrine of evolution to mental activities, who emphasized freedom of the will, and who did much to popularize biological science.

case history: reconstruction of the past life of an individual (normal or abnormal) in order to determine the underlying causes for present behavior. The past history of a patient up to the time of institutionalization is called the anamnesis; the progress of the patient while under treatment, the catamnesis (follow-up).

case load: the number of clients for which a clinical psychologist or social worker is responsible.

case study method: the individual approach to the problems of a person. Tests and measures, interviews with the client, information obtained from dependable sources, and appraisals of assets-liabilities differentiate the case study method from other procedures. The method is primarily intended to be helpful to the client, not to collect data for scientific research.

caste: social status which determines rigid and inescapable roles for occupation, marriage, and participation in group life.

castration complex: psychoanalyst's term to describe the fear of genitals because of forbidden erotic desires. The female is said to believe that the penis has been removed; the male, that it may be (Abraham, 1925).

catabolism: disintegration of tissues. It is the antithesis of anabolism, which is the repair of tissues or constructive metabolism.

catagelphobia: dread of being ridiculed.

catalepsy: loss of consciousness, with extreme rigidity of muscles. Hysterics sometimes induce this state by rapid exhalations.

catamnesis: the record of a patient following the admission to the institution and covering the period of hospitalization and the out-patient supervision.

cataplexy: muscular rigidity caused by intense emotional upheaval or by hypnotic suggestion.

catastrophic experience: total loss of self-confidence, the feeling of emotional security, and self-respect.

catastrophic threat: apprehension of being alone and helpless in a potentially hostile universe (Freud, 1937).

catatonia: a mental disorder in which odd postures, stuporous states, muscular spasms, indifference to the environment, mutism, negativism, waxy flexibility or spring resistance are symptoms. Kahlbaum (1874) introduced the term, and both Kraepelin (1893) and Bleuler (1924) established it in the literature of psychiatry. It is one of the forms of schizophrenia (dementia praecox).

cathexis: term in psychoanalytic theory referring to the concentration of psychic energy in a particular outlet. Ego-cathexis refers to the direction of the libido upon the self (narcissism); object-cathexis, towards a person or thing; and phantasy-cathexis, towards the inner world of daydreams.

Cattell, James McKeen (1860–1944): American psychologist who, under Wundt, commenced experiments on reaction times and, under Galton, on individual differences. He was among the first to use psychological tests on large groups.

cathode-ray oscillograph: apparatus whereby a magnetic field deflects a beam of electrons. It has been used in studies of cortical action currents by Kornmüller (1933), who reports two types of currents: (1) that which occurs when the experimental animal is quiet; and (2) that which occurs when a stimulus is applied by the investigator. The latter type is found only in specific areas of the brain.

causal relationship: that which exists because of a determined order of sequence, not by chance or whim.

causation, multiple: referring to the theory that so many complex factors determine human behavior that it is futile to look for a single cause for any personality trait, reaction, or disorder.

cell: the unit of the organism (Schwann, 1839). Brain cells were first mentioned by Purkinje (1837), and Golgi (1873) first developed a method of staining which made nerve cells visible under the microscope for close study.

Celsus, Cornelius: medical historian who lived about 10 A.D. Many of his views on mental disorders are thought to have come down from Hippocrates.

cenophobia: morbid fear of large halls, auditoriums, or edifices with high ceilings.

censor: psychoanalytic term for the coercive influence of the ego and the super-ego upon the unwelcome impulses of the id; hence these impulses are barred from consciousness or compelled to assume disguises (*dream symbols, reversal formation, displacement,* and the like). By a process of mental catharsis, the patient may achieve a release from all these tensions.

center: an area in the brain where, presumably, certain functions are localized. Broca (1861) located the speech center, and thus initiated the search for centers involved in other functions.

central nervous system: the brain and the spinal cord.

central tendency: the measure which typifies the distribution of scores; hence *mean, mode,* or *median.*

cephalgia: headache.

cephalic index: ratio of breadth and length of the skull.

cephalo-caudal axis: the imaginary line from head to tail, the head region being the major gradient in embryological development (Child, 1921).

cerebellar ataxia: lack of integrative synergia in voluntary (striated) muscular activity. The condition arises from a lesion in the cerebellum. Locomotion is uncertain and wobbly (*cerebellar gait*), and the muscles do not function in reciprocal innervation.

cerebellum: the part of the brain which lies below the cerebrum and above the medulla oblongata and the pons Varolii. It mediates the integrative synergia of the striated musculature (Tilney, 1938). Its functions were described by Rolando (1809).

cerebral cortex: the gray matter, or neopallium, of the cerebral hemispheres. The infra-granular layer of the neopallial cortex, appearing only in mammals, is the oldest from a phylogenetic standpoint; and the supra-granular layer is the most recent, the rudiments of which are found in the brains of great apes. The pyramidal cells of this layer (Purkinje, 1837) are said to mediate the higher mental functions.

cerebral dominance: the tendency of one hemisphere of the cerebrum to be more involved in the mediation of various functions than the other hemisphere is.

cerebral dysrhythmia: the presence of abnormal brain waves in the electroencephalogram. Delta waves found under waking conditions, and a 3-per-second wave found only in epilepsy, are examples of this phenomenon. Some authorities have suggested that *cerebral dysrhythmia* is a more appropriate term than *epilepsy*.

cerebral localization: the reference of definite functions to specific parts of the brain. Broca (1861) was the first surgeon to report the localization of the speech function; and Fritsch and Hitzig (1870) reported other localization of the various mental functions. Flourens (1824) developed the theory that the cerebrum functions *in toto*. The general outlines of the doctrine are still open to question (*e.g.*, Lashley, 1929, vs. Kornmüller, 1933).

cerebration: reflective thinking.

cerebrology: Rosanoff's term (1927) for neuropsychiatry.

cerebrotonia: Sheldon's term (1942) for the temperament associated with the ectomorphic physique. Owing to the excessive development of the nervous tissues (*ectoderm*), the cerebrotonic is thoughtful, aloof, restrained, solitary, and quiet in behavior.

cerebrum: the principal area of the brain, consisting of the two hemispheres.

certainty: the ultimate degree of assurance regarding the validity of a belief or an opinion.

cervical: pertaining to the region of the neck.

chain reflex: an automatic type of response in which the response constitutes the stimulus for a second response, and so on.

chalone: endocrine secretion which inhibits or slows various functions. Some pharmacologists have suggested that *hormone* be used to denote an excitant; *chalone*, an inhibitor; and *autocoid*, both secretions.

chance forms: meaningless materials, such as inkblots, upon which the individual projects interpretations, thus revealing psychodynamic trends in the personality. The Rorschach Inkblot Test is one of the most widely known examples.

character: personality evaluated by reference to a moral code (G. W. Allport, 1937).

character analysis: application of psychoanalytic procedures to a normal person, as for purposes of training.

character neurosis: according to psychoanalysts, a psychoneurotic disorder in which the principal symptom is the compulsive repetition of characteristic actions resulting in humiliation, suffering, and failure.

Charcot, Jean Marie (1825–1893): French neurologist who identified hypnosis with hysteria. He was the leader of the Salpêtrière group that opposed the conclusions of the Nancy psychiatrists (Bernheim and others) on this issue. The Nancy group explained hypnosis in terms of the psychology of suggestion. Charcot made many contributions to psychiatry and neurology (1872–1893). Freud studied under him in 1885–1886.

charlatans: unrecognized practitioners of pseudopsychology (*phrenology, physiognomy,* and the like) who, by plausible and unscientific procedures, deceive the credulous.

chasmus hystericus: hysterical yawning.

chemoreceptor: the olfactory and the gustatory receptors. The Schneiderian membrane (containing the olfactory cells) secretes a solution which reacts when gaseous particles affect it; hence olfaction is classed as a chemical sense. Some physiologists describe a common chemical sense (C. Morgan, 1943), which is differentiated from pain and pressure (Crozier, 1916), and the receptors for which seem to be concentrated in exposed moist tissues, though found elsewhere in the body.

Cheyne-Stokes nystagmus: rhythmical oscillations of the eye-

balls in time with a crescendo-diminuendo type of respiration. It was described by John Cheyne (1777–1836)
and William Stokes (1804–1878).

chiaroscuro effect: differential shadings in an inkblot or work
of graphic art. Rorschach (1922) reported that responses
determined by chiaroscuro—F(Fb)—indicate dysphoria.

chiasm: the joining and crossing of the two optic nerves just
in front of the tuber cinereum.

chirognomy: pseudo-science of determining a person's character from the shape of the hands and the lines of the
palm.

child analysis: the application of psychoanalytic techniques
to the study and treatment of children. Freud reported
the analysis of a phobia in a five-year-old boy, and
Melanie Klein has continued to develop this application
of psychoanalysis.

child psychology: that division of psychology which is concerned with the development of children from birth to
adolescence. Preyer (1881) wrote one of the first scientific accounts of child development, and G. S. Hall
(1891) founded the first journal of child psychology in
the English language.

chiromancy: the pseudo-science whereby a person's future is
foretold by reading the lines of the palm or the shape of
the hand.

choc: Binet's term (1887) for responses to a situation which
causes an emotional shock and for which there are no
prepared reactions.

choice reaction: an experiment in which the subject responds
to one stimulus but not to another (Donders, 1868). Ach
(1905) reported that the "choice" factor soon disappears, and that the reaction is little more than an appre-

hension of the stimulus, and then the movement (pressing the key to stop the chronoscope).

choler: yellow bile, which is one of the four classical humors described by Hippocrates. The others are black bile, blood, and phlegm.

choleric: the classical temperament (humoral doctrine) characterized by labile emotions, quickness to anger, and irascibility. It was thought to arise from a relative excess of bile.

chorea: non-rhythmical, spasmodic twitchings of the muscles, particularly in the face, limbs, and shoulders, which occurs more often in youth than in maturity. The patients are often irascible and difficult to manage during the course of the disease. The condition is popularly known as St. Vitus' dance.

chorea, Huntington's: a severe disorder which makes its onset at about age thirty or forty and is characterized by an increasing rate of choretic movements, with great mental deterioration. The disorder has been traced to a family which landed in Boston in early Colonial days, and it is known to be hereditary. The course of the deterioration covers ten or fifteen years, and no cure is known. It was described by George Huntington (1850–1916), an American physician.

chorea lasciva: the term which Paracelsus (1567) proposed to replace St. Vitus' dance. He believed that the etiology lies in an emotional shock or the sight of taboo behavior.

chorea, Sydenham's: an infectious type of chorea occurring in elementary school children who live in poverty-stricken environments. In school these pupils are high-strung, alert, and tense. The most obvious symptom is head-shaking. The disorder was described by Thomas Sydenham (1624–1689), an English physician.

chromatic aberration: The result of unequal refraction of light from various parts of the spectrum.

chromatic scale: an octave proceeding by semitones instead of the intervals of the diatonic scale.

chromatopseudopsia: color-blindness.

chromatopsia: a pathological condition resulting from effects of certain drugs or from disorders of the retina in which objects are perceived in inappropriate colors.

chromesthesia: the association of images of colors with various stimuli, such as letters or musical tones (Galton, 1883).

chromosome: a minute body in the cell. In mitosis, the chromatin is resolved into the chromosomes, which contain the genes (determiners of heredity). In the human being, the female has 48 chromosomes; and the male, 47 plus a rudimentary chromosome (Y). The term was coined by Waldeyer (*c.* 1890), who discovered that a certain stain made these bodies visible under the microscope.

chronaxy: the time required for an electrical impulse, of a defined strength, to traverse a nerve fiber and excite a muscular contraction. Lapicque introduced the concept.

chronic: of continued duration.

chronoscope: a device for measuring the time interval between a stimulus and a response. The first practical chronoscope was developed by Wheatstone in 1840, and the one which was used in the early experimental work by psychologists was devised by Hipp in 1842.

cilia: hair-like processes whereby certain protozoa move about; also, the hair-like processes on certain epithelial tissues.

ciliary body: the part of the vascular tunic of the eyeball between the choroid membrane and the iris, whereby the accommodation of the lens is mediated. Muscle fibers in the ciliary body contract and pull the body forward.

circular psychosis: manic-depressive disorder, alternating type, with periods of excitement followed by depressions.

circumstantiality: Bleuler's term (1930) for irrelevance in the talk of manic patients. Mr. Jingle in Dickens' *Pickwick Papers* illustrates it.

clairvoyance: the reputed ability to apprehend various situations without the mediation of known sense organs.

clang: an assemblage of tones (Titchener, 1897). A tone is a simple clang; a chord or a discord, is a compound clang. This denotation was given by Helmholtz (1863).

clang association: the repetition of a word (often a neologism) which resembles the sound of the stimulus word of a free-association test. According to some theorists, the sounds of nature (thunder, falling water, and the like) "ring out" sounds from human observers; hence the origin of language is explained.

class: a stratification in group life which sets high, but not impassable, barriers for upward or downward mobility.

classification: orderly arrangement of data.

claustrophobia: morbid fear of being in small, enclosed spaces.

clavus: an intense headache which is described as a sensation of having a nail or dagger driven into the brain.

climacterium: the menopause, or cessation of menstruation.

climacterium virile: Kurt Mendel's term (1910) for an alteration in the physiology of the male which occurs between ages fifty and sixty. Accompanying the climacterium, there may be symptoms of depression and anxiety.

clinical: pertaining to the intensive study of an individual, in which all the various psychological techniques pertinent to a given person are used for the purpose of analyzing difficulties and planning a program of re-adjustment.

clinical crib: apparatus in which the human infant may be viewed through a one-way screen, the purpose of the experimenter being that of collecting data on infant behavior (Gesell, 1928).

clinical psychology: the branch of psychology which applies scientific principles to an intensive study of the assets and liabilities of an individual, the purpose being that of aiding the re-adjustment, or furthering the wholesome development, of the individual. Tests and measures are used as helpful tools in gathering data, but much of the benefit comes from the practical experience of the clinical psychologist.

clitoris: the female counterpart of the male's penis, an erectile organ situated on the ischiopubic rami. According to Freud, the erotic phantasies of some adult women are rooted in clitoris sensuality originating in the infantile discovery of this organ, which they wish to be the penis. He adds the statement that the clitoris becomes an erogenous zone before the vagina does.

cloaca theory: the psychoanalytic theory that expulsion affords erotic gratification to the infant. Later on the infant may learn that retention is also pleasurable. Thereby traits of free-spending or miserliness may be developed.

clonus: alternate contractions and relaxations of muscles.

c. n. s.: the central nervous system.

coarctation: condition of emotional indifference as a result of constrictive tendencies (Rorschach, 1922).

cocainism: a term used by Erlenmeyer (1886) to describe the physical and the psychological results of addiction to cocaine. The drug acts at first as a stimulant; then as a narcotic. The addict reports paresthesias ("cocaine bugs"), which are sensed as ovoid bodies on or under the skin. Addiction results in emaciation and decline of intellectual and ethical traits.

cochlea: the cavity of the inner ear, which makes $2\frac{1}{2}$ turns and is about one inch long. The organ of Corti (containing the receptors) lies in the cochlea. It is shaped like the shell of a snail and is approximately a quarter inch from front to back.

co-conscious: Morton Prince's term (1914) for the re-arousal of memories ("passive neurograms") which function unconsciously to govern parts of the behavior of a person. They are co-existing states of consciousness of which the personal consciousness is not aware. He traced the doctrine to Leibnitz, and utilized it as a frame of reference for his account of multiple personality.

coefficient of alienation: a ratio indicating the lack of relationship between two arrays of scores.

coefficient of contingency: ratio between variables expressed in categories rather than numbers.

coefficient of correlation: an index of the degree of relationship between variables. Galton (1885) first described a technique for indicating correlation, and Pearson (1920), who developed a mathematical formula for correlation, wrote on the early history of the procedure.

coefficient of correlation: Pearson: the ratio between two or more sets of variables, expressed as a pure number, between $+1.00$ and -1.00.

coefficient of multiple correlation: a number expressing the ratio between one set of variables and a weighted series of variables (two or more).

coefficient of partial correlation: a number indicating the ratio between two sets of variables with other variables held constant.

coefficient of reliability: a number showing the ratio between a set of variables and another set of variables which might determine the consistency of the measures. Three techniques are used: retest reliability, equivalent forms of tests, and split-half (or odds-evens).

coefficient of validity: a number expressing the ratio between a set of measures and the criterion.

coenesthesia (cenesthesia): the vague pattern of organic sensations which makes up the feeling-tone (pleasant or unpleasant) of an individual at any given time (McDougall, 1923).

Coghillian sequence: the successive stages in the development of *Amblystoma* as described by Coghill (1929), the most primitive behavior of the tadpole being a mass reaction, and the specific patterns developing therefrom by a process of individuation. The course of individuation is from head to tail and from central to peripheral axes. This observation controverts the theory that the primitive mechanism is the single reflex and that behavior is built up additively.

cognition: all the intellectual activities, as distinguished from conation and affectivity. This division of mental activities was made by Ward (1886), who identified cognition with awareness of changes in the sensory continuum, that is, with intellection or knowledge.

cohesion: the unification of the various parts of a Gestalt by the principle of closure, whereby the Gestalt acquires a degree of stability (Koffka, 1925).

cold spot: a minute area which responds to an appropriate stimulus creating a sensation of coldness (Blix, 1882). The procedure usually followed is to explore the skin surface with a blunt cone which has been cooled a few degrees below skin temperature. Roughly, there are ten cold spots to one warm spot. Cold spots can be stimulated by warm stimuli (paradoxical cold, von Frey, 1895).

collective unconscious: Jung's theory (1928) about an inherited, racial unconscious mind, from which individual conscious and unconscious minds emerge. It displays itself in the disordered thinking of the psychotic, and occasionally in the dreams or the neurotic behavior of the non-psychotic individual. It consists of deep instincts and archetypes (primitive patterns of thought).

Colombier, Jean (1736–1789): French psychiatrist who tried to arouse public opinion about the need for better care and treatment of mentally disordered persons.

color: visual qualities differentiated on the basis of hue, saturation, or brilliance. Titchener (1897) reported that the normal individual can differentiate among 32,820 sensory elements of colors.

color-blindness: inability to discriminate colors. Achromatopsia (total color-blindness) is rare; dyschromatopsia (partial color-blindness) occurs in 4% to 7% of males and 0.5% females. Deuteranopia is green-blindness; protanopia, red-blindness. The phenomena of color-blindness (Daltonism) were first described by John Dalton (1794).

color contrast: the effect of a background of colored paper upon a gray patch superimposed thereon, the gray taking on the hue of the complementary of the background (van Musschenbroek, 1768).

color mixer: apparatus on which colored disks may be rotated, thus fusing light waves (Maxwell, 1855). Some colors blend; others cancel (Newton, 1704). Later investigators have worked out various laws of color mixing, especially by using disks which can be interlaced (Maxwell, 1855, method).

color pyramid: Titchener's graphic representation of the manner in which primary colors combine to form the 32,820 individual elements of visual sensation (1897). At the four sides are red, green, blue, and yellow; black at the bottom, white at the top.

color zones: the differential sensitivity of various parts of the retina to various colors (Young, 1801). The actual discovery of color zones is usually attributed to Purkinje (1825).

coma: state of unconsciousness from which the individual cannot be aroused by orders or other external methods.

commissural fibers: nerve fibers which unite the two hemispheres of the brain or the two sides of the spinal cord.

common sensibility: Hamilton's term (1859) for tactual sensations.

community: a primary, inclusive social grouping, with identifications of interests and with suspicion towards outgroups, the members living within a short distance from one another and finding within the grouping an opportunity to satisfy their needs.

comparative psychology: the division of psychology concerned with likeness and differences in the behavior of various lower organisms. Aristotle is credited with the original observations, and Darwin (1859) gave great impetus to the science. Thorndike (1898) was the first to use the exact technique of laboratory experimentation in this field.

compensation: a means of achieving a measure of satisfaction when the primary motive is blocked (Adler, 1917). Compensations may be either direct or indirect. In direct compensation (over-compensation), the individual redoubles efforts to surmount the barrier; in indirect compensation, the individual seeks to discover goals which may be achieved and which will, thereby, lessen the feelings of inferiority. Social feeling is (according to Adler) the true and inevitable compensation for the weakness of individuals.

competition: striving for individual triumph over other persons who are also seeking to triumph. The term refers also to rivalry between motives as well as to struggles between persons. Darwin's theory of struggle for survival (1859) led to the belief that it is an innate drive or instinct; many contemporary thinkers attribute it to the results of social pressures.

complacency: contentment, complete satisfaction. According to Raup (1925), the basic drive is that of achieving, or maintaining, complacency.

complementary color: the color which, when mixed in proper amounts, gives grayish white (Newton, 1704). Grassmann (1853) demonstrated that every color has a complementary.

completion test: Ebbinghaus' procedure (1905) of presenting the subject with material from which certain letters, words, or phrases have been omitted, the missing parts to be supplied to make a meaningful whole. He believed that such a test is a satisfactory way of measuring intelligence.

complex: an emotionally charged constellation of ideas, which may be either conscious or unconscious (Freud). McDougall (1923) would restrict the term to denote morbid, unwholesome trends; and use *sentiment* for wholesome, desirable ones.

Complex Psychology: C. G. Jung's term for his system of psychology (1925), which, however, is best known in America as Analytic Psychology.

complication experiment: Wundt's adaptation (1862) of

astronomers' method of determining reaction time when either a visual or an auditory stimulus were likely to be given. Wundt's experiment required the subject to make one motor response after he had identified the stimulus which he was directed to respond to from among several stimuli presented simultaneously.

compound tone: Titchener's term (1897) for a tone which a trained introspectionist can analyze into the lowest partial or fundamental and the upper partials, thus repeating in sensation the mathematical analysis of the ratios.

comprehension test: a series of questions about practical situations, devised by Binet (1905) for inclusion in his scale for measurement of intelligence.

compromise-formation: a term used by psychoanalysts to denote both symptomatic acts and manneristic acts (Healy, 1930), which appear to be unintentional, trivial, unmotivated, but which are determined by repressions. The ego and/or the super-ego combine with the id to allow them expression in temporary, insignificant outlets.

compulsion: irrational behavior which the individual feels that he must carry out, though it serves no conscious purpose other than to remove the disquietude which would arise if it were not performed.

compulsion neurosis: according to the psychoanalysts, a squandering of psychic energy in compulsive-obsessive behavior (useless acts or absurd thoughts). The compulsive-obsessive trends either reveal repressed wishes or indicate penances for guilt.

compulsion repetition: a psychoneurotic disorder in which the individual occupies himself with trivial behavior, though eager to go on to more important tasks. Psychoanalysts say that it is an attempt to escape from infantile feelings of anxiety or guilt.

Comte, Auguste (1798–1857): French philosopher who introduced the term *sociology* and who regarded the mind as the product of socialization rather than as a function of the brain. He was interested in the influences of social and political events upon human behavior.

conation: a term introduced by Ward (1886) to denote that part of the mind which is implied by such words as *willing, desire, aversion, motivation,* and the like.

concentration: the act of focusing attention upon a restricted range of elements in a total situation, these elements contributing to the achievement of a purpose or need of the individual.

concept: a mental activity which brings two or more situations, experiences, or objects into a relationship; also, the sum-total of past experiences brought to bear upon a given situation.

concept development: the genesis of meanings, particularly with reference to the growth of experience whereby stimuli acquire significance for the individual.

concept, egocentric: Piaget's term (1929) for the personalized meanings which young children assign uncritically to physical events. In a broader sense, it refers to any meaning which is centered in the individual as the point of reference in the universe.

concept generalization: the process whereby concepts are widened to subsume classes. In valid concept generalization, the individual notes points of likeness and difference among the separate objects or experiences, and then tests by the method of varying the concomitants to check upon the logic of the common thread running through them.

conceptual color: the artist's use of color to bring out the meaning, rather than to reproduce exactly the colors of the objects in the actual scene. Perspective, lights, shadows, and the like involve the use of conceptual color by the painter.

concussion: the result of a blow on the head, the effects being a loss of consciousness, weakened pulse, and the like. A partial shock may affect recall of events immediately prior to the trauma (retrograde amnesia) or those which follow immediately afterwards (anterograde amnesia), even though the individual may not lose consciousness (as in the case of an athlete who receives a blow on the head). Both types of amnesia are often reported by those who experienced severe concussion.

condensation: a psychoanalytic mechanism whereby much pent-up (repressed) psychic energy is given expression in a limited outlet. Nicknames, neologisms, certain gestures, and dream symbols are examples.

Condillac, Etienne Bonnot de (1715-1780): French philosopher who applied the doctrine of mechanism to empirical psychology and developed sensationistic elementarism. This is the theory that all mental life arises from simple sensations, and hence that any complex state can be resolved into the sensory elements out of which it was built up.

conditioned reflex: Anrep's translation (1927) of Pavlov's discovery (1890) that a response will be elicited by a stimulus which frequently preceded the adequate (unconditioned) stimulus. The best-known example is that of the dog which salivates at the sound of a bell, this sound having frequently been made just before food was presented.

conditioned response: the response to a situation which originally was inadequate to elicit it, but which, through repetition or strong emotional re-enforcement, acquired almost as great a potency as the situation originally the only adequate one. It is an extension of the Pavlovian description of conditioned reflexes made in order to account for more complex (often socialized) types of responses.

cones: receptors in the retina which respond in daylight vision (von Kries, 1894). These cells were first identified by Kölliker (1854) as differing from rods (which respond in twilight vision, as von Kries demonstrated).

confabulation: in Rorschach Inkblot protocols (1922), the tendency of the subject to be carried away by his illogical, more or less abstract type of thinking.

configuration: an organized whole that cannot be broken down into elements without losing its meaning, and that, consequently, is more than the sum of the elements out of which it is composed. Ehrenfels (1890) introduced the concept of form-qualities into psychology, and Wertheimer (1912) founded Gestalt Psychology, which developed the doctrine and grounded it upon an experimental basis.

conflict: in the psychoanalytic sense, a condition of psychic tension resulting from a repressed wish or from ambivalent instinctual drives. Allport (1923) differentiates between conflicts between two or more persons (overt conflict), and the struggle between rival impulses within the individual (covert conflict).

conformity behavior: that type of behavior in which (Allport, 1933) common segments of habits (institutionalized) are involved and which fits the J curve. That is, all except a relatively small number conform to the folkways, laws, or mores imposed by society.

confusion: either a disturbance or a clouding of consciousness (Bleuler, 1930). Among the causes are the following: fever, intense emotions, mental deficiency, and men-

tal disorders. Deliria are confusional states with hallucinations and delusions; twilight (crepuscular) states are
more or less well-systematized confusions. Autopsychic
confusions relate to personal identity; somatopsychic,
to the body of the patient; and allopsychic, to other
people and to the environment (Wernicke, *c.* 1875).

congenital: any condition or trait which exists at birth.

conoid body: the pineal gland.

Connectionism: Thorndike's system (1913–1914), which emphasizes the connections (S–R bonds) between the stimulus and the response.

connectors: the nervous mechanisms which mediate between
receptors and effectors.

Conolly, John (1794–1866): English psychiatrist who developed the method of treating patients without the use
of restraint. His theories about the value of non-restraint
were debated heatedly for many years.

consanguinity: blood relationship; descent from a common
ancestor.

conscience: the organized system of habits which are evaluated by reference to an ethical code. The code sets arbi-
trary standards whereby actions are adjudged either right
or wrong. According to psychoanalysis, it is the same as
the super-ego.

consistency reaction: the self-consistency of a person with
reference to the sum-total of all traits or the tendency of
the person to manifest a given trait under all circumstances (Woodworth, 1940).

consonance: the pleasing harmony resulting from the play-
ing of a note with its third, fifth, eighth, etc. Helmholtz
said that it is a learned preference; Stumpf, innate.

constancy hypothesis: the one-to-one correspondence between the stimulus and the sensation, a point of view

which Condillac formulated (1754) and against which Gestaltists have protested.

constancy of the IQ: the tendency of the intelligence quotient to remain unchanged between successive tests of the same individual over a period of years. Some psychologists refer to it as a "dogma" and point out that Binet himself did not subscribe to it (1909); others defend the theory of a great degree of stability in the intelligence quotient.

constant error: the error due to the apparatus, the reaction-time of the observer, or some other factor which causes the results to deviate from the true value. In psychophysics, Fechner was the first to report it (1860).

constellation: a psychoanalytic term for a group of ideas with a strong, but not repressed, affective tone. In a complex, the affects are repressed.

constitution: the totality of the anatomy and the physiology of the body. The term is used by psychoanalysts to connote the established habits (mechanisms) of the individual.

constitutional excitement and depression: mental disorders which are not caused by adventitious factors but which arise from the physiological condition of the patient (Bleuler, 1930).

constitutional psychopathic states: Kraepelin's term (1883) for an ill-defined category of disorders in which he placed such symptoms as the following: uncontrolled excitement, despondency, homicidal impulses, chronic thievery, pyromania, sex perversions, and wanderlust. He believed that such individuals are the result of bad heredity, and hence degenerates. He distinguished a class of disorders which he called *psychopathic personalities.* These include the pathological liar, the swindler, malingerers, born criminals, and unstable individuals. The classification has been criticized by many psychiatrists.

constitutional types: personality make-ups which correspond to morphological characteristics. Kretschmer (1921) identified the asthenic build (tall and slender) with schizothymic traits (introversion, formalism, idealism); the pyknic (rounded, short, heavy body-cavities), with cyclothymia (moody, but usually happy; extraverted, realistic); athletic (normal); and dysplastic (deformed, out of proportion)—the latter two tending towards introversion. (*Leptosome* and *asthenic* are the same.) Sheldon (1940, 1942) identified the following: ectomorph (fragile build) associated with cerebrotonia (intellectualism); mesomorph (bone and muscle), with somatotonia (assertiveness, athletic); endomorph (digestive viscera), viscerotonia (love of ease). Many other systems have been proposed, the most influential of the older ones being that developed by Lombroso (1876) to account for habitual criminals.

constriction: applied by users of the Rorschach Inkblot Test to individuals who lack spontaneity and ease; overly repressed.

contagion, social: the spread of a fad or an attitude, particularly when the emotional component is large, from one person to another. According to Tarde (1895), contagion is explained by the theory of imitation; but later investigators have criticized this theory (*e.g.*, F. Allport, 1923).

contamination: the organization of a concept by joining two or more irreconcilable concepts (Rorschach, 1922).

content psychology: Wundt's system, in which the contents of the mind (sensory elements) are isolated by experimentation (1862). Opposed to content is the act psychology of Brentano (1874). Content versus act was once an important controversial issue in psychology.

context theory: Titchener's explanation (1909) of how meaning is derived by means of images which are brought to bear upon the perception of a sensation, the appropriate image giving the name to the sense impression. It was developed as a refutation of the imageless-thought theory (Würzburg School), but it was first mentioned by Berkeley (1709).

contiguity, law of: Aristotle's principle of association of ideas which states that when two or more ideas are experienced together the revival of one tends to revive the others.

contiguous receptor: a receptor which is stimulated only when some form of energy comes into direct contact with it or with its accessory processes (hence contrasted with distance receptor).

continence: abstinence from sex relations.

continuous data: variables which are separated only by infinite gradations.

continuum: a field of experience which, though it may be broken into elements, is a whole.

contrast, law of: Aristotle's principle of association of ideas which states that the revival of one idea tends to effect the revival of its opposite.

contrast, simultaneous: the spatial juxtaposition of opposed sensory impressions (usually colors) whereby the value of each is enhanced.

contrast, successive: the temporal juxtaposition of two or more opposed sensory impressions or other mental processes, whereby the intensity of each is enhanced.

contrectation: the impulse to touch members of the opposite sex indiscriminately (H. Ellis, 1910).

control, experimental: the procedure whereby provision is made to equalize the effects of variables which otherwise would invalidate the experiment.

controlled analysis: a psychoanalysis by a student who works under the tutelage of an accredited analyst.

controlled association: a response which is limited by the instructions given before the stimulus is presented. Spearman (1927) stated that difficult controlled-association tests (opposites; analogies) are among the best measures of general intelligence.

convergence: the inward turning of the eyes to focus upon a stimulus within a twenty-foot distance. Wundt (1859–1861) conducted the first important experiments dealing with the relation between convergence and depth perception.

conversation: a more or less lengthy talk-exchange among two or more persons. Piaget (1925) described the collective monologue, in which the auditor's presence stimulates the speaker but in which the talk is not adapted to the interest of the listener (a type of soliloquizing in public); and the adapted-information type, in which the auditor's interests are fully taken into account by the speaker.

conversion: a radical change in behavior patterns which is more or less enduring and which (usually) implies a reorientation to religion (Starbuck, 1899). Some religionists distinguish between two types of conversion: the struggle to escape from sin, and the struggle to achieve the larger life.

conversion hysteria: a psychoneurotic reaction to conflict in which the id and the super-ego requirements are satisfied by the conversion of the repressed wish into a painful or unpleasant physiological symptom.

conviction: the ultimate in assurance regarding the validity of a belief.

convolution: a convex fold of the brain.

convulsant: any drug or method of shock which produces muscular spasms.

convulsion therapy: the artificial induction of convulsions in order to effect a cure or palliation of a mental disorder. The method was first used by Sakel (1924).

coöperation: the subordination of egocentric interests to the welfare of the group in joint endeavors.

coördination: according to Dewey (1896), the organization of means with reference to a comprehensive end. It also means the integration of antagonistic muscles (reciprocal innervation; synergy).

copiopia: hysterical eyestrain.

coprolalia: filthy talk by mentally disordered individuals.

coprophagia: the eating of excreta by disordered individuals.

coprophilia: extreme interest in the act and the products of excretion, which, according to psychoanalysis, is a normal phase of the anal-erotic stage of development.

cord: a tendon; the spinal cord.

Coriat, Isadore (1875–1943): American psychiatrist who was deeply interested in abnormal psychology, described a case of multiple personality, and stated that some neuroses have no sex etiology (contrary to the Freudian view).

corium: the deep layer of the skin.

cornea: the transparent area (one-sixth the surface circumference) in the anterior of the eyeball. It is continuous with the sclerotic membrane. Normally a sensitive region, it may be touched in certain forms of major hysteria and catatonia without pain being displayed by the patient.

Cornelius, Hans (1863–   ): German psychologist who,

with Meinong and others, worked on the problem of
form-qualities (Gestaltqualitäten).

corpora **quadrigemina:** four rounded eminences in the mid-
brain, the superior (anterior) mediating vision; the inferior (posterior), hearing.

Corti, Alfonso (1822–1876): Italian histologist who investigated the structure of the inner ear. He described what is
known as the organ of Corti, a complicated structure
which contains the receptor endings of the cochlear nerve
fibers.

Coué, Emile (1857–1926): French pharmacist who developed a technique of self-suggestion for therapeutic purposes ("New Nancy School"). He taught that heterosuggestion is really auto-succession.

counseling: the psychotherapeutic relationship in which an
individual (the client) receives direct help from an ad-
viser (directive counseling) or finds an opportunity to
release negative feelings and thus clear the way for positive growth in personality (non-directive counseling).
The former is the traditional type; the latter was introduced by Rogers (1942).

craze: a fashion which is adopted with great suddenness,
attracts wide attention, and then is quickly dropped.
Those who participate in a craze have considerable,
though temporary, enthusiasm for it.

creative synthesis: Wundt's term (1891) for the apperceptive process in which elements are brought together into
more or less meaningful relationships, ranging from mere
agglutination up to a concept. J. S. Mill (1869) introduced the concept of "mental chemistry" to account for
this fusion of ideas.

creative thinking: the achievement of a new relationship
among the parts of experience, which, according to

Wallas (1926), has four stages: preparation, incubation, inspiration or illumination, and verification. The creative idea (third stage) comes as a flash of insight or a sudden thought.

cretinism: a type of mental deficiency which is associated with hypofunctioning of the thyroid gland. Cretins are small, with short arms and legs, dry skin, sallow complexion, protruding abdomens, and relatively large faces.

criminal psychology: the application of psychological techniques to the detection, conviction, and re-adjustment of the social offender. Münsterberg (c. 1900) was the first to apply psychology to court-room procedures.

crisis: Mesmer's term (1766) for spasmodic convulsions which he induced in his patients (by mesmerism) and which he considered to have great therapeutic value.

criterion: anything which is used to validate a test, interview, rating scale, and the like. School grades, for example, are the criterion for the validation of a test of scholastic aptitude.

critical ratio: the difference between two normally distributed sets of scores divided by the standard error.

critical score: the score on a test (or battery of tests) which separates the unsuccessful from the successful candidates for preferment (as for a job).

cross-transfer: the advantage which accrues to the unpracticed side from practice involving the other side (as in handwriting or other motor functions).

crowd: a number of individuals under the influence of common emotional excitement, primitive impulses, and singleness of purpose (Le Bon, 1913). It is variously used; hence the denotation is uncertain.

crowd mind: the doctrine that a totally different mentality takes possession of individuals when they form groups.

The vogue of this concept has been great in Europe (Hegel's philosophy and Nazi practices giving support to it), but in America it has found only a few adherents (McDougall, 1928, being one of the exceptions).

crush: a sudden, intense affection, usually on the part of a young pupil towards the teacher.

cry, epileptic: the sound made by the sudden expulsion of air from the lungs of the grand mal patient in the initial phase of an attack. It was once believed to be the anguished cry of the individual as demons took possession of his body.

cryanesthesia: inability to obtain a sense impression of cold.

cryesthesia: the sense of cold, the receptors of which are cold spots (Blix, 1882).

cryotherapy: treatment by reducing the temperature of the body to 80 or 90 degrees Fahrenheit for a day or two. This variety of shock is said to be a palliative in some types of mental disorders.

cryptogenic: of unknown origin.

cryptomenorrhea: the experience of all the subjective accompaniments of menstruation but without the flow.

cryptomnesia: the revival of former experiences without awareness of the circumstances under which they originally occurred.

crystal gazing: the projection of mental images upon a crystal ball (or any shiny surface) while making strong anticipatory responses (expectancy) and while under a trance-like influence.

cue: an element of an antecedent situation which has potency to redintegrate all or part of the original response (consequent).

cul-de-sac: a blind alley in a maze; an impasse in trial-and-error behavior.

culture: the mores, folkways, institutions, and traditions which distinguish one group, nation, or race from another.

culture, personal: the level of achievement of an individual in the mastery of all that constitutes the culture of his group or nation or race.

culture-epochs theory: G. Stanley Hall's extension of the principle of biological evolution, in which he stated that the individual recapitulates the cultural development of the human race in his development.

culture lag: the tendency for well-established habits to persist after they have become outmoded by the general advances in culture.

cumulative record folder: the folder which contains all data for a pupil from the time of entrance into school until graduation. Personal evaluations by teachers, course marks, biographical notes, and test scores may be included, thus furnishing invaluable material for longitudinal studies of some phases of child and adolescent psychology.

cunnilingus: a form of perversion in which the tongue is applied to the vulva or clitoris.

cunnus: the external genitalia of the female.

curve, normal probability: the graphic representation of the theoretically possible distribution of an infinite number of scores which vary by chance, having a bell-shaped appearance. The mathematical properties of this curve were described by Gauss (1809), a German astronomer.

custom: the totality of established practices regarding socially acceptable behavior.

cutaneous sensation: the totality of awareness arising from the application of various stimuli to the skin surface. Weber (1834) began the exploration of this field; Blix (1882) and Goldscheider (1884) located separate points which respond, respectively, to cold, warmth, and pressure; and von Frey (1894) located pain spots.

Cuvier, Georges Leopold C. F. (1769–1832): French scientist who served as chairman of a committee to investigate the claims of phrenology for recognition (Gall and Spurzheim being involved as subjects of the report). The committee (on which Pinel was a member) returned an adverse report (1808).

cyclic disorder: one which has periods of remission and exacerbation.

cyclothymia: Kretschmer's term (1918) for alternations in moods, associated with the pyknic build. Kahlbaum had introduced the term (1882) to denote a condition of alternating moods of joy and depression.

cynicism: the philosophy founded by Antisthenes (*c.* 425 B.C.), who taught that natural impulses ought to be repressed and that man should cultivate his intellect. He established the belief that feelings, emotions, and appetites are base, unworthy parts of human nature. The term also implies a compensatory dislike for popular esthetic and ethical values by some one who is struggling to overcome a feeling of inadequacy to cope successfully with other persons for status.

cynophobia: intense fear of dogs.

cyclopean eye: the localization of binocularly-seen objects in a single, median position. In target-shooting the tendency has to be overcome, though it is normally evident in uniocular vision.

Cyrenaicism: the crassly hedonistic philosophy first taught by Aristippus (*c.* 400 B.C.). He believed that the highest good is to extract from each fleeting moment the maximum of pleasure. According to Freud, the id is governed by this type of principle. Psychologists have made a great deal of use of the doctrine of the Cyrenaics in theoretical interpretations of the learning process. A pleasurable outcome of an act is supposed to favor its repetition; a painful or annoying outcome tends to extinguish the act from an individual's repertoire of responses (Thorndike, 1913, for example).

cytoplasm: all the protoplasm of the cell, with the exception of the endoplasm, the fluid substances in the meshes of the protoplasm (*paraplasm*), and the nucleus.

D

D: Rorschach symbol for a response to a large, commonly selected detail in the inkblots.

d: Rorschach symbol for a response to a small, uncommonly selected detail in the inkblots.

dactylogy: the science of spelling out words by the fingers, as by deaf mutes.

dactylomegaly: abnormally large fingers.

damp: to check the vibrations of a tuning fork.

Dalton, John: an Englishman whose color-blindness was described in 1684. Color-blindness is often called Daltonism; a color-blind individual, a Daltonian.

dancing mania: an outbreak of hysterical dancing by persons under the influence of religious ecstasy, which occurred in Aix-la-Chapelle in 1347 and spread through the Netherlands. After a few weeks it died out, though there were recurrences during the next century.

danger situation: one which, according to psychoanalysis, causes the ego to adopt symptoms or to impose severe inhibitions, the principal causes being anxiety about castration, loss of love, and social status (Freud, 1924).

Daquin, Joseph (1733–1815): French psychiatrist who influenced Pinel and who did much to advance the cause of humane treatment of mental patients.

dark adaptation: the adjustment of the eye to a low intensity of light (Aubert, 1865).

Darwin, Charles Robert (1809–1882): English biologist who stimulated the genetic approach in psychology (1859), developed a theory of evolution (Darwinism),

and made a careful study of emotions in man and animals
(1872).

Darwin, Erasmus (1721–1802): grandfather of Charles
Darwin. He wrote on associationism (1794), and he
sought to systematize the accounts of mental disorders.

Darwinian tubercle: a blunt projection on the upper part
of the outer ear, once considered to be a stigma indicating atavism.

data: items collected in a psychological investigation or experiment. They may be qualitative (statistics of attributes) or quantitative (statistics of variables). Data not
expressed in statistical or logical form are called raw
data. Those which may take any value within the range
are known as continuous data; those which may take only
certain variate values are discrete data.

day-blindness: low visual acuity in daylight, as a result of
scotoma, nutritional disorders, or other conditions affecting the sensitivity of the retina.

day-dreaming: vicarious gratification for repressed or
thwarted wishes by indulgence in fantasy. In schizophrenia, the day-dream may be substituted for reality in
the behavior of the patient.

daymare: an intense condition of fear during the day, thought
to be indicative of the imminence of a convulsive disorder
or to indicate some other type of organic pathology.

Dd: Rorschach's symbol for a rarely selected detail on the
inkblot test. Loepfe used this symbol for a normal detail
selected by children under age 12 or 14.

dd: Klopfer's symbol (1942) for a response to a minute detail
on the Rorschach inkblots.

deaf mute: a person unable to hear or to speak, other than
by unintelligible gutturals. Laura Bridgman (1829–1889)

is the most frequently cited example in the literature of psychology.

death instinct: Freud's term (1914) for the drive to injure one's self or other persons and to destroy. It (the *Thanatos principle*) has its counterpart in the biological principle of catabolism; and it has a greater force than the life (*Eros*) principle.

debility: general weakness (*asthenia*).

decadence: a psychoneurotic condition in which abnormal, eccentric, morbid, sensuously mystical interests predominate. The psychological connotation of the term arises from a 19th century group of French writers.

deceit test: any of a large number of measures of honesty and trustworthiness, first used extensively by Hartshorne and May (1928) in the Character Education Inquiry.

decibel: one-tenth of a bel; hence a convenient unit for measuring intensity levels of sound.

decile: one of the ten groups of scores which are organized by nine equidistant points on the x-axis of a frequency distribution.

decussation: the X-like crossing of nerves, the principal ones being the optic chiasm and the crossing of nerve fibers in the medulla.

deduction: the application of general principles to specific instances; reasoning from the general to the concrete.

deep reflex: one which is elicited by percussion of tendons or bones or points of insertions of muscles.

defecation: the excretion of feces, which, according to psychoanalysis, is an act of great importance in the determination of personality formation. The infant discovers that the act has erotic aspects; hence it becomes a primary interest in the first year of life. Retention, in order to heighten pleasure, is learned by some young infants.

defense mechanism: loosely, the maintenance of the sense of personal worth by resorting to fictions. In psycho-analysis, the unconscious attempts to dispose of unwelcome instinctual tendencies by the ego. Various mental symptoms may be adopted, such as delusions, hallucinations, obsessions and compulsions, and morbid fears.

deficiency, mental: lack of intelligence.

degenerate: one whose moral behavior is at complete variance with the mores of the community. The term is often used by laymen, but it seldom occurs in textbooks on psychiatry.

degeneration: a reversion to a more primitive type of behavior in sexual outlets, as a result of organic pathologies. According to Morel (1857), mental disorders are the result of "hereditary degeneration."

degrees of mental deficiency: idiots, imbeciles, and morons. In England, these are subdivided into low, medium, and high; and *feeble-minded* is used with about the same connotation as *moron* in America. (Tredgold, 1909).

déjà entendu: a disorder of recognition in which the individual mistakenly believes that he has previously heard a given tale.

déjà vu: the illusion of having previously seen something which, actually has never been encountered before. It is associated with fatigue, sleepiness, or psychotic conditions.

delayed response: a response which ensues after a time interval has elapsed following the application of the stimulus. In Pavlov's technique (1890), the continuous ringing of the bell (substitute stimulus) before presentation of food to the dog will establish a delayed conditioned response, the time interval being approximately that which elapsed between the start of the bell and the food. When the time gap is unfilled, a weak (trace) reaction may be established.

deliberation: reflective thinking.

Delboeuf, Jean L. R. (1831–1896): Belgian psychologist who worked on the problem of sensation differences, and whose views influenced Titchener.

délire: a term used by French psychiatrists to designate a disorder of affects.

delirium: mental disturbance resulting from fever, intoxication, disease, or trauma. The disturbance is characterized by hallucinations, rare illusions, disorientation, excitement, and the like.

delirium tremens: disorder caused by excessive indulgence in alcoholic drinks and described first (1813) by Sutton. It is said to occur after several years of addiction and to be partially the result of avitaminosis (Bleuler), the attack often being precipitated by a special occasion. Prominent symptoms are hallucinations of small, moving objects or animals; memory disturbances; confabulations; pseudohumor or intense fear. The course lasts from a day to more than a week.

delusion: unfounded belief retained in spite of all evidence to demonstrate its untenability. A delusion arises out of inner needs (Kraepelin); hence it is not tested by reference to canons of logic. Allopsychic delusions relate to the environment; autopsychic delusions, to the personality of the patient; somatopsychic delusions, to the patient's body. Delusions are classified as systematized or unsystematized; permanent or transitory; bizarre, irrational, or self-consistent; grandiose, persecutory, erotic, nihilistic.

dementia: impairment of mental functions as a result of acquired (not hereditary) factors (Tuke, 1892). The term is usually restricted to disorders associated with brain pathologies, such as the results of drug addiction, paresis, senility, and the like; but it is also used in connection with the deteriorative changes in some schizophrenic patients, even by those who regard this disorder as functional.

dementia praecox: Kraepelin's term (1898) for a deteriorative mental disorder affecting the intellectual processes and making its onset in the post-adolescent years. He expressed the opinion that the etiologic factors might be metabolism pathology. It takes the following forms: hebephrenia (Hecker, 1871); catatonia (Kahlbaum, 1874); paranoid; and paraphrenia (Kahlbaum, 1874). Bleuler's term *schizophrenia* has largely replaced *dementia praecox*.

Democritus (460–370 B.C.): Greek philosopher who developed a consistent theory of materialism.

demonomania: the obsession that one is influenced by evil spirits or witches. In the Western World, this mass delusion was initiated by the publication (1478) of *Malleus Maleficarum*, and it culminated in the execution of witches in Salem, Massachusetts (1692–1693). Morbid fear of witches, demons, or evil spirits, is called *demonophobia*; and the folk-lore systematizations of beliefs regarding them, demonology.

dendrite: the short branch of the nerve cell which conducts the impulse to the axon. Golgi (1873) devised a method of staining neurons to make dendrites visible under the microscope. Kappers (1908) named the process of growth of dendrites *neurobiotaxis*.

dependency: in mental hygiene, a lack of self-reliance, and hence a tendency to seek the aid of other persons in important decisions.

depersonalization: the loss of a sense of personality, of reality, or of identity. Reil described this disorder in 1796.

depression: melancholia, gloom, dejection. One of the earliest examples in the literature is the case of King Saul (I Samuel 16). In agitated depression, there is great activity, without the flight of ideas which accompanies mania or the stupor which usually is a concomitant of depression. In reactive depression, the dysphoric condition disappears after the problem-situation has been resolved.

depth psychology: that which deals with so-called unconscious phenomena, as contrasted with the conventional emphasis upon objective psychology or analysis of conscious processes. The term is often applied to psychoanalysis because of its emphasis upon deep, unconscious determinants of behavior.

dereistic thinking: that which is characterized by disregard of logic, reality testing, and experience (Bleuler, 1924). According to Bleuler, it is the type of thinking which is found in daydreams, mythology, and paranoid schizophrenia, the motivation coming from the innermost nature of the person.

derived primary attention: according to Titchener (1896), secondary attention, which often results after an initial period when attention must be forced.

dermographia: a condition in which markings made on the skin with a blunt instrument raise welts which are visible for periods of from five minutes to a day later. It is considered to be attributable to abnormal disturbance in the equilibrium of the vasomotor mechanisms of the skin.

desensitization: reduction of tension pertaining to a defect, real or imaginary, as a result of psychological counseling or psychiatric treatment. The patient is taught how to view with equanimity a situation hitherto considered to be intolerable.

desire: either a want or an aversion, the connotation being that something in the present experience of the individual has upset equanimity and that purposeful striving is initiated as a result. The term is sometimes used to refer to a more or less conscious upheaval in complacency, but it does not imply such a definite goal as a wish. There appears, however, to be no consistency in the use of such terms as *want, drive, appetite, motive, wish,* and *desire,* each writer formulating his own definitions.

deterioration: continuous impairment of a function or the totality of functions. It is marked by loss of interest, poor social adjustments, or faulty ethical behavior as well as by reduction of physical vigor. Among the tests of mental deterioration are those of Babcock (1930) and Goldstein-Sheerer (1941).

determinism: the doctrine that physical and mental conditions preclude the possibility of freedom of choice. In the ethical system of the Stoics, this theory was first expressed; and in modern times, it has been emphasized by the Freudian school of psychiatry.

detour: an indirect, not obvious way to the goal, which must be found by the human being or the animal in a problem situation. According to Thorndike and others, the detour is discovered in a process of blind trial and error; according to Köhler and others, by insight.

deuteranopia: green-blindness. According to G. Wilson (1855), this was the type of color-blindness which Dalton (the first to report his own case, 1794) had.

development: the process of maturation of an organism; hence the sequential alterations which occur from conception to maturity. Some writers distinguish this term sharply from *growth*; others consider *growth* to have more limited connotation. Hence *growth* is said to mean augmental changes; *development* (the more inclusive term), qualitative, gradual, permanent changes in mental and/or physical aspects.

developmental psychology: the application of psychological theory and principles to a study of the progressive changes which take place from conception to death, the data being drawn from phylogeny as well as from ontogeny.

deviate: one whose behavior or physique differs markedly from the average. The term is usually restricted to apply to undesirable traits or configurations of traits.

deviation: the distance of a score from some measure or reference point, such as mean, mode, median. The average deviation is obtained by dividing the sum of absolute deviations from the central tendency (usually the mean) by the number of scores. The standard deviation is the square root of the mean of the sum of the deviations squared. The quartile deviation is one-half the range between the 25-%-ile and the 50-%-ile.

dextrality: handedness, or preference for the use of the right side more than for the other in motor activities.

dextrosinistral: the use of the right hand in writing, but with a preference for the use of the left hand.

diadokokinesis: the condition of being able to make coördinated muscular movements in rapid sequence.

diagnosis: identification of a disorder by a study of various symptoms.

diagnostic test: one which assists in the location of specific difficulties or patterns of errors. In educational psychology, a diagnostic test is used to appraise the specific disabilities of a pupil in a given subject, and thus to furnish a basis for remedial instruction.

diaphragm: muscular (at circumference), tendinous (in center) wall separating the thorax from the abdomen, and the principal muscle in inspiration-expiration.

diathesis: predisposition, hereditary or adventitious, to a mental or a physical disorder.

dichoglottic stimulation: Henning's term (1916) for simultaneous application of two different substances to taste receptors.

dichorhinic stimulation: Henning's term (1916) for simultaneous application (by means of a double-olfactometer) of different odors.

dichotic stimulation: Stumpf's term (1916) for the application of diverse stimuli to both ears simultaneously (the stimulation of one ear being called *monotic*).

dichotomy: two exclusive categories, the data in the one not being in the other. The data of psychopathology are traditionally represented as being a continuum approximating the Gaussian frequency curve; recently, some writers have suggested that a dichotomy of distributions may exist, the one distribution including the normal, and the other, the pathological.

dichromatopsia: red and green blindness.

diencephalon: the between-brain, or the optic thalami and the third ventricle together with associated structures.

difference limen: the point of just noticeable difference between two stimuli. The classical experiments of the difference limen were reported by Weber in 1846.

difference tone: Tartini's term (1714) for the third tone which seems to accompany two tones of different pitch sounded together. Helmholtz (1856) recognized the importance of the discovery.

differential psychology: the application of psychological theory and procedures to the study of individual differences. This field of psychology was founded by Galton in 1883.

differentiation: Pavlov's term (1890) for the well-established conditioned reflex which can be aroused only by the conditioned stimulus most frequently used in the training periods. At first, the dog would salivate when the metronome clicked at almost any rate, but eventually the salivation would occur only when the rate used over and over again in the training was heard. Thus, the conditioned reflex is said to pass from a condition of irradiation to one of differentiation (or specificity).

diffuse sclerosis: hardening of arteries in large areas of the brain, with consequent deterioration in mental activities.

digit-span test: a measure of the span of unrelated digits (presented visually or spoken) which a subject can repeat correctly. The test was devised by Jacobs in 1887.

dilantin: a drug used in the treatment of epilepsy to reduce the frequency of seizures.

dilapidation: a condition of grave impairment of functions; severe dementia.

Dilthey, Wilhelm (1833–1911): German philosophical psychologist who (1883) taught that psychology and natural sciences are entirely unrelated, the facts pertaining to the one being unlike those of the other. Psychology must be teleological, and it must proceed by philosophical (non-experimental) methods to build up a valid body of knowledge.

dimensions of consciousness: according to Boring (1933), the successors to the Wundtian-Titchenerian attributes: attensity (clearness), extensity, intensity, protensity (temporal aspect), and quality.

diplegia: paralysis affecting both sides of the body.

diplopia: a condition of muscular imbalance in which one object is seen as two. When it occurs in one eye, the person may be malingering, hysterical, or afflicted with a cataract.

dipsomania: uncontrollable craving for alcohol.

directive counseling: the use of advice, orders, suggestions, threats, cajoling, and the like, in an interpersonal relationship dominated by the counselor, who asks certain questions and takes the responsibility for assisting the client to formulate the answers, plan a new mode of adjustment, and overcome difficulties. It is the opposite of non-directive counseling, in which the client is encouraged in free expression of negative feelings and in finding his own solution for his difficulties.

discrimeter: apparatus for measuring the ability of a human subject to distinguish between two or more stimuli by making the correct response. A serial discrimeter (measuring speed of finger movements in response to a series of stimuli visually presented) is included in the Stanford Motor Skills Unit (1928).

discrete data: those which are discontinuous, and hence do not have intermediate values.

discrimination: the act of making judgments about differences among stimuli presented simultaneously or sequentially.

disinhibition: Pavlov's term (1926) for the loss of restraint of a conditioned reflex (inhibition) when an extraneous stimulus is presented (*e.g.*, the buzzing of a fly). This is also called inhibition of the inhibition.

disorder: a generic term for any pathological condition.

dispersion: the scattering of the measures within the range and about the central tendency. The principal indices of dispersion are the following: quartile deviation (Q);

average deviation (AD or MD); and standard deviation (SD or sigma).

displacement: a Freudian mechanism (1900) whereby part or all of the unconscious (instinctual) impulse and phantasy are represented in the conscious by a surrogate, thus displacing the emotional energy from one object to another.

disposition: according to McDougall (1923), the totality of the instinctive tendencies of an individual. He taught that hereditary factors influence the quality and the quantity of instincts, and hence the dispositions vary.

dissociation: a concept proposed by Janet (1889) and developed by M. Prince (1905) of psychic tension, which, when reduced in force, causes certain mental elements to split apart from the rest. The basic theory originated in the teachings of Charcot (1872), who believed that in hysteria the stream of consciousness breaks up into diverse elements. The gradual break up of unified consciousness is called dissolution; the sudden break (as in a psychic trauma), disruption. Dissociated elements lie in the co-conscious (Prince, 1914), or in the unconscious (Freud, 1895), where they exert a potent influence upon the behavior of the individual.

dissonance: the effect produced to notes within the octave which do not fuse (Stumpf, 1890); hence the antonym of consonance (Helmholtz) or fusion (Stumpf).

distoceptor: a receptor which responds to stimuli; inability to hold a mental set until the completion of an activity.

distress: a condition of persisting affective disquietude.

distribution: the branching of a nerve fiber. Also, the arrangement of scores or measures on a psychological test or experiment.

dizygotic twins: those which are the result of fertilization (by spermatozoa) of two separate ova. Monozygotic twins (identical) are the result of fission of a single fertilized ovum.

Do: Rorschach's symbol for an oligophrenic detail selected on the inkblot test.

dolichocephaly: long, narrow head; having a cephalic index of 77.6 or less. The cephalic index is the ratio of the breadth of the skull to the length. Some writers refer to skulls above 80 as brachycephalic; those below 80 as dolichocephalic.

dominant character: that which suppresses the recessive character (Mendel, 1866) in the development of the organism. In the classical studies on the coloration of sweet pea flowers, Mendel referred to the color appearing in most of the hybrid generation as the dominant character; that which appeared in only a few, the recessive character.

Donders, Frans Cornelis (1818–1889): Dutch oculist who investigated eye movements (1875) and reaction time in discrimination between two stimuli (1868).

dorsal: back.

double-aspect theory: the view (Spinoza, 1665) that mind and body are merely separate manifestations of the one underlying principle—God. His doctrine is strictly deterministic, and it implies that God maintains a continuity of relationship between mind and body.

doubt: uncertainty preceding belief or disbelief (McDougall, 1923). In American psychology of religion, it is a period of disquietude in adolescence, which is normally followed by a religious conversion (Hall, 1891).

drainage theory: McDougall's belief (1929) that nervous impulses are shunted out from areas of higher resistance to those in which the resistance is relatively the least.

drapetomania: wanderlust, as among patients with senile dementia.

draw-a-man test: Goodenough's (1926) non-language measure of intelligence of children, the subjects being rated on keenness of observation as revealed by their drawing of a man.

dream: mental activity during sleep. Freud's theory (1900) is most widely known in modern times, though many diverse theories have been proposed in all ages. According to this theory, the manifest content symbolizes the expression of libidinal (or unconscious) wishes (which comprise the latent content). The Censor imposes disguises of the latent processes, and hence they may be obscured by the symbolizations (until they are made clear by the technique of psychoanalysis). Then their wishful nature is revealed.

drifting reaction: Boisen's phrase (1936) to characterize the simple type of schizophrenia. According to this conflictual point of view, the patient has an intolerable loss of self-respect, and hence drifts aimlessly.

drill: repetitive practice on motor or ideational material, usually in the sense of establishing factual items or skills as habits (or conditioned responses).

dromomania: wanderlust, as among patients with senile dementia.

drug deliria: excitement, confusion, hallucinations, stupefactions, and/or delusions induced by excessive use of such drugs as bromides.

dual personality: two distinct personalities in one individual, usually with amnesia for each other, but with more or less well-integrated separate personalities (Prince, 1905). The case of Mary Reynolds (1815) is the oldest in the literature. The personalities are said to alternate, to be co-conscious, or to be one-way amnesic.

dualism: the doctrine that mind and body are separate, unlike entities. Among the theories of the philosophers, the following have had an influence upon the development of modern psychology: interactionism (Descartes, 1650); epiphenomenalism (Hobbes, 1651); double-aspect theory (Spinoza, 1665); and psychophysical parallelism (Leibnitz, 1695).

DuBois-Reymond, Emil (1818–1896): German physiologist who studied the electrical phenomena of the nerve impulse and who taught Hall, Sully, and Wundt.

duct gland: a gland with a tube or channel for discharging secretions on an external or internal surface of the body. (For example, lachrymal, parotid, or sweat glands).

ductless gland: glands which do not have ducts or channels for secretion upon a surface. There are two classes of ductless glands: the endocrine glands (*e.g.*, thyroid, pituitary, pineal, and the like); and gland-like tissues, such as the spleen, coccygeal, and carotid glands, and the lymph nodes.

duplicity theory: the theory (von Kries, 1894) that rods mediate vision at low illumination (achromatic); cones, daylight vision (chromatic and achromatic).

dura mater: the membrane which forms the outer covering of brain and spinal cord.

duration: the temporal attribute of sensation, which Titchener (1905) called protensity.

dynamic psychology: that which emphasizes motivation (conation). The term often refers to a systematic formulation which incorporates some of the theories of psychoanalysis, though in a broad sense American functionalism (as opposed to content psychology) is dynamic.

dynamogenesis: a term used by Brown-Séquard (1860) to denote a principle according to which changes in the nervous system (nervous impulses) invariably find an outlet in motor activity. Baldwin (1901) spoke of mental dynamogenesis, by which he meant that sensory consciousness tends to result in motor consciousness. The doctrine was influential in early studies of sensory vs. motor reaction-times.

dynamograph: apparatus for measuring muscular strength.

dys-: Greek prefix which destroys the good sense or increases the bad sense of the root to which it is attached. Almost all of the terms with this prefix refer to organic pathologies, though writers are not consistent in this respect.

dysacousia: impairment of hearing, usually accompanied by pain when stimulated by some frequencies.

dysaphia: impairment of the sense of touch (pressure).

dysarthria: defective articulation resulting from a cerebellar disorder.

dysbulia: distortion of appetites, needs, drives, or motives, which is inimical to the health of the patient.

dyschiria: extreme awkwardness in manual tasks.

dyschromatopsia: severe color-blindness.

dysdiadochokinesis: great awkwardness in performing coordinated muscular movements in rapid succession.

dysergasia: A. Meyer's term (1910) for any marked disturbance of psychobiological functions.

dysfunction: impairment of any or all of the normal functions of the organism.

dysgeusia: serious disorder of the taste sense. As a rule the patient complains that all foods have a vile taste.

dysgnosia: impairment of perceptual functions, as a result of cerebral pathology.

dysgonadal syndrome: any type of precocious sex behavior.

dyskinesia: impairment of power to make voluntary (striped muscle) movements.

dyslalia: disorder of articulation: Some experts in speech used the term to designate articulatory disorders in which there are no demonstrable lesions in the nervous system, and in which there may or may not be malformations of speech organs.

dyslexia: impairment of ability to read, as a result of cerebral lesions.

dyslogia: inability to express thoughts in understandable speech.

dysmenorrhea: disorder of menstrual functions, particularly (in psychology) as it affects efficiency of work.

dysmimia: impairment of the ability to imitate gestures or postures.

dysmnesia: impairment of memory functions.

dysmorphia: misshaped body; dwarfism, gigantism, acromegaly, and the like.

dysnoia: depressed moods; despair; the impairment of ability to think clearly.

dysopia: generic term for any grave pathology of the eye or the accessory apparatus of the eye.

dysorexia: craving for unnatural food.

dysosmia: impairment of the olfactory sense. It is usually referred to as an omnious symptom.

dyspepsia: indigestion, such as that caused by emotional tension, anxiety, or fits of temper.

dysphasia: impairment of ability to speak clearly, as a result of cerebral lesion.

dysphemia: a generic term for grave speech disorders such as stuttering.

dysphonia: an unnatural sound to the voice.

dysphoria: gloom; anxiety; despair. The term refers to any grave abnormality in feelings and emotions (affectivity).

dyspituitarism: a generic term referring to any disorder caused by a pathology of the pituitary gland.

dyspraxia: impairment of well-established habits, as a consequence of a stroke or of other pathologies of the central nervous system.

dystrophia adiposogenitalis: a disorder (Frölich's syndrome) resulting from pathology of the hypothalamus and characterized by excessive fat, undeveloped genitalia, and absence of hair (or little hair) on pubes.

dystrophy: malnutrition.

DZw: Rorschach's symbol for a response to a large white space on the inkblot test. A small, rarely selected white space he designated as DdZw.

E: the experimenter.

ear: organ of hearing. The outer ear includes the pinna (or auricle) and the external meatus; the middle ear, the tympanic membrane, ear-ossicles (malleus, incus, and stapes), Eustachian tube, fenestra ovalis, fenestra rotunda, and accessory processes; the inner ear, the utricle and the saccule (vestibule), semicircular canals, cochlea, and accessory processes. The organ of Corti (1851) includes the receptors for hearing. Theories of the physiology of the ear have been set forth by Bell (1808), Helmholtz (1863), Rutherford (1886), Waller (1891), Wever and Bray (1930), and others. The gross anatomy of the ear was first described by Empedocles (*c.* 450 B.C.); the histology of the inner ear by Corti (1851), Reissner (1851), and Kölliker (1854).

Ebbinghaus, Hermann (1850–1909): German psychologist who investigated memory processes experimentally. He found that there is a steep increase in the number of repetitions necessary to learn series of nonsense syllables as the lists are lengthened, and that forgetting takes place most rapidly after the learning, and with a decreasing rate as the time-interval increases between learning and recalling. He devised the completion test (1897).

eccentricity: total lack of conformity to the folkways and the mores of the group. Maudsley (1867) describes eccentrics as comprising a borderland group between mental health and mental disorder.

ecdemomania: wanderlust.

ecdysiasm: impulse to disrobe in public; exhibitionism.

echographia: a type of aphasia in which written questions are copied but not answered by the patient.

echolalia: senseless repetition of words or sounds, without the intent to convey meaning to the auditor. It is a common symptom in the catatonic form of schizophrenia. Some writers have widened the meaning of the word to include the use of language by infants and children for play purposes.

echopathy: a disorder characterized by senseless repetition of words or of actions by others. The patient seems to have a morbid compulsion to imitate.

echopraxia: a common symptom in the catatonic form of schizophrenia, in which the patient mimics the observer.

eclampsia: a convulsion during pregnancy, labor, or the immediate after-period.

eclectic psychology: that which draws from various "schools" or divergent theories; hence a presentation of psychological facts and theories without any commitment to a specific frame of reference.

ecology: in social psychology, the relationships between people and their physical environment; migrations of people and the adaptation of their institutions to fit the demands of climate, geography, soil, water supply, and the like, of their new environment.

economics, mental: the psychoanalytic principle which states that adjustments requiring the least expenditure of effort take precedence over those which would necessitate greater effort, even though the latter might conceivably be better.

ecstasy: an exalted condition which may take the form of immobile postures or excited behavior, usually with complete indifference to surroundings and with visions (Pratt, 1920), as in states of religious fervor.

ectoderm: the outermost layer of the embryo, from which the central nervous system (and other tissues) are developed. It is also called the epiblast.

ectomorphy: Sheldon's term (1940) for a body-build characterized by long, fragile bones, and highly developed nervous system, lying, as it were, with little protection by other tissues. Associated with this build is the cerebrotonic temperament (Sheldon, 1942). The cerebrotonic is said to be restrained in behavior, to prefer solitude, to be intent and ambitious, and to be inclined towards timidity.

ectomia: excision, as of a portion of the brain. Franz (1907) first reported retention of well-established habits in cats and monkeys that had been subjected to partial ectomy of the brain.

edema, cerebral: excess fluid in the ventricles or outside the brain substance and within the membranes covering the brain.

educational age: the age of a pupil as determined by a battery of subject tests or a general achievement test based upon the school curriculum, expressed in terms of the chronological age of the average pupil to make that score.

educational psychology: application of psychological facts, theories, and methods to a study of such topics as learning, motivation, individual differences, memory, intelligence, guidance, appraisal, and the like, as they relate to educational procedures. The "father of educational psychology" is Herbart (1776–1841). The early important textbooks were written by Bain (1878), Claparède (1905), and Thorndike (1913–14).

E.E.G.: electroencephalogram. Clinical application of the E.E.G. was established by Berger (1924), though the phenomena of electrical concomitants of brain activity was known as early as 1874.

effect, law of: Thorndike's controversial principle (1913) which states that a satisfying outcome stamps in, and an annoying outcome stamps out, a modifiable connection between a stimulus and a response. This is a statement of the principle of psychological hedonism, traceable to the ancients and brought into modern psychology by Hobbes (1651).

effector: a response mechanism, such as a muscle or gland.

efferent fiber: one which transmits the nervous impulse from the brain or the cord to an effector.

efficiency: a term borrowed from mechanics to denote the ratio between output (and accuracy) on the one hand and expenditure of energy on the other hand.

ergesis: insomnia or a condition of extreme alertness.

ego: in the Freudian sense (1927), the organization forced upon the id (which obeys the pleasure principle) by the demands of the environment (reality principle). It is partly conscious and partly unconscious; it goes to sleep, but it still censors the id; and it has to serve the demands of the id, the external world, and the super-ego (conscience). In the non-Freudian sense, it refers to the self (*e.g.*, James, 1890).

egocentricism: a concept originating in the work of Piaget (1924) which states that young children tend not to adapt their speech to the background of their auditor, not to test their conclusions regarding natural phenomena, and to disregard the realities of situations. In language development, for instance, the child of two uses monologues; next comes the stage of the collective monologue; and finally, that of adapted information. Concepts of the physical universe display similar egocentric trends. Freud has said that (from the standpoint of psychoanalysis) egoism is the counterpart of narcissism (direction of the libido upon the individual himself).

egomania: the ultimate in conceit.

egregorsis: inability to sleep.

Ehrenfels, Christian von (1859–1932): student of Brentano and originator of the concept of form-qualities (1890). The form-quality is a unique phase of consciousness which is observable in the organization (temporal and spatial) of elements into configurations or wholes.

eidetic image: an unusually vivid memory image. This concept was developed by E. R. Jaensch (1925), who reported that eidetic images are like hallucinations (though the individual knows that they are memory images), that they occur most frequently in young children, and that differences in imagery are based upon constitutional factors (Walther Jaensch).

Einstellung: the mental set which determines the selection of stimuli and the response.

ejaculatio praecox: ejaculation before intromission or quickly thereafter.

ejaculatio retardata: abnormal delay in ejaculation, often as a result of depression or anxiety neurosis.

electric-shock therapy: treatment of mental disorders by electric shocks to the head of the patient (Cerletti and Bini, 1938).

electro-biology: hypnotic phenomena. The term was used in 1850 by Dods and Grimes to denote a mysterious power which, allegedly, they were able to impart through mesmerism. It was popular among laymen in the United States and England as a "science" of hypnosis.

electroencephalography: the recording of electrical phenomena associated with brain activity (Berger, 1924). The record of brain waves is the electroencephalogram.

elementarism: the type of psychology which analyzes mental activities into elements of sensation, image, and feeling. Wundt (1858 *et seq.*) established the tradition of making introspective analyses of the elements of consciousness, though some prefer to refer to Wundtian psychology as content (*Inhalt*).

elements: (Titchener, 1897) sensations, images, affections— which are mental experience reduced to its lowest terms (according to content psychology).

Electra complex: term used in Freud's early writings to denote a fixation of a daughter upon her father. The term has been replaced by Oedipus complex, which subsumes both daughter-father and son-mother love-relationships.

Elliotson, John (1791–1868): English physician who invented the stethoscope, and who founded (1842) a hospital for the use of hypnosis (*mesmerism*) in surgical operations.

emancipation: achievement of independence from parental control and support. According to psychoanalysis, a recrudescence of narcissism after puberty assists the youth in breaking the fixations.

embolalia: neologisms interspersed among the words of sentences uttered by the patient.

embryo: the human organism during the first six weeks of prenatal life (after which it is termed a *fetus*, the first two weeks being the germinal stage).

embryology of mind: Carmichael's term (1941) for studies of fetal behavior of animals.

emergency theory of emotions: Cannon's term (1929) that emotions prepare the body to meet extreme situations.

The emotion is the result of innervations from the hypo-thalamus.

Emmert's law: the statement (1881) that the size of the after-image is directly proportional to the distance to which it is projected.

emmetropia: normal vision.

emotion: a broad term variously defined, but usually refer-ring to a wide pattern of sensations within the body. Can-non's definition (1929) refers to emotion as a stirred-up condition during periods of difficulty in making adjust-ments, and manifested in a variety of somatic and visceral reactions. In psychoanalysis, the term subsumes the ex-pression of instinctual drives (conscious or unconscious). Theories of emotions differ as widely as definitions do.

emotional age: a measure of the emotional maturity of a person as expressed in terms of the chronological age of the average individual who has achieved a given degree of freedom from infantile and childish modes of emo-tional behavior.

empathy: a term used by Lipps (1903) to denote the act of projecting oneself into a work of art or a natural scene. This concept was incorporated into many theories of es-thetics. Psychoanalysts use the term to denote an objec-tive, impersonal recognition of the significance of another person's behavior (as opposed to sympathy and under-standing).

Empedocles (*c.* 490–435 B.C.) : Greek philosopher who dis-covered the existence of the cochlea, and who taught that objects give off an effluvia which stimulates the senses.

empirical psychology: that which proceeds by the method of experiment and scientific objectivity. Fechner is often referred to as the founder of strictly empirical psychol-ogy, and Brentano as the psychologist who combined the empirical method with psychological theory. Rational psychology is the antithesis of empirical, and it proceeds by the method of deduction (Aquinas, 1257).

employment psychology: the use of psychological tests in the selection of personnel, the application of psychological principles to training and promoting employees, the development of efficient procedures in management-employee relationships, and similar uses of psychological methods and facts in business and industry.

encephalomalacia: softening of the brain, with concomitant impairment of mental functions.

encephalitis: inflammation of the brain. Encephalitis lethargica was fully described by Economo (1929), though the first reported case occurred in 1915. It takes a variety of forms, the etiology is obscure, and the symptomology is complex. Among the manifestations mentioned by psychologists are the following: apathy, alteration of moral character, disruption of learned functions, parkinsonism (mask-like countenance), and disturbances of reflexes; among the sequelae are the following: headaches, insomnia, memory disturbances, tremors, and the like.

encephalon: the brain.

end-brain: the telencephalon (anterior portion of the prosencephalon).

end-brush: the arborization or terminal expansion of the axon process of the neuron. It was made visible by the Golgi method of staining for microscopic examination (1873).

end-organ: a term used by von Frey (1894) to denote the mosaic of receptors in the skin (pressure, cold, warmth, and pain).

end-plate: expansion of the motor fibers or axons on a group of muscle fibers.

end-pleasure: the orgasm. According to psychoanalysis, the sex act is divided into fore-pleasure (involving the various erogenous zones) and end-pleasure (the activity of the genitalia).

end-spurt: increase in output (and speed-up) as the goal is approached.

endocrine gland: a multicellular organ which does not have a duct (or channel) and which secretes directly into the blood-stream, thus affecting other organs of the body. The terminology is not consistently used, but some writers refer to the excitatory secretions as autocoids; the inhibitory secretions as chalones. Others refer to the secretions as hormones (whether inhibitory or excitatory).

endocrinotherapy: treatment of disorders (*e.g.,* cretinism or involution melancholia) by the use of hormones.

endogenous: arising from within the body.

endolymph: liquid in the membranous sac in the inner ear (this sac being surrounded by perilymph).

endomorphy: roundness of bodily build, with flabby muscles and large viscera (Sheldon, 1940). Correlated with the endomorphic build is the *viscerotonic temperament* (Sheldon, 1942), which is characterized by preference for good living, sloth, good-fellowship, and dependence upon other people. According to the theory, this build is a result of development of the innermost layer (endoderm) of the embryo.

endophasia: silent reproduction of a word or a sentence without overt activity in the speech organs. *Endomusia* is the silent reproduction of a melody without overt speech behavior.

endowment: the capacity of an individual as determined by his heredity.

engram: a latent memory trace (said to be left in the brain as a result of any given former experience).

enneurosis: innervation (discharge of the nervous impulse into an effector).

enosimania: pathological condition in which dreadful happenings are anticipated by the patient.

entoptic phenomena: subjective visual phenomena, such as flying particles in the humor (*muscae volitantes*), corneal specks, shadows of the iris, projections of retinitis, and the like. These phenomena were elaborately described by Helmholtz (1867).

enuresis: inability to control urination; specifically, bed-wetting. Gesell (1940) establishes the norm at 42 months for remaining dry at night without being picked up.

eonism: adoption of dress and mannerisms of a member of the opposite sex. The term is coined from the name of a Frenchman (d'Eon) who achieved notoriety by this type of behavior.

epicanthus: the fold of skin over the point of juncture (inner) of the eyelids. A form of mental deficiency known as *Mongolism* (*Tartarism*) is so-named because the pronounced epicanthus resembles that of the Orientals.

epicritic functions: Rivers' term (1908) for higher mental activities. He broadened the concept of *epicritic sensibility* (Head, 1905) to include cerebral functions.

epicritic sensibility: Head's term (1905) for cutaneous receptors which lie close to the surface and which mediate fine discriminations in each modality (pressure, pain, warmth, and cold).

Epicurus (341–270 B.C.): Greek philosopher who upheld a refined type of hedonism, was the first to formulate the doctrine of freedom of the will, and advocated the suppression of all emotions (since they bring pain).

epilepsy: convulsive disorder: a condition of cerebral dys-rhythmia. Lucretius described (in literary terms) the classical form (*c.* 70 B.C.). The *grand mal* form has the following stages; aura (in many cases), tonic stage, clonus, and coma. In *petit mal,* there is a loss of consciousness for a brief period, temporary confusion, but seldom a fall. In the Jacksonian type, there is a twitching of a group of muscles. In the psychic equivalent, there is a psychogenic convulsion which superficially resembles a grand mal attack. Some grand mal seizures are followed by a furore, during which the patient may commit crimes of violence; many are followed by a period of stupor.

epileptoid personality: Rosanoff's term (1905) for an individual who is extremely irritable, selfish, uncoöperative, apathetic, stubborn, (sometimes) fanatical in theological opinions, loud and boisterous, and inclined to violent temper outbursts.

epinephrin: hormone secreted by the medulla of the adrenal gland.

epinosic gain: the personal advantage gained by a real or a psychoneurotic illness. The patient receives sympathy, escapes from work, and is waited upon; hence Freud speaks of the wish to become ill. According to psychoanalysis, the patient may relive the Oedipus situation while receiving attentions from physicians and nurses.

epiphenomenalism: Hobbes' term (1651) for a solution of the mind-body problem, his view being that consciousness is a by-product of nervous impulses in the brain.

equilibrium: the balance of bodily and mental processes. Cannon (1931) preferred to use the term homeostasis to denote the constant states or equilibria maintained by physiological processes; Raup (1925) referred to the optimum mental equilibrium as *complacency*.

equipotentiality: the capacity of any part of the embryo (if transplanted) to develop into any tissue or group of tissues in the mature organism. According to Lashley (1929), any portion of the cerebrum is potentially as ready as any other part to mediate any type of learned activity (excluding the sensory and the motor areas of the cortex).

Erb, Wilhelm Heinrich (1840–1921): German physician who investigated birth palsies.

erectile tissues: multicellular groups containing expansile capillaries which, when stimulated, become erect (*e.g.*, penis, breasts, clitoris), and hence are included in the erogenous zones (Freud).

erethism: heightened responsiveness of the nervous system; excitability.

ereutrophobia: morbid fear of blushing, which may accompany extreme self-consciousness.

ergasiology: A. Meyer's term (1915) for the study of psychobiological functions. *Ergasia* refers to the whole personality and the totality of its biological substratum.

ergograph: Kiesow's apparatus (1890) for studying the effects of muscular fatigue. In the usual form, the apparatus consists of a spring which is pulled repeatedly by the middle finger, the number and the strength of the pulls being recorded.

Erlenmeyer, Friedrich Albrecht (1849–1926): German psychiatrist.

erogenous zones: according to psychoanalysis, libido cathexis proceeds as follows: general (polymorphous perverse), mouth, anus, and (finally) genitalia. Since the earlier outlets tend to keep some of the capacity to respond to erotic stimulation, there are various zones (used in fore-pleasure) other than the genitalia.

eros instinct: Freud's concept (1920) of all the instincts involved in self-preservation and sex pleasure, and opposed by the death (*thanatos*) instinct.

erotomania: obsessive interests in sex; nymphomania or satyriasis.

error, experimental: that which results from such factors as imperfections in the apparatus, variations in reaction time, sampling, variables which cannot be adequately controlled, and the like.

error, refractive: imperfections in the eye which cause astigmatism, hyperopia, myopia, or presbyopia.

error, statistical: various mathematical figures which indicate how far an obtained measure differs from the true measure.

erythrophobia: morbid fear of blushing; also, hypersensitivity to reds, a symptom reported as occurring in some patients who have had cataracts removed.

Esdaile, James: an English surgeon who (1846) wrote about many operations which he had performed upon Indian patients through the use of hypnotic anesthesia.

Esquirol, Jean Etienne Dominique (1772-1840): French psychiatrist who was taught by Pinel. He was the first to study hallucinations carefully (having originated the term); he was interested in mental disorder as it relates to criminal behavior; and he was one of the first psychiatrists to undertake statistical investigations of the incidence of various psychoses.

essential hypertension: high blood-pressure associated with worries, business responsibilities, and prolonged excitement.

esthesiometer: apparatus for determining the two-point

threshold. In his classical investigations (1834), Weber used the compass, measuring the least distance at which his subjects could differentiate between oneness and twoness.

esthetics: the study of beauty and ugliness, which has attracted the attention of experimental psychologists as well as theorists. Fechner is often called the "father of experimental esthetics" (1865 *et seq.*).

etiology: causative factors, predisposing and precipitating, which result in a disorder.

eu-: Greek prefix denoting a normal, healthy, or desirable condition.

eubolism: normal metabolism.

euesthesia: sense of well-being.

eugenics: the application of knowledge about heredity to the improvement of the race by limiting offspring to the healthy. Galton (1869) became interested in problems of human heredity, and, in 1904, founded a laboratory (in London) for research in eugenics. He emphasized not only the elimination of the unfit, but also the improvement of human stock by an application of the principles of heredity.

eumetria: the expenditure of the adequate amount of energy to complete successfully a given task, without undue fatigue or excess movements.

eunoia: the healthy mind.

eunuchoid build: a bodily build resembling that of the eunuch (castrated male), and resulting from underdevelopment of gonads. A variety of types has been described, some writers emphasizing the infantile or childish appearance, the feminine type of hips, scanty hair in pubic area, and hypogenitalism.

euphonia: a clear, pleasing voice.

euphoria: in a broad sense, happiness or contentment. The term is used in psychopathology to denote an unreasonable degree of elation symptomatic of a mental disorder (Bleuler's *morbid euphoria,* 1924).

eupraxia: good muscular coördination in learned functions.

Eustachio, Bartolomeo (1500–1574): Italian anatomist who described the canal connecting the middle ear and the pharyx (Eustachian tube).

euthanasia: painless death for incurable illnesses, serious mental deficiency, and victims of extreme accidents.

euthenics: improvement of the race through a program of raising the quality of the environment, extending the benefits of medical knowledge and skill, establishing playgrounds and better schools in all communities, and the like.

euthymia: a pleasant disposition.

eviration: the adoption of feminine mannerisms by a man (Krafft-Ebing, 1908).

evolution: the phylogenetic changes which have resulted in the development of the species (Darwin, 1859). The fundamental principle is natural selection, with the principles of struggle for existence and of variation the subsidiary ones. The theory gave great impetus to the development of comparative psychology and to the use of the genetic method in the field of human psychology.

excitation therapy: Janet's concept (1925) of a procedure in restoring the level of psychic energy necessary for eliminating the depression of affects and building up a zest for living.

exercise, law of: Thorndike's law of learning (1913) which states that repeated use of a connection between a stimulus and a response (S-R bond) strengthens, and disuse weakens, it.

exhaustion disorders: a loosely defined category of psycho-neuroses and psychoses in whch the causative factors are tentatively identified with prolonged fatigue, malnutrition, and the like. Jelliffe and White (1923) mention the difficulty of separating infectious from exhaustion disorders.

exhibitionism: in the narrow sense, exposure of genitals. According to psychoanalysis, the exposure is usually done in the presence of a person who represents the Oedipus situation. In a broad sense, the term is used to connote various attention-getting activities.

Exner, Sigmund (1846–1926): German physiologist who made important contributions to the psychology of vision, and who defended the doctrine of cerebral localization of function.

exorcism: treatment of mental patients by the use of incantations or threats, the theory being that the disorder is caused by a demon who has taken possession of the body of the patient. (Matthew 8:28 cites an example of exorcism.)

exogenous disorder: one which arises from factors outside the nervous system (*e.g.*, a head injury).

exophthalmus: a disorder caused by hyperthyroidism, the principal symptoms being a protrusion of the eyeballs, muscular tension, irritability, and hyperkinesis.

expansiveness: the uncontrolled delusions of great self-importance, wealth, and power which are symptoms in paresis. (Shakespeare's *Timon of Athens* is an example of a literary use of these symptoms.)

expectation: a condition of readiness (or set) to make a certain type of response to a situation, thus causing misperceptions, such as those which are used by stage magicians or which occur in daily life. The term usually connotes the emotional condition of preparedness for a given type of response. Titchener (1896) described it as an attitude based upon kinesthetic and organic sensations, usually accompanied by a feeling-tone.

experience: a broad term referring to the totality of all the activities whch have occurred during the life of the individual, whether they are conscious or unconscious (verbalized or unverbalized). In the Titchenerian sense (1897), it denotes the conscious response to stimuli (devoid of inferences, expectations, and other distortions; mind is defined as the totality of human experience considered as dependent upon the nervous system.

experiment: observation under controlled conditions, all variables being identified and only one factor being varied at a time; hence involving pre-arrangement and usually (not always) implying a laboratory situation.

experimental neurosis: the artificial induction of a conflictual situation which disorganizes the established patterns of behavior in an animal (Pavlov, 1909). Rats, dogs, goats, and sheep are among the animals which have been used in experiments of this type, particularly by American psychologists since 1935.

experimental psychology: the application of experimental methods (originally those used in physics and physiology) to the study of mental activities. Wundt (1879) is generally called the "father of experimental psychology."

expiation: the performance of an act in order to lessen the tension arising from a sense of guilt. According to psychoanalysis, the motivation comes from repressed incestuous or homosexual cravings.

extensity: Titchener's term (1924) for the spatial dimension of sensation. Lotze (1852) introduced the doctrine of *local sign*, which states that a characteristic of the receptor functions is to locate the point of stimulation; Hering taught that extensity is based upon nativistic conditions (1864); Wertheimer (1912) re-introduced the concept of primary, unlearned extensity in sensation-perception; and (in 1710), Berkeley taught that extensity (in visual sensations) is based upon empirical factors.

exteroceptor: a receptor which responds to stimuli from without (as contrasted with interoceptor and proprioceptor).

extinction, experimental: the elimination of a conditioned reflex by the repeated presentation of the conditioned stimulus without reinforcement (Pavlov, 1890).

extirpation experiment: removal of a portion of the cortex in an animal that has learned a maze (or a mode of escape from a puzzle-box, and so on), the purpose being to measure the relationship between the amount and the area of brain tissue removed and the retention of the capacity for performing the given act. Franz is among the earliest investigators in this field (1907). Mutilations and removal of sense organs and motor mechanisms also belong under this heading.

extratensive: the *Erlebnistypus* (Rorschach, 1923) characterized by emotional ability and responsiveness to the outside world, capacity for good social rapport, and a practical interests in affairs. On the Rorschach Inkblot Test, the predominance of color responses over fantasies of movement reveal this tendency.

extraversion: Jung's term (1923) for an attitude-type characterized by an extreme degree of sociability, aversion to meditation and introspection, fluid affects, and responsiveness to the environment. In psychoanalysis, the term refers to the outward direction of the libido.

eyedness: the dominance (muscular) of one eye over the other in such activities as threading a needle, sighting a rifle, looking through the manoptoscope (apparatus for determining eyedness) and the like.

eye movements: the saccadic movements of the eyes, as in reading a line of print. J. Müller (1826) was the first to write a scientific description of eye movements.

F: Rorschach symbol for responses determined by the form of the inkblot. These responses are classified as good form and poor form.

f: frequency.

fables test: simple tales with a moral, included in the Terman Revision of the Binet Scale (1916), the subject being required to interpret the meaning implied.

Fabre, Jean Henri (1823-1915): French entomologist who wrote extensively on the social behavior of insects.

face sheet: the summation of essential data included in the case history.

facial asymmetry: imbalance between expressions and morphology of the right and the left halves of the face, which is infrequently mentioned as a possible sign of cerebral-hemisphere dominance (*e.g.*, by C. K. Ogden, 1926).

facial expressions: static and dynamic patterns of the face, which are important as social stimuli (F. Allport, 1924). Darwin (1872) developed a theory which includes the following principles: (1) survival of associated habits once used by primitive ancestors as fulfillment of needs or as defenses; (2) the result of direct action of the nervous system, the motor outflow thus causing the expressions; and (3) antithesis, the expressions being arranged in polarities (*e.g.*, elation-sadness).

facial nerve: the VIIth cranial nerve.

facilitation: the increase in the efficiency of an act. Asynergies, incoördination, errors, response times, and dissatisfactions are reduced as facilitation is increased.

facilitation, social: the increase in output as a result of the sight and the sound of other persons engaged in the same type of behavior (Allport, 1924). Triplett (1897) was one of the first to report an experimental study of the influence of a co-acting group upon individual behavior. Two factors have been differentiated: (1) the mere presence of other persons who exert an influence upon output; and (2) the influence of rivalry or competition.

facilitation, retroactive: the strengthening of a stimulus-response connection as a result of a similar type of learning-situation taken up after the first connection has been formed. It is the antithesis of the factor of retroactive inhibition.

factor: one of the elements which, as a result of interaction with other elements, produces a given result. In heredity, the factors are the genes; in statistical analysis of test results, a factor is a determiner of the intercorrelations. In test results, a factor is some element which can be distinguished from all the other elements which determine the score. Thurstone (1935) has described a procedure for a statistical determination of the least number of factors required to explain intercorrelations among tests.

faculty: a mental function, such as reason, intelligence, memory, and the like. The existence of separate faculties has long since been discarded, but the terminology still continues to be used.

faculty psychology: the traditional point of view expounded by the Scholastics and developed in systematic form by Wolff (1734) which divides the mind into separate divisions. Wolff's book was used throughout Germany and France, and it supplanted the Aristotelian point of view in psychology, as well as introducing a concept which is still influential through the terminology of the science.

Wolff divided the mind into the faculties of knowing and feeling. The faculty of knowing he subdivided into sensation, perception, imagination, memory, and intellection; the faculty of feeling, into pain, and pleasure, the will manifesting itself through this faculty of feeling (or desire).

fad: a sudden, intense enthusiasm for an activity, manner of dress or ornamentation, book, and the like, which is of short duration. Couéism, for instance, was a fad. Eventually a fad may become incorporated into the social inheritance of the group (*e.g.*, *mob*, once a fad for *mobus vulgus*). Some social psychologists differentiate *fads* (defining them as of slow development), *crazes* (sudden in development, quick in passing), and *booms* (like crazes, but involving economic interests, not diversions). (La-Pierre and Farnsworth, 1936).

Falret, Jean Pierre (1794–1870): French psychiatrist who prevailed upon law-makers to substitute *mental alienation* for the confusing terminology used in courts of law, and who specialized in the study of emotional disorders.

familial trait: a characteristic which appears in successive generations of a family, and which may be due to genes or to cultural influences.

family constellation: the diverse psychological environments arising from the birth order of children in the same family. According to Adler (1930), the first child is likely to be spoiled; the second, to develop a strong interest in successful competitive endeavors; and the youngest, to be the victim of a "begging" style of life.

family romance: according to psychoanalysis, the Oedipus situation, which is an inevitable aspect of growing up.

fanaticism: unreasoning enthusiasm and unwarranted, illogical opinions. The fanatic may be a true paranoiac or a schizophrenic, paranoid type.

fantasy: daydream; autistic or deisristic thinking. Weyer (1579) was among the earliest psychiatrists to appreciate the role of fantasies in mental disorders.

Farrand, Livingston (1867–1939): American anthropologist who assisted Cattell (1896) in a program of mental testing.

far-sightedness: hyperopia. The condition is due to shortness of the eyeball or a defect in the lens, and it is at least partially correctable by convex lenses.

fashion: a loose term usually limited to modes of dress which are currently accepted. New fashions originate in "style centers" and are disseminated by advertisements which appeal to the wish for prestige.

fascination method: the technique of inducing hypnosis by having the subject stare at a bright, glittering object, such as the hypnotist's eyes, a revolving mirror, or a small piece of metal.

father fixation: in the early writings of Freud, the *Electra complex*, which is an intense love of daughter for father. In the later writings, the Oedipus complex was broadened to include both son-mother and daughter-father love-relationships.

fatigue: the reduction of output, loss of efficiency, and/or development of boredom. Mosso (1890) developed the ergograph for obtaining an objective record of fatigue in a voluntary activity (weight lifting), and many theories have been advanced to account for the results of continued activity. Mental fatigue is an elusive topic, and it defies a lucid definition. The refractory period of a neuron (Gotch and Burch, 1899) is said to bear a superficial resemblance to whatever the term *fatigue* connotes.

Fechner, Gustav Theodor (1801–1887): German physicist who is known as the "father of psychophysics." He described (1860) the three classical methods of measuring consciousness: (1) a refinement of Weber's technique (1829) for just noticeable differences; (2) the method of average error in judgment; and (3) the method of right and wrong judgments. He also restated Weber's law of just noticeable differences in mathematical terms.

feeble-mindedness: oligophrenia; mental deficiency.

feeling: (Titchener, 1896) an elementary mental process which differs from sensation and which has the dimension of pleasantness-unpleasantness. Other writers identify it with a vague pattern of sensations, principally organic, which furnish the hedonic tone.

feelings, tridimensional theory: Wundt's theory (1903) that feelings have three dimensions: pleasantness-unpleasantness; excitement-numbness; and tension-release.

feeling type: one of the function-types described by Jung (1923), in which affects dominate and which, together with the thinking type, comprises his *rational* class (intuitive and sensation function-types being the *irrational*).

fellatio: the act of achieving an orgasm by inserting the penis into the mouth. According to Freud, the mouth is the first specific erogenous zone; hence the perversion is an example of failure of libidinal development beyond this level.

fenestra ovalis: oval-shaped aperture into which the footplate of the stirrup (stapes) is inserted; opening in middle ear.

fenestra rotunda: a round aperture closed by a small membrane; a part of the middle ear.

festinating gait: the incoördinated walk of a victim of

paralysis agitans. The walk is hurried and uncertain as to direction.

fetishism: erotic attachment to an object which symbolizes the person to whom it belongs. Hair, shoes, handkerchief, and the like, may have fetishistic value. The hand or the foot of the beloved one may also serve as fetishes. Psychoanalysts borrowed the term *fetish* from a French anthropologist (de Broses) who wrote on idols and talismans (1760).

fetus: the prenatal organism after the sixth week (in man) following conception.

fever therapy: treatment of neurosyphilis by the method of injecting malaria parasites into the blood of the patient. Wagner-Jauregg was awarded the Nobel prize in medicine (1927) for developing this procedure.

fibrillation: the development of fibrils or tiny nerve filaments. S. T. Bok (1915) described the manner in which neuroblasts send fibrils away from the field of nervous activity (stimulogenous fibrillation). The outgrowths towards the center of nervous activity form the dendrites (called *neurobiotaxis*, Kappers, 1917).

fiction: according to Adler (1907), the compensatory achievement of a type of superiority which seems to be a real accomplishment, not a vicarious satisfaction.

figure and ground: Rubin's term (1912) referring to the tendency of one part of a perceptual configuration to stand out (figure) clearly and the rest to form a background. The figure-ground relationship is of particular interest in Gestalt psychology.

filial regression: Galton's principle (1869) which states that the offspring of abnormal parents tend to approach the norm.

final common pathway: Sherrington's term (1906) for the

motor nerve fiber into which a number of nervous impulses are converged.

first cranial nerve: the olfactory nerve.

fistula: a canal which is not allowed to heal and through which secretion passes, as the saliva from the Pavlovian dog used in the conditioning experiments (1890).

fixation: abnormal attachment of the libido to some person, object, or level of psychic development; hence, according to psychoanalysis, a mechanism causing a reduction in the amount of libido for dealing with reality (Freud, 1905). The term is also used to refer to an unreasoning attachment to some individual who is a parent substitute.

fixation point: any point upon which one or both eyes are focused when motionless. *Binocular fixation* refers to the act of focusing both eyes simultaneously, and it was first described by J. Müller (1826). Donders (1846) stated that the retinal points are constant for any object in the field of vision for any given head or eye position. *Fixation time* refers to the interval for which the eye is stationary while the individual is engaged in the act of reading.

fixed idea: an obsession.

flaccid: completely relaxed muscles.

flagellantism: self-whipping under the influence of ecstasy or drugs. Beginning in the thirteenth century, this form of "mass hysteria" spread from Poland to Italy, and it has continued into modern times.

flexibilitas cerea: flexibility of limbs and neck of some patients with catatonic schizophrenia and with severe hysteria.

flexor muscle: a muscle that bends or flexes a limb.

flicker: perception of flashes or cycles of light when the frequency of cycles is below the fusion frequency. In motion pictures, flicker disappears when the frames are run at from 15 to 20 a second (unless the light is very bright).

flight into illness: escape from an intolerable reality by adopting the symptoms of an organic disorder.

flight of ideas: increased speed of associational processes, as in certain types of mental disorders and intense episodic situations.

Flourens, Marie, J. P. (1794-1867): French neurologist who experimented upon animals by removing portions of the brain, and who developed the doctrine (1824) that the cerebrum functions *in toto*, not in separate parts or centers.

focus of eyes: the act of binocular adjustment on a central point so as to effect clear, fused retinal images. The near point of accommodation for normal eyes is a fixation point on the median line about three inches distant from the face.

Foerster, Richard (1825-1902): German ophthalmologist who, with Aubert, investigated the phenomena of the visual field (1856).

folie: French term for an adventitious mental disorder.

folie du doute: chronic indecision; abulia.

folk psychology: Wundt's term (1900) for the application of psychological techniques to the investigation of racial characteristics, especially those of primitive people.

folklore: the body of legends, customs, manners, and beliefs of primitive people which have survived into modern times.

folkways: Sumner's term (1907) for customs derived by trial and error which are considered to be the "proper" way of doing things, such as principles of child guidance, education, and other forms of social behavior. Folkways are said to be subject to considerable alteration as compared to mores.

fontanelles: unossified areas on the cranium of the neonate.

foramen: an opening in a bone.

forced movements: Loeb's term (1890) for the tropistic behavior of plants and animals. He developed the theory that behavior may be accounted for in terms of strictly mechanistic principles, the stimulus causing chemical alterations in the protoplasm and thus forcing the movements.

forebrain: the prosencephalon.

fore-consciousness: according to psychoanalysis, that part of the mind which is amenable to voluntary recall.

fore-pleasure: according to psychoanalysis, the anticipatory erotic stimulation preceding the orgasm (*end-pleasure*). The various erogenous zones pre-dating the genital stage are said to be part of the fore-pleasure.

forgetting: oblivescence of learned material; loss of retention. The classical experiments of forgetting were made by Ebbinghaus (1885), who concluded that the rate of forgetting is most rapid at first; slower with the passage of time after the initial learning period.

formal discipline: the traditional doctrine in education that certain subjects possess mind-training value, and hence that they do not require other justification for being included in the curriculum.

form-board: a measure of intelligence which consists of blocks to be fitted into a recess. The first form-board was devised by Seguin (1842), and many types have been constructed by subsequent investigators.

fornication: extra-marital coitus.

Foster, Michael (1836–1907) : English histologist who, with

Sherrington, named the junction between neurons the *synapse* (1907).

Fournier, Jean Alfred (1832–1914): French physician who devised various tests of the ataxic gait.

fovea centralis: the depression in the macula lutea which (in the human eye) contains no rods, and which is the point of clearest vision.

fraternal twins: dizygotic twins, who may be of the same or the opposite sex and who do not have identical sets of genes.

free association: the uninhibited sequence of ideas elicited by the analyst, no hampering or directive instructions being given to the patient. Jung (1910) developed a method (initiated by Cattell and Kraepelin) of presenting the patient with one hundred standard words for free association.

free-floating affects: the psychoanalytic doctrine that the affect belonging to a repressed idea may become attached to an altogether different idea as a result of its detachment from the original.

frequency: the number of complete vibrations a second of a vibrating body.

frequency distribution: the arrangement of scores on a psychological measure in order of magnitude. A graphic representation is called a frequency curve or histogram.

frequency, law of: recall or recognition whch is attributed to the number of repetitions employed during the learning period. Reliance upon the drill method of instruction exemplifies the use of this principle of learning.

Freud, Sigmund (1856–1939): Austrian physician who, as a young man, worked on problems of brain neurology, and who, starting in 1895, developed the principles of psychoanalysis. In 1903 he founded the Viennese Psychoanalytic Society for the discussion of his theories and procedures. Many of his concepts have been incorporated into academic psychology, and in recent years some American psychologists have become interested in developing experimental psychoanalysis.

friction: a term used in counseling and psychotherapy to denote incompatibilities of personality among members of a family constellation.

frigidity: absence of sex desires in a woman. According to psychoanalysts, it may be attributed to the castration complex, repressed incestuous feelings, or homosexual tendencies.

fringe of consciousness: metaphorically, that part of consciousness which lies around the area in the focus of attention. The concept was introduced by Prince (1916) to denote thoughts and feelings of which the person is only vaguely aware.

Frölich, Alfred (1871–   ): Austrian neurologist who (1901) described the pathologies consequent upon dysfunction of the anterior lobe of the pituitary gland. Frölich's syndrome is characterized by a eunuch-like fatness, abnormalities in secondary sex characteristics, and the like.

frotteur: one who achieves erotic gratification by contact, other than coitus, with another person. The contact may be accidental, as in a crowd; or it may be purposeful, as when fully clothed partners in the act rub together.

frustration: the condition of being thwarted in the satisfaction of a motive. Writers on dynamic psychology tend to stress the thesis that the primitive reaction to frustration is aggressive behavior, usually accompanied by hate towards the person or the situation blamed as the source of frustration or by a generalized hostility. Dollard (1939) developed this frustration-aggression hypothesis.

frustration tolerance: Rosenzweig's concept (1938) of an ability to endure frustration over a relatively long period of time without making efforts either to resolve the tensions indirectly or to satisfy the motive directly. This is a learned ability, though hereditary factors contribute strongly to one's level of frustration tolerance.

fugue: a temporary period of disorientation and loss of identity. It may be caused by drugs (headache nostrums), intense mental conflicts, and various psychiatric disorders.

function-engram: Jung's term (1923) for the archetype which invests the individual's symbol with its real significance.

function-types: Jung's expressive types (1923): feeling, intuition, sensation, and thinking. Function-types are to be distinguished from attitude-types: introversion and extraversion.

functional autonomy of motives: G. Allport's term (1937) designating the lack of dependence of various motives upon so-called primitive drives. It is the antithesis of the theory that all motives may be reduced to a limited number of innate drives, out of which, presumably, they were developed.

functional disorder: a term loosely used to refer to disorders which do not have a demonstrable organic etiology. The dichotomy of functional-structural is cited as an example of the confusion stemming from Cartesian dualism (1650).

functionalism: the type of psychology which emphasizes activities rather than the contents of consciousness. It was founded by J. R. Angell (1894) as a protest against the

Wundtian-Titchenerian emphasis upon analysis of mental states. Dewey was also an able proponent of functionalism.

fundamental tone: the lowest in a compound tone.

fungiform papillae: the low, mushroom-like papillae which are covered with secondary papillae. They are found on the tongue surface.

furor: the transitory mania and disorientation which occurs at the end of a classical attack of grand mal epilepsy. In the furor epilepticus, Mary Lamb is said to have killed her mother. Cicero defined it as a condition in which the individual is completely irresponsible for criminal acts.

fusion: according to psychoanalysis, the union of the life (*eros*) and the death (*thanatos*) instincts which occur in the normal person but which is lacking in those with mental disorders.

fusion, tonal: Stumpf's term (1890) for the tendency of certain tones to fuse into a single tone which is perceived as something different from any of its constituents. Fusion of tones is a function of the ratio of the separate tones which blend together.

G: Rorschach's symbol (1923) for a response the content of which is the whole inkblot (*Ganz*).

gait: manner of walking. The following types of gaits are often mentioned (in clinical psychology): ataxic (the foot being raised high and brought down on the whole sole); cerebellar (staggering); cow (caused by knock-knees); frog (hopping manner of the victim of poliomyelitis); paretic (shuffling); spastic (feet scarcely raised, toes dragging, legs almost unbent); waddling (duck-like manner of victims of certain types of paralysis).

Galen, Claudius (130–200): Greek physician who lived in Rome, and who established many facts about human anatomy. His writings (and those attributed to him) were the only textbooks on medicine and mental disorders for about fifteen hundred years.

Galileo (1564–1627): Italian scientist who re-established the science of physics, and whose views upset the anthropocentric conception of the universe.

Gall, Franz Josef (1758–1828): anatomist (German-born; worked in Vienna) who introduced the doctrine of phrenology (1808). Actually, he wrote and lectured on craniology and physiognomy, whereas Spurzheim (his collaborator) coined the term *phrenology*. The doctrine teaches that each mental faculty has a precise cerebral localization and that it is revealed by the degree of protrusion or recession in the skull immediately above it.

Galton, Francis (1822–1911): English investigator who founded eugenics, established the concept of individual differences, devised pieces of apparatus (*e.g.*, a bar for judgments of just noticeable differences in lengths, a whistle for determining auditory threshold, and used a method (later perfected by Pearson) of correlation.

Galvani, Luigi (1737–1798) : Italian physicist whose investigations into the field of electricity opened leads followed by modern investigators of electroencephalography and electrophysiology.

gamete: a germ cell.

gamma hypothesis: Dunlap's concept (1932) designating a response which has no effect upon a repetition of the same response when a similar situation is encountered.

gamma-movement: Kenkel's term (1913) for change in apparent size of an object when the intensity of the illumination is altered.

gammacism: childish talk by an affected person or a mental patient.

ganglion: group of nerve cells, bound together by connective tissues, which lie outside the brain and the spinal cord. Some of the older neurologists refer to masses of nerve cells in the mid-brain as basal ganglia.

Ganser, Sigbert Joseph (1835–1931) : German psychiatrist who described a syndrome (*Ganser syndrome*) occurring in hysteria or malingering, the individual's behavior being nonsensical, his answers to questions being grossly absurd, and his general demeanor being ridiculous. In legal practice, the syndrome is regarded as an attempt to gain leniency through the assumption of symptoms of mental disorder.

gargalanesthesia: insensitivity to tickling.

gargoylism: gross abnormalities in bony structure of the body, opaque corneas, enlargement of liver and spleen together with mental deficiency (described by Tredgold, 1912).

gelasmus: hysterical laughter.

Gemeingefühl: Weber's term (1846) to denote common sensibility (tickle, pain, warmth, cold, and all other sensibilities that supplement the sense of touch or pressure). The sense organs are found in the skin, eyes, ears, muscles, tongue, and other areas of the body.

gene: the bearer of heredity, which lies in the chromosome. Knowledge of the functions of genes (particularly in Drosophila melanogaster) was developed by T. H. Morgan and associates (1916 *et seq.*).

general factor: Spearman's concept (1912) of a central factor or ability which is displayed to a large degree in some functions and to a lesser degree in others, and which accounts for the intercorrelations among tests of intelligence. In order to denote it precisely, he referred to this factor as *g*. Physiologically, it is correlated with nervous energy; psychologically, with number facility, mental speed, verbal facility, and the like. It manifests itself in two ways: eduction of relations (similarities, differences, whole-part relationships); and eduction of correlates (the relationship of one situation or object to another).

general paralysis: the older term for paresis. Differentiating criteria for this type of disorder were expounded in 1851 by Delasiauve, and Krafft-Ebing (1897) showed that general paralysis is caused by syphilis.

generalization: the mental activity of forming a judgment or concept pertaining to an entire category of data, the observations or the items of experience underlying which are limited to a representative sampling. In mental measurements, the individual is required to formulate a valid generalization from fragmentary data presented in the test.

genetic psychology: the branch of psychology which deals with growth and development from conception to maturity as well as the gradual decline in psychological functions (Quetelet, 1835). Darwin (1877) wrote on the psychology of the infant; Preyer (1881) described the mind of the child in systematic fashion; Hall (1904) was the pioneer in adolescent psychology, and he was also among the first to deal with the psychology of later maturity and senescence (1922).

genius: a broad term referring either to an abnormally high order of general intelligence or to special talent of an unusual degree. The classical study of genius was made by Galton (1874), who strongly believed in the inheritance factor.

geophagia: the eating of dirt.

Georget, Etienne (1795–1828): French psychiatrist who (at age 25) wrote an important textbook on dementia.

geriatrics: branch of medicine which deals with the physical disorders associated with advanced age.

geriopsychosis: Southard's term (1916) for mental disorders occurring in old age.

germ-cell: Weismann's term (1893) for the reproductive cell, which preserves a continuity in spite of changes occurring in the somatic cells. Thus, somatic cells might be injured without any effect upon germ-cells. De Vries (1900) developed the theory that germ-cells may mutate, and so create new species.

gerontology: psychology and biology of the aged. The first journal devoted exclusively to this field was started in 1945.

Gestalt: pattern or configuration. The implication is that the whole is not analyzable into separate parts, but that it is an integration.

Gestalt psychology: a point of view initiated by Wertheimer (1912) which emphasized the unitary nature of mental functions as opposed to *elementarism*. *Gestalten* are unitary, integrated structures; they may be dynamic (redintegrating to closure, emerging as "insights," perceived as strong in some parts and weak in others, and the like), or static (that is, enduring; without temporal qualities).

gigantism: unusually large stature as a result of hyperfunctioning of the anterior lobe of the pituitary.

Giraldès, Joachim Albin (1808–1875): Portuguese surgeon who studied the brains of hydrocephalic mental defectives.

glaucoma: hardening of the eyeball, resulting in a restricted field of vision and in a colored ring seen when the patient looks at lights.

glia cells: cells which form the supportive framework of nervous tissues.

glioma: a tumor. In the brain, a glioma is a multicellular structure composed of glia cells. It may occur in the retina, and hence impair visual acuity or result in blindness.

globus hystericus: a lump in the throat which impedes free breathing and results in a choking sensation, and which occurs during an attack of hysteria.

glossolalia: unintelligible jargon uttered in a condition of religious excitement. The earliest account is to be found in Acts 2:4, and the phenomenon has been studied by Weinel (1899) and Davenport (1906).

glove anesthesia: insensitivity in the hand, not conforming to the distribution of sensory nerves, and hence considered to be a symptom of hysteria. This symptom was described by Charcot (1879). It has been pointed out by recent students that the questions of the physician may indirectly suggest symptoms of this type.

goal: that for which the individual strives.

goal gradient: the effect of nearing the goal upon the incidence of errors and the rate of performance in the maze-learning of the rat (Hull, 1932).

Goethe, Johann Wolfgang von (1744-1832): German poet who developed an influential theory of color vision (1810).

golden section: an esthetically pleasing division of a geometrical figure, the proportion of the parts so divided being about 3:5.

Golgi, Camillo (1844-1926): Italian histologist who discovered a method of staining nervous tissue (1873). Cells with short axons and dendrites found in the cortex of the cerebrum are among the important discoveries named in his memory.

Goll, Friedrich (1829-1903): Swiss anatomist who studied the structure of the spinal cord, and in whose memory the posterior-interior column has been named.

gonads: testes or ovaries.

grand mal: the major type of epilepsy. In the classical attack, the following stages may occur: aura or warning, cry, fall, tonus, clonus, sleep, and furore. Hippocrates (*c.* 400 B.C.) vigorously opposed the current belief that it is a "sacred disease" and stated that it has natural causes; Lemnius (1651) had to oppose this persisting superstition about its etiology.

graphic rating scale: a procedure for indicating on a linear scale the rater's judgment regarding the status of an individual on a given trait, the scale including the entire range of degrees in which the train may appear (or seem to appear).

graphology: (Baldo, 1662) a pseudo-science which purports to analyze personality from handwriting. Hull and Montgomery (1919) report that there is no correlation.

graphomania: production of voluminous writings, usually incoherent and meaningless, in certain types of mental disorders. Bleuler (1930) includes the symptom under deteriorative paranoia and paranoid schizophrenia.

gray: in the Hering theory, the series between white and black having neither hue nor saturation (1874); according to G. Müller (1897), a cortical gray results when black and white are in equal proportions (a view which Titchener adopted in 1923).

gray matter: the cortex of the cerebrum and the inner portion of the spinal cord.

green: sensation resulting when the normal eye is stimulated by about 505 millimicrons wave-length.

group, co-acting: a collection of persons attending to a common stimulus (Allport, 1923). In a face-to-face group the stimulus is the presence of other persons; in the co-acting group, the presence of others may facilitate or lower the efficiency of performance of a task.

group mind: a view, generally regarded by modern psychologists as fallacious, that there is a mental structure (or mental dynamics) in a group of persons unlike that found in the individuals who compose the group. The hypothesis is a variant of realism, and its critics are nominalists. Le Bon (1895) was a leading proponent of the group or crowd mind.

growth: augmentation of structures from embryonic stage to maturity. The modern theories emphasize the dynamic factors in growth, the view being that specialized tissues emerge, by a process of individuation, from the primitive mass (Coghill, 1915); hence that it is not an additive process of building up multicellular specialized tissues. Growth of axons has been described by Bok (1915) and of dendrites by Kappers (1908), these processes being developed by individuation through stimulation from the neuroblast.

guidance: the use of psychological techniques of appraisal for the purpose of assisting the individual, either through directive or non-directive counseling, to make a better adjustment to his environment. In a guidance clinic, the functions of the staff members are usually specialized, and various experts appraise the individual from the standpoint of their particular fields of competence. The minimum staff of a clinic includes a psychologist, a psychiatrist, and a social worker.

guilt feeling: according to psychoanalysis, tension existing between the ego and the super-ego; in the psychology of religion (Starbuck, 1899), the sense of sinfulness which leads to conversion (usually occurring at age 16 or thereabouts).

gustation: sense of taste. The taste receptors are mediated by portions of the seventh, the ninth, and the tenth cranial nerves.

gutterophonia: a throaty sound in speech.

gynecomania: male impulsiveness to assault women; satyriasis.

gynephobia: aversion to association with women on any social level.

gyrus: convolution of fold of the cerebrum or the cerebellum. The gyri serve as convenient landmarks to specify areas of localization of various sensory and motor functions.

H: Rorschach symbol for a response in which the content is a human being. When part of a human being is perceived, the symbol is Hd.

Haab, Otto (1850–1931): Swiss ophthalmologist who defined an abnormality of vision in which the pupils contract in near-vision, but convergence and accommodation do not change. Haab's sign is an index to a cortical lesion.

habit: a learned response, in which the muscular coördinations, associations, or emotional element has, through training, become fairly well established, rapid, and almost automatic. The concept received great emphasis in the writings of Bain (1856), Carpenter (1874), and James (1887); and it attracted so much popular attention that the term soon lost any precise denotation which they may have intended to give it.

habituation: the condition of making more or less automatic responses to stimuli which have been repeatedly presented. The term is used in a loose, general sense.

habitus: bodily build. Usually the term implies that the general morphology of the body is correlated with a personality type.

habromania: an extreme degree of euphoria, implying serious mental disorder and dilapidation.

hadephobia: the delusion that one has committed the unpardonable sin (Mark 3:29), and hence is doomed to an eternity in a literalist's conception of hell.

Haeckel, Ernst Heinrich (1834–1919): German biologist who (1884) developed the theory that ontogeny recapitulates phylogeny. This view impressed G. S. Hall greatly, and he developed a corollary (1904) to the effect that the mental development of the individual recapitulates the mental development of the race. This principle of Hall's is called the doctrine of *culture-epochs*.

hair cells: processes in the organ of Corti (and elsewhere in other organs) which are responsive to stimulation; hair-like processes of sensory nerve endings.

hair esthesiometer: apparatus devised by von Frey (1896) for investigations of sensitivity to pressure. In the original apparatus, horse and human hairs were fastened to the ends of sticks, and then applied to various points on the surface of the skin.

Hall, Granville Stanley (1844–1924): first president of the American Psychological Association (1892); founder of the *American Journal of Psychology* (1887); pioneer in child and adolescent psychology, and in psychology of senescence; important contributor to educational and religious psychology.

Haller, Albrecht von (1708–1777): German scientist sometimes called the "father of experimental physiology." His classical investigations dealt with the irritability of living tissues and with the rate of the nervous impulse (1762).

hallucination: traditionally defined, a percept-like response in the absence of any external sensory cues and accepted without question of its objective validity. Hallucinations may occur in any modality, but they are most frequent in the auditory field. This point of view was introduced by Esquirol (1838), who also coined the term *hallucination*. Inquiries (*e. g.*, the 1889 questionnaire of the English Society for Psychical Research) indicate that mental images like the Esquirol type of hallucinations are of fairly wide occurrence (though seldom in the life of one person). The use of various drugs to induce hallucinations has been reported. Hoffmann and others have emphasized the factor of pathologies in ideational centers; James (1890) seemed to favor the hypothesis of dissociation; some writers refer certain hallucinations to pathological conditions in sense organs or sensory nerves.

hallucinosis: Wernicke's term (1870) for prolonged and intense hallucinatory conditions.

halo effect: tendency to assign a high (or low) rating on all traits because the individual is considered to be high (or low) on one trait. Thorndike (1920) warned against this persistent error which invalidates the use of rating scales unless raters are cautioned against it, traits are clearly defined, or one trait is rated at a time.

hamartophobia: Hall's term (1904) for a sense of sinfulness experienced by adolescents which may lead them to a religious conversion or to despair.

Hamilton, William (1788–1856): Scottish philosopher who was a leader in associationism (1830). It has been noted that his principle of redintegration is somewhat analogous to the concept of the conditioned response.

handedness: preference for the use of one hand more than the other in various activities. A *dextrosinistral* individual is one who, having a preference for using the left hand, has been taught to write, draw, hold a fork, throw, and the like, with the right hand. The *index of dextrality* refers to a ratio of preference for right or left hand in a variety of tasks.

Hans, Clever: a horse exhibited in Berlin as a genius in calculations. The apparent superiority of this horse (one of a group known as the Elberfeld horses) excited so much amazement that the Minister of Public Education asked Stumpf to investigate. He reported that the animal was able to respond to minimal and unintentional cues given by its trainer.

haphalgesia: inability to bear the weight of bed coverings or clothes because of hypersensitivity to tactile sensations. The disorder may occur in hysteria; it most frequently occurs in serious organic pathologies.

haphemetria: explorations of the cutaneous senses, particularly, the use of the esthesiometer (von Frey, 1896) in the investigation of thresholds for the sense of pressure.

haplopia: normal fusion of retinal images, focus, and accommodation. This condition is the opposite of diplopia.

haptic: tactile.

haptodysphoria: neurotic aversion to touching certain common objects because of gooseflesh, involuntary tremors, and other concomitants of autonomic disturbance.

harp theory: a popular term for the Helmholtz theory of hearing (1863) which states that the rods of Corti are large at the tip and small at the base of the cochlea and that some are attuned to vibrate when stimulated by low frequencies, others by higher frequencies, and so on (like the strings of a harp or piano).

Hartley, David (1705-1757): English physician who developed a physiological explanation for the association of ideas (though he was a dualist), and who, therefore, is often referred to as the founder of British associationism.

Hartmann, Karl Robert Eduard von (1842-1906): German philosopher who (1869) laid the basis for the concept of the unconscious mind.

Harvey, William (1578-1657): English physician who (1629) announced his epochal discovery of the circulation of the blood (thus exploding the myth that animal spirits move it back and forth in the body).

Head, Henry (1861-1940): English neurologist who made

a thorough study of aphasia (1920). With Rivers, he developed a theory of cutaneous sensation (1905) which states that there are three divisions: protopathic, epicritic, and deep. (Epicritic: fine discriminations; protopathic: response to intense and painful stimuli, as in the viscera and in areas lacking epicritic receptors; deep: a part of the protopathic modality—in the viscera.)

heat: sensation (discovered by Altruz, 1896) when cold and warmth receptors in adjacent areas are simultaneously stimulated. Subsequently, investigators added the view that pain receptors must also be stimulated to give this ambiguous sensation.

hebephrenia: Hecker's term (1871) for a mental disorder occurring early in life, resulting in rapid deterioration, and distinguished by a disorganization of emotions.

heboidophrenia: a term introduced by Stransky (1909) to designate the simple type of dementia praecox.

Hecker, Ewald (1843-1909): German psychiatrist who described and named the disorder called *hebephrenia* (1871).

hedonic tone: the prevailing affects judged on the pleasantness-unpleasantness dimension. Hedonia is the condition of unusual cheerfulness; anhedonia, of despair.

hedonism: the ethical doctrine that the *summum bonum* is found in the pursuit of pleasure. The doctrine of psychological hedonism used in many theories of the learning process may be traced to Epicurus (306 B.C.).

Helmholtz, Hermann Ludwig Ferdinand von (1821-1894): German scientist whose researches in optics and audition contributed much to psychology as well as to physiology. His volumes on vision (1867) are considered to be his greatest achievement, and this field of study led him into psychology. He was the first to measure the rate of the

nervous impulse (1850), and he developed the famous
Young-Helmholtz theory of color vision (1852).

Helmont, Jan Baptista van (1577–1644) : Flemish physician
who introduced a doctrine (later exploited by Mesmer)
that there is a fluid called animal magnetism by means of
which persons can influence the behavior of others. Mesmer announced (1781) that the "discovery" was original
with him.

hemeralopia: blindness or indistinctness of vision in sunlight.
The condition is associated with albinism, malnutrition,
deterioration of pigment cells in the retina, general weakness, and similar pathologies.

hemi-: Greek prefix referring to a unilateral condition. Many
of the terms with this prefix allude to hysterical symptoms described by Charcot (1879) and Janet (1907);
others refer to conditions arising from lesions in the
nervous system.

hemiablepsia: unilateral or bilateral blindness in one-half of
the visual field, as a result of lesions in the optic com-
missure.

hemiageusia: an organic disorder in which half the tongue
is insensitive to taste.

hemianacusia: unilateral deafness.

hemianalgesia: insensitivity to pain on one side of the body.
According to Charcot (1879) and Janet (1907), it is
one of the major symptoms of hysteria.

hemianesthesia: loss of cutaneous sensitivity, especially to
pain, on one side of the body. The term usually refers to
hysterical reactions.

hemianopia (hemianopsia): vision in only one-half of the
visual field. Janet described the first case in 1894, and
demonstrated the hysterical nature of the symptoms. He

suggests that the reaction may originally have been associated with a temporary condition of visual impairment.

hemianosmia: inability to respond to olfactory stimulation in one nostril, as a result of organic impairment.

hemiataxia: inability to effect muscular coördinations on one side of the body; as a result of lesion in the nervous system.

hemiballismus: tremors and muscular weakness affecting one side of the body; unilateral chorea. The condition has an organic basis.

hemidiaphoresis: perspiring on only one side of the body. Also called *hemihidrosis*.

hemihyperesthesia: unilateral increase of sensitivity. Unilateral reduction of sensitivity (raising of the threshold) is called *hemihypesthesia*. Some modern students believe that Charcot and Janet unintentionally suggested to their patients that they had this, and analogous, symptoms.

hemiplegia: paralysis of one side of the body. In the hysteric, according to Janet (1907), the symptoms are exaggerated, and they do not conform to the neurological patterns. In organic hemiplegia, reflexes are affected, other signs of lesions are present, and the patient gains no advantage by his symptoms.

hemophilia: a condition, usually hereditary, in which the blood does not coagulate when the individual is cut. Writers observe that it is transmitted through the mother and that it seldom occurs among females.

hemothymia: pathological excitement by the sight of blood; sometimes a motive in sadistic killings.

Henning, Hans K. F. (1885–   ): Dutch physiologist who classified olfactory sensations (1915) and taste sensations (1916). The Henning olfactory prism groups elementary odors as follows: fragrant, etheral, spicy, putrid, burned, and resinous. The Henning taste tetrahedron includes the following elementary taste sensations: saline, sweet, sour, and bitter. Titchener adopted both the olfactory and the gustatory classifications of Henning.

Henri, V.: French psychologist who, with Binet, wrote on individual psychology (1895) and on various tests of higher mental functions.

Heraclitus: Greek philosopher (5th century b.c.) who taught that nature is in a state of ceaseless change.

Herbart, Johann Friedrich (1776–1841): German philosopher and educationalist who is called the "father of educational psychology." He was among the first to state that psychology is not a branch of speculative philosophy, but a science.

heredity: a broad term referring usually to the sum total of biological influences which at the time of conception determine an individual's capacity for growth and development. Both biological and social heredity are differentiated by some writers and confused by others. Galton (1869) taught that biological heredity is of maximal importance in determining the psychological make-up of the individual, and he founded an institute (1904) to promulgate his views.

heredity-environment controversy: the debate between advocates of nature versus nurture. Much of the controversy is centered about the concept of the IQ constancy.

Hering, Ewald (1834–1918): German physiologist who developed an influential theory of color vision (which is a rival to the Young-Helmholtz theory). He postulated (1878) three pairs of chemical (or metabolic) substances in the retina, each of which changes in either of two directions when stimulated appropriately (assimilation and dissimilation). The substances give rise, respectively, to the following sensations: white-black; red-green; and yellow-blue. He also reported (1877) his discovery of psychological zero in the thermal sense (the point of reference for judging warmth and cold being the temperature of the skin).

hermaphroditism: bisexualism; having both ovaries and testes.

herpes: red spots in the skin due to inflammation of small blood vessels. The condition is said to occur in some individuals as a result of intense emotional stress.

hetero-: Greek prefix which signifies *other, different.*

heterochiral: referring to the other hand, as that which is not trained but which may be tested for the effects of cross transfer.

heteroeroticism: attraction to members of the opposite sex.

heterogeneous: composed of a diversity of elements.

heterokinesia: a psychotic or psychoneurotic condition in which the patient obeys requests by making movements other than those which he intends to perform.

heterolalia: using words which were not intended by the speaker. According to psychoanalysis, this is an example of a purposeful accident, the true intent being unconscious, and hence the slip of the tongue occurs. It is also explained as being the result of extreme self-consciousness and embarrassment.

heterometropia: a condition of refractive disparity between the two eyes.

heterorexia: the eating of unnatural food substances; parorexia.

heterosexuality: normal sex adjustments to members of the opposite sex.

heterosuggestion: suggestion given by another person (as contrasted with autosuggestion). The term usually refers to the dominance of the subject by the hypnotist.

hexadactylism: having six fingers or toes (considered to be a Mendelian trait).

hidrosis: perspiring. In conditions of nervous tension, the individual may exhibit hyperhidrosis (excessive sweating).

hierarchy of habits: an integration of habits (usually motor skills) in the performance of a complex act (*e.g.*, typing), the simpler parts being automatic, effortless, and rapid.

higher mental functions: a loose term used by Binet (1902) to refer to complex functions such as attention, orientation of ideas, imagination, logical memory, and judgment.

hippus: reflex spasms in the pupils.

His, William (1831–1904): German histologist who discovered neuroblasts and the manner in which axons and dendrites grow from the cell body (1886).

histogram: a graphic representation of a frequency distribution of scores by means of rectangles of widths or heights proportional to the frequency in each interval.

Hitzig, Eduard (1838–1907): German neurologist who (with Fritsch) located certain motor areas in the human brain (1870).

Hobbes, Thomas (1588–1679): English philosopher who laid the basis for stimulus-response psychology (1651), exalted reason, and emphasized determinism in psychology.

holergasia: A. Meyer's term for a general disorder of psychobiological functions; hence a psychosis.

Holmgren, Alarik Frithiof (1813–1897): Swedish physiologist who devised a test for color-blindness. The Holmgren worsted test consists of a series of skeins which are to be matched with red, green, and rose.

Holt, Edwin B. (1873-1946): American psychologist who introduced the work of Bok (1915) and Kappers (1917) and developed the theory of the reflex-circle (the response to one stimulus being the stimulus for the next response).

homeostasis: Cannon's term (1932) for the constant states maintained by physiological processes.

homoerotic: attraction to members of the same sex for outlets for erotic desires.

homogenitalism: libidinous desires for members of the same sex.

homosexuality: a term used in psychoanalysis to denote the second stage in personality development, which is that of attraction to members of the same sex (the first being autoeroticism; the final being heteroeroticism). The term is used in a wide connotation, and it does not imply actual erotic contact.

Hoover, Charles F. (1865-1927): American physician who developed a test for differentiating between organic and hysterical hemiplegia.

hormone: secretion of an endocrine gland.

horopter: a term coined by Aguilonius (1613) to denote apparatus for determining each point in the field of binocular vision which is seen either as one or two (because of convergence).

hue: the color of a visual stimulus, which is determined by the wavelength.

Hume, David (1711-1776): Scotch philosopher who taught that the only contents of mind are sense-impressions and ideas (faint copies of sense-impressions). He rejected the concept of causality and emphasized the association of ideas (a mere sequential flow).

Huntington, George (1850-1916): American psychiatrist

who described a hereditary form of chorea (*Huntington's chorea*). It makes its appearance in the fourth decade of life, and it results in slow physical and mental deterioration.

Husserl, Edmund (1859–1938): German psychologist and philosopher who introduced the doctrine of phenomenology into psychology. This doctrine has been defined (Lanz, 1924) as the study of "objects in their relation to consciousness in a state of supreme impartiality, when the face-value and systematic significance of the objects concerned does not come into consideration."

Hutchinson, Jonathan (1828–1913): English physician who described the peg-shaped teeth (Hutchinson's teeth) of the congenital syphilitic.

hydrocephalus: a type of mental deficiency resulting from an excess production of cerebrospinal fluid in the ventricles of the brain. The head is usually very large (except in internal hydrocephaly), general physical condition is poor, and the mental defect varies from idiocy to borderline. The exact cause is unknown.

hydrotherapy: the use of water in any form (steam, ice, or liquid) for relief of pain and for tonic or sedative effects. The continuous bath (of neutral temperature) and the cold-sheet pack are often used to quiet excited patients.

hylozoism: the doctrine that matter is endowed with mind.

hypacusia: impairment of hearing.

hyper-: Greek prefix which denotes "an excess of" or "an unusual amount of."

hyperacusia: abnormal keenness of hearing.

hyperactivity: hyperkinesis.

hyperacuity: an exceptionally low threshold of stimulation in any or all sense organs.

hyperalgesia (hyperalgia): extreme sensitivity to pain.

hyperanakinesis: rapid twitchings in a limb or the facial muscles.

hyperaphia: tactile sensitivity in an extreme degree.

hyperaphrodisia: the condition of satyriasis or nymphomania.

hyperasthenia: extreme weakness, as in a patient with a severe organic disorder or with a condition of psychoneurotic lethargy and loss of muscular tonus.

hyperbulia: a psychoneurotic haste in making decisions.

hypercryalgesia: an extreme degree of sensitivity to cold.

hypererethisia: a condition of being intensely irritable and impatient, as in hyperthyroidism, fatigue, onset of a cold, and the like.

hyperesthesia: a low threshold for stimulation of sense organs.

hypergeusia: an extreme degree of sensitivity to tastes.

hyperhedonia: pathological optimism and joy, as in hebephrenia.

hyperhidrosis (hyperidrosis): excessive activity of the sweat glands.

hyperkinesis: intense, restless activity, as in hypomanic conditions and similar states.

hypermetropia (hyperopia): farsightedness. The eyeball is abnormally short or the lens is imperfect; hence the image tends to fall behind the retina.

hypermnesia: remarkable ability to retain, recall, and recognize past experiences. It is said to occur during periods of intense emotional excitement. Some writers have commented upon the possibility of eidetic imagery as an explanation of unusual ability to reproduce rote materials.

hyperorexia: a morbidly acute appetite; bulimia.

hyperosmia: unusually acute sense of smell. In the psychotic, this leads some patients to believe that enemies are injecting gases into their rooms or placing noxious substances in their food.

hyperphasia: a rapid, incoherent jumble of words.

hyperpituitarism: acromegaly, which is a condition marked by a large head, thick lips, prominent nose, large chest, short arms and legs, and huge hands.

hyperpraxia: rapid and exaggerated movements in performing habitual acts by manic patients.

hyperprosexia: an unusual degree of attentiveness to, or concentration upon, a portion of the total situation present to senses or to an ideational element.

hypersthenia: a feeling of abnormal muscular prowess, as in a patient with exalted delusions.

hypertarachia: extreme nervousness, irritability, and impatience.

hypertension: high blood-pressure. In the condition known as *essential hypertension*, prolonged worries and anxieties are mentioned as the principal causative factors.

hyperthermalgesia (hyperthermoesthesia): extreme inability to endure warmth or heat.

hyperthyroidism: excessive activity of the thyroid gland, which causes loss of weight, hyperhidrosis, irritability, and hypertonicity.

hypertonus: a failure of reciprocal innervation between flexors and extensors, which results in a condition of rigidity, exaggeration of reflexes, and an inability to perform acts involving muscular coördination.

hypesthesia: a general loss of sensory acuity.

hyphedonia: loss of zest for, and pleasure in, life.

hypnagogic state: the condition when one is about to fall asleep or is just waking up, when rare illusions and hallucinatory experiences may occur. The term was first used by Maury (1861) in his discussion of the similarity between dreams and hallucinations.

hypnocatharsis: the use of sleep-producing drugs or hypnotic suggestions to induce dreams which will effect release of tensions, painful memories, or fears.

hypnogenic: the suggestions used by the operator and the paraphernalia (bright object, or flashing mirrors, couch, and so on) in the induction of hypnosis.

hypnosis: Braid's term (though he preferred *neurohypnotism*, 1843) for a trance-like condition induced by suggestions. Charcot (1872) upheld the view that it is a pathological state analogous to hysteria (Salpêtrière school); Bernheim (1884) explained hypnosis in terms of suggestion (Nancy school). Most contemporary psychologists agree, in essence, with Bernheim's conclusions.

hypo-: Greek prefix meaning "a deficient amount of."

hypochondria: a morbid concern about one's health, and, in many cases, a concentration of attention upon various symptoms of physical disorder.

hypofunction: deficiency in the functioning of any organ or system of the body.

hypogeusia: insensitivity to taste stimuli.

hypogonadism: deficiency in the functioning of testes or ovaries, and hence abnormalities in the secondary sex characteristics.

hypoglossal nerves: the twelfth pair of cranial nerves, which innervate the muscles of the tongue.

hypognathous: a protruding lower jaw.

hypokinesis: lethargy; disinclination to move; diminished energy.

hypomania: the mildest degree of the manic phase of a

manic-depressive psychosis. Acute mania and hyperacute mania are the extreme degrees of this disorder.

hypophonia: inability to speak above a whisper.

hypophrenia: mental deficiency.

hypophysis cerebri: the pituitary gland.

hypopituitarism: deficiency in the secretions of the pituitary gland. The conditions frequently mentioned in the literature are the result (in part) of hypofunctioning of the anterior lobe of the pituitary—namely, dwarfism and Frölich's syndrome. A psychosis resembling schizophrenia has been reported in connection with hypopituitarism (Tucker, 1933).

hypoplasia: underdevelopment of some part of the body (Kretschmer, 1925).

hypothalamus: that part of the forebrain which regulates body temperature, and which mediates the motor expression of emotions in animals (Masserman, 1943).

hypothymia: inability to make adequate emotional responses.

hypothyroidism: inadequate functioning of the thyroids. If the condition exists from birth, it is known as cretinism; if it occurs later on, it is known as myxedema.

hypotonia: flaccidity of the musculature.

hysteria: a disorder once thought to occur only among women and to be caused by the migration of the uterus. It was brought into prominence by Charcot's studies (1872–1893), which promulgated the theory that morbid heredity is an important causative factor. Freud (1885) became interested in hysteria and developed the theory that it is caused by a psychic trauma of which the patient has no conscious recollection. The term is often used to connote conditions of emotional instability and of suggestibility (Babinski, 1908). When the unconscious (repressed) conflict finds expression in a physical disorder, Freud calls it *conversion hysteria.*

hystero-epilepsy: Charcot's term (1872) for the form of hysteria in which motor symptoms (convulsions, tremors, and tics of a violent type) predominate.

ictus: in music, an accentuated beat; also, a stroke of apoplexy.

iconolagny: form of sex perversion in which gratification is achieved by looking at lewd pictures or in interpreting works of art in a pornographic manner.

id: in Weismann's biology (1889), the chromatin granules of the cell; in psychoanalysis, the source of instinctual drives. George Groddeck (1916) proposed to Freud that the concept of the unconscious be revised to include the id, a dynamic concept referring to unlearned, basic drives which obey nothing but the pleasure principle. It appears in the infant and in certain types of mania in pure form. The id is uncontrolled by reality, morality, prudence, or social responsibility. These make up the ego, which exercises an administrative function over the id.

id-ego conflict: one of the most severe forms of intrapsychic disharmony, in which primitive instinctual drives are neither inhibited nor repressed, but find a partial outlet in psychoneurotic symptoms (according to psychoanalysts).

idea: a broad term referring to a concept or mental image.

idea of reference: an obsession (or delusion) in which the individual is the center of reference in the environment, chance remarks or glances being construed as having an allusion (usually a disparaging one) to the individual.

ideal types: Spranger's doctrine (1928) that there are six basic value-directions: economic, esthetic, political, social, religious, and theoretical.

idealism: the point of view in systematic psychology which states that personality (or the self) is the primary datum, and which, therefore, is opposed to the concept of materialistic mechanism (radical behaviorism). The doctrine stems from the philosophy of Plato.

ideation: reflective thinking; the activity of organizing concepts (or images) into meaningful relationships.

idée fixe: obsessional belief which dominates, to the exclusion of everything else, in the thinking of the individual (Janet, 1889).

identical elements: Thorndike's explanation (1913) for transfer of training, the carry-over of advantage gained in a practiced function to an unpracticed function being attributed to the similarity of elements in the functions. According to this theory, there is no necessity for assuming that generalization takes place.

identification: the enhancement of prestige by the assumption of enviable or admirable qualities in other persons or in the institutions to which one belongs. According to Freud (1900), it is an unconscious and emotionalized mechanism whereby unfulfilled wishes obtain vicarious gratification.

ideology: a systematized philosophy of the state, which, according to dissenters, is a rationalization for questionable practices. The term also denotes the science of ideas.

ideomotor action: the tendency of motor activity to follow immediately after the idea of action. The term was introduced by Carpenter (1874), and the concept was developed by James (1890) as the basis for psychology of volition. Now the concept has been largely discarded.

ideophrenia: a mental disorder with strong obsessional trends.

idiocy, amaurotic family: a rare type of mental deficiency with blindness, the disorder having been traced to immigrants who landed in America during Colonial days. It is also known as Tay-Sach's disease.

idioglossia: the formation of meaningless words, particularly the use of words within a family circle which were once employed by the children.

idiopathic disorder: one which does not arise from, and is not sustained by, another disorder. Thus, idiopathic epilepsy is the primary form of the convulsive pattern for which no specific organic cause has yet been located.

idioretinal light: photisms, sensations of light which arise from chemical processes in the retina, not from stimulation by lightwaves. (Helmholtz, 1856).

idiot: the lowest grade of mental defective, usually characterized by physical stigmata. According to the (British) Royal Commission on the Feeble-minded, an idiot is "a person so deeply defective from birth or from an early age that he is unable to guard himself against common physical dangers." Binet (1905) defined idiocy as a condition of such want of intelligence that the individual can make no use of language (beyond parrot-like sounds) and that his aptitudes are roughly equal to those of a two-year-old normal child or less. Seguin (1846) wrote on the education of idiots.

idiot-savant: a loose term applied to mental defectives (usually imbeciles at least) who have a relatively fair amount of skill in handicrafts, cards or checkers, a method of rapid calculation (usually by eidetic imagery) or the like. The case of J. H. Pullen (1833–1916), known as the "mad Genius of Earlwood Asylum" and famed for his mechanical contrivances, is an example.

illiteracy: the condition of inability to read and/or write as a result of lack of opportunity to learn or of mental deficiency. Loss of ability to read (because of organic lesion) is alexia; loss of ability to write (organic lesion), agraphia.

illness, adjustive: psychneurotic (usually hysterical) escape from situational difficulties by flight into illness, thereby lessening the tensions by an evasive adjustment.

illusion: a misinterpretation of sense impressions. The types of illusions often mentioned are as follows: those which arise from the physiology or anatomy of sense organs; those arising from the configuration of the stimuli; and those which arise from anticipatory or expectancy adjustments. An illusion was analyzed by Aristotle (crossed-finger), and illusions became a topic of interest to modern psychologists after Necker (1832) had described reversible-perspectives.

image: according to Titchener (1897), the element of ideas, differing from sensations in three ways: the qualities are unclear (pale, misty), intensity is less, and duration is brief. According to objectivists, the image is a conditioned response, not a mental element. The concept of the image was introduced into psychology by Hume (1748), who sharply distinguished between sensation-perceptions on the one hand and images-ideas on the other.

image, eidetic: an unusually vivid image which possesses many of the characteristic features of an actual sense-impression (E. Jaensch, 1925). Eidetic images are relatively common among young children; rare among adults.

imageless thought: a controversial theory (Würzburg School) which states that thinking is an abstract, image-less activity. Marbe (1901) introduced the theory; in America, Woodworth was its chief proponent; Titchener, its principal critic.

imagery types: Galton's conclusions (1883) regarding the incidence of various types of mental images (visual, auditory, gustatory, motor, olfactory, tactual) which were reported to him in response to his famous questionnaire. He asked the informants to rate on a point-scale the vividness of images in each modality, and thus introduced the theory of individual differences as well as of imagery types into psychology.

imaginary companion: a fantasy common among bright children from age three or four to six. It occurs most often when the child has no contemporaries with whom to play, and it usually fades out when real playmates are found.

imagination: the re-organization of past experiences into new combinations.

imago: an autistic image of the ideal person with whom to fall in love. According to psychoanalysis, it has its genesis in the parent of the opposite sex and undergoes many alterations during the course of the years. It accounts for sudden attachments.

imbalance: a condition of unequal strength in the eye muscles, as a result of which the retinal images do not fuse unless correctional lenses are worn.

imbecile: according to the well-known definition of the Royal Commission on the Feeble-minded: "one who, by reason of mental defect existing from birth or from an early age, is uncapable of earning his own living, but is capable of guarding himself against common physical dangers." Binet (1908) states that imbeciles cannot write intelligibly or read with comprehension, and that the level of intelligence does not exceed that of a normal child of six or seven years of age.

immature: the condition of not yet having attained full

growth. Immature behavior usually refers to that which is inappropriate for the individual's level of chronological development.

immediate memory: the repetition of a list of words or digits without error after a single presentation. Jacobs (1887) was among the first to determine experimentally the immediate memory span (amount that can be grasped upon a single presentation).

implicit behavior: subdued muscular activity, as contrasted with overt behavior. According to Watson (1919), thinking is a process of implicit behavior, such as lip and tongue movements, slight gestures, and the like. This view accords with the motor theory of consciousness.

impotence: inability to achieve an orgasm. It may arise from organic or psychic factors.

impressions: the neural events which are initiated when a stimulus affects a receptor. According to Avenarius (1888, 1890), psychology is the science dealing with the experiencing individual (who receives impressions); physics, with the nature of reality considered apart from the experiencing individual; hence the principal datum of psychology is the immediate impression, from which all the complexities of mental life are developed.

impulse: a sudden drive to action; particularly a relatively simple drive of short duration. The term is used with varying connotations by different writers, and thus it has acquired diverse meanings, the one point of agreement being that it implies a sudden, intense drive.

impulsiveness: the train of acting suddenly and without foresight or prudence. The stimulus initiates a train of behavior which is already in a condition of a prepared reaction, and in which the cognitive aspect is subordinated to the conative-affective aspects.

incest: coitus within the range of family ties, which, by mores and law, prohibit marriage. According to psychoanalysis, the universal taboos of incest and parricide have their genesis in the Oedipus complex; and incestuous phantasies, conscious and unconscious, are potent determinants of psychoneurotic and psychotic conditions.

incidental learning: that which is acquired as a by-product of the intentional learning. According to Kilpatrick (1923), the really important outcomes of schooling are the results of incidental learning (attitudes, preferences, ideals, interests, and the like), whereas subject-matter mastery is soon lost because of lack of use of it.

incoherence: the absence of logical connections among sequential parts of a belief or delusion. The logic of the transitions is not obvious to the observer; but, in theory (Hart, 1912), the connections lie in the private logic of the patient. The extreme degree of incoherence in speech is called a salad of words or a word hash, but proponents of the theory of psychological determinism object to the superficiality of these descriptive phrases.

incompetent: in the legalistic sense, inability to manage one's personal affairs because of mental deficiency or grave mental disorder.

incoördination: inability to control muscular movements in purposeful activities, such as walking, writing, speaking, or standing. Nicolas Friedrich (1825–1882), a German physician, described the most common type of hereditary ataxia, which involves cerebellar lesions and appears at about age ten. The effects of various drugs upon the loss of coördinations is well known. In tabes dorsalis incoördination is the outstanding symptom (locomotor ataxia).

incoördination tests: typical tests for ataxia are as follows:

the patient's ability to touch the end of the nose with the index finger, the eyes first being open, and then closed; the eyes being closed, the patient's ability to bring the index fingertips together in front of the chest; the Romberg test, in which the patient's ability to stand at attention, eyes closed, without swaying.

incubus: in the Middle Ages, the popular delusion of hysterical women that an evil spirit cohabited with them during sleep.

incorrigible child: unmanageable; resistant to the authority of parents. The term is usually applied to a young girl whose precocious sex behavior leads her to encounter difficulties with school authorities or the police.

identification: Freud's term (1900) to denote an unconscious process in which the individual introjects the characteristics of another person or persons.

identity hypothesis: Fechner's theory (1860) that, since body and mind can be measured, they are basically identical.

individual differences: the measurable unlikeness of people, which, in a random sampling of any given trait, provides data for a bell-shaped curve. The concept of individual differences was introduced by Galton (1883), and it has become one of the central topics in psychology. According to the standard theory, any given trait is distributed in Gaussian fashion in a continuum, all differences, therefore, being qualitative. G. Allport (1937) has raised questions about this assumption and has presented reasons for believing in the uniqueness of each person.

Individual Psychology: the point of view established by Adler (1911) and emphasizing the urge for superiority, the inferiority feeling, and compensatory goals. At one time, Adler was closely associated with the Viennese Psychoanalytic Society, but he left in order to found his own system.

individualism: the condition of independence from the stereotypes of the group.

individuation: Coghill's term (1929) for the emergence of specific structures and functions from the embryo *Amblystoma*.

induction: the process of reasoning in which observations of particular data furnish, by analogy, a basis for inferences regarding the whole of which these data are a part (Bacon, 1620). J. S. Mill broadened the term to include the uniformity of nature, whereby it is valid to make general inferences from particular observations by the methods of agreement, difference, residues, and concomitant variations (1843).

industrial psychology: a branch of applied psychology in which techniques of tests and measurements, rating scales, interviews, attitude studies, job specifications, training programs, accident clinics, and the like are related to problems of industry.

inertia: the tendency for mental activities to perseverate.

infancy: the first eighteen months of life.

infantile sexuality: the psychoanalytic doctrine that the unconscious sex wishes of the adult are closely related to sex wishes of the first five years of life. Thus, the psychoneurotic adult or the immature adult unconsciously seeks gratification of infantile sex drives through wit, dreams, phantasies, and other mechanisms.

infantilism: an extreme degree of immaturity and dependency.

infatuation: an intense erotic attachment of short duration. According to psychoanalysis, it is attributable to an

Imago, which is the idealized, autistic representation of a partner in erotic satisfactions.

inferiority feeling: Adler's concept (1911) denoting the loss of a feeling of superiority which follows defeat, organ inferiority, or low social status. Birth order is a frequent determinant, the oldest child having the least of it; and the second child, usually impressed with the feeling (or complex). Adler believes that the sex conflicts (major determinants according to Freud) are secondary outcomes of the inferiority feeling in psychoneurotics.

inheritance: the transmission from one generation to another of (a) social institutions, culture, mores and folkways, personal advantages arising from the privileged status of parents, and the like; and (b) of the genetic constitution which determines physical growth and development.

inhibition: the restraint of a response. According to Pavlov (1890), it is observed in its simplest form in the delayed reaction, in which the dog is trained to respond to a conditioned stimulus repeatedly given at a set time-interval before the adequate stimulus. Eventually, the conditioned stimulus will, after the set time-interval, elicit the reflex. An extraneous stimulus (buzzing of a fly, for instance) will inhibit the inhibition. He also found that newly established conditioned reflexes are in a state of irradiation, any extraneous stimulus being likely to elicit them; but, after continued training, discriminations are established with reference to the conditioned stimulus (the process of differentiation). The establishment of sphincter controls in the human infant is considered to be the first important lesson in inhibitions.

initial spurt: the vigor displayed in mental and physical activities before the individual settles down to a more or less steady work curve.

initial torpor: the ".warming up" period in undertaking a
new activity immediately after having left a different
type of activity. The effect is known as proactive inhibition (Ebbinghaus, 1885).

inner ear: the vestibular apparatus, semicircular canals, and
cochlea.

inner speech: implicit muscular activity in the articulatory
apparatus.

insane: mentally deranged. The term has a legal, not a medical or psychological, reference at the present time.

insania: Cicero's term (*c.* 75 B.C.) for a condition of mental
disorder marked by a loss of poise, emotional control, and
balance; but not so severe as a furore, in which the individual is legally irresponsible by reason of complete derangement.

insanity, types of: (1) abortive: Westphal's term (1877)
for unusually strong obsessions and fixed ideas; (2) artificial: H. Tuke's interpretation (1880) of hypnosis
(Braidism); (3) ideal: Arnold's designation (1782) of
a derangement of ideational functions; (4) moral:
Prichard's designation (1835) of what is now referred
to as psychopathic behavior; and (5) puerperal: a term
said to have been used by Hippocrates to denote mental
disorder following childbirth.

insomnia: inability to sleep.

insight: the sudden achievement of a meaningful relationship among the various parts of the situation. Hobhouse
(1901) criticized the trial-and-error theory of learning
(Thorndike's) by stating that animals can learn the relations of objects in a problem situation, and hence work
out a solution. Köhler (1924) reported well-known experiments dealing with the ability of anthropoid apes to
learn by insight.

inspiration-expiration ratio: a concept introduced by Stör-ring (1906) for use in records of the rate of breathing and used by Benussi (1916) as a technique for lie detection. Woodworth (1938) recommended that the duration of inspiration be divided by the duration of the whole cycle, and that the ratio be referred to as the I-fraction.

instinct: often defined as a complex pattern of unconditioned reflexes or as an unlearned, inner drive to biologically purposeful action. This troublesome word was introduced into human psychology by Preyer (1881), and it received great impetus from James (1890). In psychoanalysis the concept is of major importance, instincts being the energy which causes tensions and drives to action. Freud wrote about the manner in which instincts are displayed, not of their actual nature.

insulin therapy: the method of shock treatment for certain mental disorders which was introduced by Sakel (*c.* 1927). He reported success with schizophrenics and morphine addicts, and his translated articles (1938) have attracted a great deal of attention in America.

integral phenomenology: the exploration of the inner life of the individual by means of personal document analysis, projective techniques, autobiographies, and similar methods.

integration: the organization of parts into wholes and the systematic arrangement of wholes in order of their importance. The concept as used in neurology refers to the coördination among receptors, connectors, and effectors. In mental hygiene, it connotes the well-organized personality.

intelligence: according to Thorndike (1903), a multitude of independent capacities, some of which are sampled by tests of intelligence; but, according to Spearman (1904), a common capacity (or group of capacities) underlying, in greater or lesser amounts, specific activities. In 1909, Binet wrote that intelligence involves the ability to maintain a direction, adaptability, and auto-criticism. Subsequently, many other psychologists have proposed other definitions none of which has been completely accepted.

intelligence quotient: Stern's technique (1912) of dividing the mental age by the chronological age in order to have a convenient expression for the ratio of intelligence to actual age. Esquirol (1828) had a vague concept relating to the IQ, when he proposed a comparison of the learning ability of mental defectives with that of normal children at the same age-level.

intelligence test: an item or series of items designed to measure the higher intellectual capacities of a person. Binet and Simon (1905) published the first practicable measure of intelligence, and Goddard (1910) adapted it for use in America. The revision of the Binet Scale by Terman (1916) firmly established the use of intelligence tests in America. Tests are classified as individual or group measures; speed (time limits) and power; verbal and non-verbal (performance).

intensity: the attribute of a sensation according to which the individual classifies it as lighter-heavier, softer-louder, smoother-rougher, and the like (Titchener, 1896), though the sensations thus compared for intensity have the same quality (*e.g.*, weight, a musical note, textiles which are touched, etc.).

intentional act: voluntary behavior, as opposed to reflex response.

intentional forgetting: according to Freud, the repression of an unwelcome memory, and hence the inability consciously to recall that which has been relegated to the unconscious.

intentionalism: Brentano's theory (1874) of the mental activity which brings the physical content into the focus of attention, the object thus being brought into the act.

interactionism: Descartes' theory (1650) that mind and body, though separate, interact, the one influencing the other. He located the place of this interaction in the pineal gland.

interest: any preference displayed when choices are offered. Strong (1927) developed a test for the measurement of interests by having the subjects choose among *like, indifference,* and *dislike* for each of 420 items, the weighted scores furnishing a basis for comparisons with persons who are successful in various occupations (chiefly in the professions).

interference: the negative transference of one function to another, as a result of which efficiency in the second is impaired. In associative interference, the exercise of a given function impedes the efficiency of learning in another function. In reproductive interference, the learning of one function impairs the efficiency of recall of another function.

interoceptor: receptor located in the viscera or elsewhere within the smooth musculature of the body. The vague pattern of interoceptive stimulation is the basis for much of what is called the feeling-tone (coenesthesis).

interpersonal relationships: the reciprocal influences which persons exert upon one another in primary (face-to-face) social groups.

interpolation: locating a point between two variables by the use of a specified procedure of statistics, as in locating centiles on the ogive curve.

introjection: a psychoanalytic mechanism connoting the process (or the result) of incorporating into the ego or the super-ego any object or person.

intromission: the insertion of the penis into the vagina.

introspection: the classical method of reflecting upon the nature of an experience for the purpose of analyzing it into its component elements. St. Augustine (396) is often referred to as the "father of psychological introspection." Baird (1913) developed the method of complete introspection, in which literally scores of pages of typescript were used to report observations of brief mental activities. Morbid introspection refers to the tendency to engage in unwholesome thinking about one's status.

introversion: Jung's term (1923) for an attitude-type characterized by a subjective point of view and a tendency to evaluate the environment with the self as the center of reference. Introversion is the antithesis of extraversion. The following function-types complicate the dichotomy: thinking, intuition, sensing, and feeling; hence there are eight possibilities for classifying any individual according to attitude-type and function-type. Freyd (1924) established a relationship between schizoid tendencies and introversion; hence much confusion has arisen about Jung's actual teachings. Freud used the term to denote the condition of being occupied with erotic phantasies which cannot be gratified in reality.

introversive: Rorschach's term (1922) for an individual who is oriented to living in a world of daydreams and who gives an excessive number of responses in terms of movement when tested by his inkblot technique .

inversion: the assumption of the role of a member of the opposite sex.

inversion of affect: the psychoanalytic doctrine of ambivalence of strong emotion, which states that, by the principle of polarities, an emotion such as love may suddenly turn to hate.

involution melancholia: a mental disorder associated with the physiological changes (especially the menopause in women) of late middle life, the common symptoms being depressed affects; hypochondria; nihilistic delusions; anxiety, often of the agitated type; and delusions of sinfulness. MacCurdy (1925) suggested that psychological factors (*e.g.*, realization of the immanence of death, feelings of frustration about accomplishments, narrowing of the range of interests) may be fully as important as the reduction of output of gonadal hormones.

intuition: the sudden achievement of a concept, without dependence upon the processes of reflective thinking (Bergson, 1911). Locke (1690) defined it as a knowledge gained by immediate, bare inspection of mental data; J. S. Mill (1843), as the axioms from which all other truths must be known.

involuntary action: that which is either reflexive or habitual, and hence performed without intent.

IQ: the intelligence quotient. (Also *I.Q.*)

iris: the pigmented circular membrane lying between the cornea and the lens of the eye. It includes two sets of musculature: the sphincter pupillae and the dilator (radial fibers) pupillae, which regulate the amount of light admitted into the eyeball.

irradiation: the spreading of excitation aroused by a stimulus (Pavlov, 1890). In the initial stages of the establishment of a conditioned reflex, any intense stimulus may elicit the response, but eventually the response can be elicited only by the stimulus consistently employed in the conditioning process. Hence, Pavlov stated, the irradiation is gradually replaced by differentiation. Watson (1924) reported that a conditioned fear for a furry animal spread to a fear of other animals and furry objects.

irrational delusion: a false belief which lacks internal consistency and which is obviously inappropriate and illogical.

irresistible impulse: a term introduced by Weyer (1579) to denote acts, usually criminal in nature, performed by an individual who had no freedom of choice, but who was directed by pathological impulses and emotions.

irritability of protoplasm: the alterations induced by stimuli. Phylogenetically, this is the characteristic of protozoa from which the specialized sense organs have been developed in the evolutionary process.

irrumation: the act of obtaining an orgasm by the mouth; fellatio or penilingus.

island of Reil: the small convolutions at the base of the fissure of Sylvius in the cerebrum, described by Johann Christian Reil (1759–1813), a Dutch anatomist.

island, tonal: inability to hear certain sound frequencies.

isolation: a Freudian mechanism whereby the obsessional neurotic represses the tensions arising from affects and seeks gratification in intellectualism, hence failing to recognize the compensatory nature of the behavior. The mechanism was defined in 1936 (English translation), and it is generally overlooked by psychoanalysts.

Itard, Jean Marie Gaspard (1774?–1838): French physician who developed a system for the education of deaf children and who described a case of a so-called feral boy (1803).

item: the unit in a psychological test or measure.

J

Jacobi, Maximilian (1775-1858): French psychiatrist who emphasized need for knowledge of the brain, and who minimized the value of non-materialistic concepts, in the treatment of mental disorders.

Jacobs, J.: among the first to investigate the memory span (1887).

Jackson, John Hughlings (1834-1911): British physician who developed the theory that epileptic convulsions result from a sudden discharge of impulses in the gray matter of the cerebral cortex.

Jacksonian epilepsy: spasms affecting small groups of muscles, without accompanying loss of consciousness but with the possibility that severe convulsions are likely to develop later.

Jackson's law: pertains to the manner in which memory functions are affected in mentally disturbed persons, recollection for events immediately preceding the onset being lost first.

Jaeger-test: measure of visual acuity in which types of different sizes are read from a card held in normal reading-positions.

Jaensch, Erich R. (1883-   ): leader of the Marburg School (Germany), which has investigated eidetic images. V. Urbantschitsch (1907) had described images as clear as percepts, but Jaensch carried the studies further. He coined the term *eidetic* (from Greek for "extremely clear and vivid") to denote images, chiefly visual, which are frequently reported by children and only rarely by adults. Jaensch incurred some odium when he and his brother became "official Nazi psychologists."

Jaensch, Walther (1889–   ): identified eidetic types occurring on a constitutional basis. The basedowoid type (B) is analogous, in minute form, to a hyperfunctioning of the thyroid; and the tetanoid type (T) is analogous, in miniature, to a disease accompanying parathyroid dysfunction.

James, William (1842–1910): "dean of American psychologists"; only man, except G. S. Hall, to be elected twice president of the American Psychological Association; author of *Principles of Psychology* (published in 1890), the book which is said to mark the turning point in the history of modern psychology; author of one of the most important theories of emotion; among the first to start a psychological laboratory, his having been in a small room with meager equipment, at Harvard about 1874–1876; described the stream of consciousness; wrote many books bearing upon psychology, but later became interested in philosophy and developed pragmatism.

James-Lange theory of emotions: the view that perception of the situation arouses motor activity and that awareness of this physiological response is the emotion. James expounded the theory in 1884; the Danish psychologist, Carl Lange (1834–1900), described it in an article published in 1885. James insisted that the theory bear both names. It has inspired a great deal of research, particularly in the field of the physiology of emotions.

Janet, Pierre (1859–   ): French psychiatrist who investigated hysteria, developed the concept of dissociation, advanced techniques of environmental and suggestive therapeutics, and upheld the concept of psychic energy. In 1906, at the dedication of the new buildings of the Harvard Medical School, he gave important lectures on hysteria.

Janet's neurosis: psychasthenia, a disorder marked by obsessions, compulsions, fears, scruples, feelings of depersonalization, and the like. It is said, by Pierre Janet, to result from loss of psychic tonus or energy.

jargon: meaningless talk by low-grade mental defectives and some psychotics.

Jastrow, Joseph (1863–1945): one of the earliest American psychologists to take his doctorate here; specialist in psychophysics; did much to popularize scientific psychology; founded the first psychological laboratory opened at the University of Wisconsin (1886).

J-curve hypothesis: the general tendency of most persons to conform in institutionalized situations, with only a small number deviating. The amount of deviation may be roughly measured; and as the nonconformity becomes more extreme, fewer individuals are found. This hypothesis, based upon observations, was reported by Floyd Henry Allport, American psychologist, in 1932.

Jehovah complex: belief that one is omnipotent and omniscient.

Jena method: Karl Brauckmann's technique for teaching deaf children to speak, the procedure being for the children to feel lip movements and thus get kinesthetic concepts.

Jendrassik effect: exaggerated knee jerk when fingers are tensely interlaced.

Jennings, Herbert Spencer (1868–   ): American geneticist who, from studies of *drosophila melanogaster* (fruit fly), drew major conclusions regarding the mechanisms of heredity.

job analysis: study of each operation necessary to perform a given piece of work.

job specification: analysis of the type of person who should be employed to perform a given piece of work.

Johnny and Jimmy: twins used in a well-known study of relative effects of maturation and training (Myrtle Mc-Graw, 1935).

Jolly reaction: abnormal fatigability of a muscle stimulated by constant faradic current, taken as one sign of possible myasthenia gravis or after-effects of encephalitis.

Jost's law: pertaining to the results of continued practice on material equally well learned at the outset, the practice being more effective for the older of two associations than for the more recently acquired.

journals: Wundt's *Philosophische Studien* (1882), in which he published many of his research reports, often referred to as the oldest psychological journal (1882). *Mind*, an English journal for philosophy and psychology, contains many of the early work of American psychologists (1876). The first American journal was founded by G. S. Hall, then of the Johns Hopkins University, and named the *American Journal of Psychology* (1887).

Judd, Charles H. (1873–1946): earned the doctorate under Wundt, succeeded E. W. Scripture in experimental psychology at Yale, and contributed much to educational psychology. He opposed E. L. Thorndike's explanation of transfer of training by identical elements and emphasized the possibility of transfer through generalization.

judgment: cognitive activity of bringing two ideas into an affirmation of similarity or difference, as in judging weights, lines, pictures, and the like. Judgment of just noticeable differences was explored by Weber and Fechner (*q. v.*)

Jung, Carl (1875–   ): leader of the Zurich school and one of Freud's earliest supporters. He is well-known for his delineation of personality types, the concept of collective unconscious, and for founding a type of emphasis known as analytical psychology.

just noticeable difference: the minimum detectable difference between two stimuli. The least-noticeable-difference experiments were first reported by E. H. Weber in 1834.

juvenile: youth or adolescent.

juvenile delinquent: from the standpoint of psychology and sociology, a youth who has been brought before police officials or presented in court, the charges having been sustained by the evidence.

K

Kahlbaum, Karl Ludwig (1828–1899): German psychiatrist who introduced the following terms into the literature: catatonia, symptom complex, cyclothymia, verbigeration.

kaintophobia: fear of change.

Kallikaks: pseudonym (literally "good-bad") of a family traced to Martin K., a soldier in the Revolutionary army who had a child by a barmaid (presumably an ament) and later had children by a normal woman. Of 480 descendants traced to his illegitimate offspring, only 46 were normal; of 496 from the normal line, only 5 were abnormal. The case was published by Henry H. Goddard in 1914.

Kalmuk idiocy: mental deficiency in which there is a superficial resemblance to the facial features of the Mongols. The Kalmuks are a Tartar tribe.

Kant, Immanuel (1724–1804): German philosopher who held decided opinions about the field and the limitations of psychology. He upheld the nativistic (a priori) doctrine of space and time perception, and he declared that sensations can never be measured. He wrote that the mind synthesizes the various elements of experience into a whole which is far more than the sum of its parts (creative synthesis).

katabolism: tearing down of tissues; hence the opposite of anabolism. Usually spelled catabolism.

Keller, Helen (1880–   ): American woman who became blind and deaf at 18 months of age and was afterwards taught by Anne Sullivan. Joseph Jastrow reported a psychological study of this case in 1894.

Kelvin, William Thomson (Lord Kelvin) (1824–1907): British physicist whose apparatus was used in the earliest studies of the psychophysics of tone.

Kiesow, Federico (1858–1941): Italian psychologist born in Germany, best known for his work on sensory phenomena.

Koffka, Kurt (1886–1941): German (later an American) psychologist who, with Max Wertheimer and Wolfgang Köhler, was one of the original leaders in Gestalt psychology (1912), and who developed the insight theory of learning (1925).

Korsakoff's psychosis: type of mental disorder occurring in acute alcoholism, the symptoms being loss of immediate memory, disorientation, and glibness (presumably to cover up memory gaps).

Kraepelin, Emil (1856–1926): "father of modern psychiatry"; systematized and classified the field of mental disorders, introducing many terms and concepts. He defined manic-depressive psychosis and dementia praecox.

Krafft-Ebing, Rudolph (1840–1903): German psychiatrist who wrote on sex aberrations and whose views are frequently cited in courts of law. He established the relationship between general paralysis and syphilitic infection.

Krause, Wilhelm (1833–1910): German histologist who identified nerve endings in the skin which are known as the corpuscles of Krause.

Kretschmer, Ernst (1888–   ): German psychiatrist who maintains that morphological and personality types are essentially the same. He described the asthenic (long, lean) as schizoid; the pyknic (short, dumpy) as cycloid. (*Leptosome* is a synonym for *asthenic*.)

Kries, Johannes von: author of the duplicity theory of vision. He reported (1894) that rods respond to light-waves

stimulating achromatic or twilight vision and that cones
respond to light-waves giving rise to daylight and chromatic vision.

Külpe, Oswald (1862–1916): leader of the Würzburg
school, which advanced the theory of imageless thought
(supported by R. S. Woodworth, American psychologist)
and which developed introspective techniques for studying higher mental functions.

Kundt, A.: German physicist who developed the dust method
for calculating tone frequencies (1866) and who made
some minor studies of geometrical illusions (1863).

kurtosis: flatness of a curve as compared to the normal frequency curve.

kymograph: apparatus recording temporal sequences. The
device usually consists of paper affixed to a revolving
drum and a stylus at right angles to the drum.

labial: pertaining to the lips. Since the mouth plays an important part in the expression of emotions (Dunlap, 1927), the musculature is often mentioned: (upper lip) *levator labii superioris, zygomaticus minor, zygomaticus major, levator anguli oris;* (lower lip) *depressor labii inferioris, depressor anguli oris, levator menti.*

labile affects: unstable feelings, emotions, and moods, characterized by quick shifts from one extreme to the other.

labiograph: apparatus for recording lip movements in speech or in thinking (implicit speech behavior).

laboratory: a place wherein by means of controlled situations, often involving the use of apparatus, scientific experiments may be conducted. William James (about 1875) set up some apparatus for the use of his students in Harvard College. Wilhelm Wundt opened the first real psychological laboratory in the world at Leipzig in 1879. Granville Stanley Hall founded the first one in America (Johns Hopkins, 1883).

labyrinthine apparatus: the cavities of the inner ear, which include the vestibular apparatus, the semicircular canals, and the cochlea.

labyrinth: a maze, such as the Hampton Court pattern used in studies of human and animal learning. Edward Lee Thorndike (1898) is said to be the first to use mazes in the study of animal learning.

lacrimal: pertaining to the tear glands.

lactic acid: an important component of the acid-base balance of the body, reported by Rich (1928) to be abnormally high in excitable persons; activity produces an excess of lactic acid. (The acid-base level is customarily measured by analyses of the urine or the saliva.)

lacuna: a gap, as in consciousness for past or present events. Presumably, a lacuna (or fugue) may be caused by drugs, mental conflicts, petit mal, inattention, or the like.

Ladd, George Trumbull (1842–1921): an American pioneer in the field of physiological psychology (1887) and one of the founders of functional psychology.

Ladd-Franklin, Christine (1847–1930): American psychologist known for a theory of color vision. According to the theory (1892), the primitive eye was responsive to light-waves for black and white; at the next evolutionary stage, for yellow and blue; and, finally, for red and green.

Laehr, Henrich (1820–1905): German psychiatrist who studied the effects of addiction to morphine.

lag: continuance of physiological activity in a receptor or in the brain after the cessation of the stimulus.

Laignel-Lavastine, Maxime (1875–   ): French psychiatrist.

laissez-faire: a minimum of governmental control. In the Lewin experiment on experimentally created "social climates" (1939), the term refers to group life without adult participation.

lalia: speech.

laliphobia: dread of the necessity of speaking by a person with a speech impediment.

lalling (lallation): meaningless repetition of sounds, as by an infant or a mental defective.

laloneurosis: a speech impediment caused by functional spasms of muscles in lips and tongue, as in fear, extreme self-consciousness, or the like.

lalopathy: any disorder of the speech functions.

laloplegia: speech disturbance resulting from a stroke. The muscles of the tongue are unaffected.

Lamarck, Jean Baptiste Pierre Antoine de (1744–1829): French naturalist who developed the theory that acquired traits are transmissible through biological heredity.

lamella: apparatus for producing deep tones. It is used in determining the lower limits for auditory sensations.

La Mettrie, Julien Offray de (1709–1751): French philosopher who upheld the doctrine of materialistic monism and who, therefore, denied the reality of mind.

Lange, Carl (1834–1900): Danish physiologist who (1885) developed a theory of emotions similar to that announced by William James (1884). The theory (said by Titchener, 1914, to have originated in the earlier writings of the French) upholds the view that the emotion is the awareness of physiological changes resulting from perception of a situation.

Langermann, Johann Gottfried (1768–1832): German psychiatrist who is said to have written the first doctoral thesis on psychiatry submitted to a German university and who contributed to psychotherapy.

Langley, John Newport (1852–1925): English physiologist who investigated the autonomic nervous system and who differentiated between voluntary and involuntary muscles.

lanugo hair: the soft, cotton-like hair of the mongoloid; also, the hair appearing on the fetus at about the fifth month.

lapsus calami: psychoanalytic term referring to the unconscious wish for a disaster.

lapsus linguae: a slip of the tongue in which the true (unconscious) meaning is revealed. Freud (1914, English translation) cited many examples.

lapsus memoriae: psychoanalytic term referring to unconscious, wishful distortion of recollections.

laryngograph: apparatus for recording movements of the larynx; hence used in experimental studies of the motor theory of consciousness.

latency period: Freudian term for the years between about five and twelve, when, presumably, the interests in sex are more or less dormant. The period begins with the repression of the Oedipus complex and ends with the onset of puberty. According to some analysts, the folk-tale of Snow White is a representation of the latency period.

latent content: Freud's term (1900) for the unconscious determinants or motivating factors of a dream. The latent content is discovered by an analysis of the manifest content.

lateropulsion: involuntary tendency to sway or walk to one side, as in the case of an individual with organic brain disorder.

law: statement of an observed uniformity to which there are few, if any, exceptions. In the biological and the social sciences there are few laws which can be affirmed with the certainty pertaining to those in the physical sciences.

Lawrence-Moon-Biedle syndrome: an inherited form of idiocy, often accompanied by webbed or supernumerary fingers and toes or with other malformations.

learning: a broad term referring to modifications of behavior as a result of experience. The theories most often mentioned are the following (*q. v.*): association; trial-and-error, conditioning; and insight.

Le Bon, Gustave (1841-1931): French social psychologist who developed the views of Tarde and who wrote on the psychology of the crowd.

Le Conte, John (1818-1891): American physicist who contributed to knowledge of vision.

Leber, Theodor (1840–1917): German ophthalmologist.

lecheur: pervert who applies mouth to genitals.

legal psychology: application of psychological principles to testimony, questioning of witness, determination of guilt, factors influencing judgment of the court, and the like. The field was established by Münsterberg (1916).

Leibniz, Gottfried Wilhelm von (1646–1716): German idealist who upheld the doctrine of pre-established harmony. According to this view, mind and body are discrete entities, causally unrelated, yet working together in harmonious concomitance.

lens: convex, transparent body lying posterior to the pupil and iris.

lenticular nucleus: an ovoid mass of gray matter in the corpus striatum. Degeneration causes Wilson's disease (1912), a syndrome marked by tremors, enfeeblement, irritability, and childish emotionalism.

Lepois, Charles (1563–1633): French physician who broke with the old tradition that hysteria occurs only among women (Hippocrates, 400 B.C.), and who denied that it is caused by the uterus.

leptokurtic distribution: a frequency curve with an abnormally high peak at the center.

leptosome: Kretschmer's term (1925, English translation) for a bodily build which is slender (asthenic) and which is associated with the schizothymic temperament.

Lesbian: female homosexual. The term comes from the name of the island of Lesbia, where Sappho lived.

lesion: an injury, structural change of pathological type, or wound to tissues.

lethomania: morbid craving for drugs.

libido: Freudian term for sexual energy. In the narrow sense, the term alludes to a drive for sex gratification; in a broad sense, it connotes the instincts of the Id. According to Jung, it is synonymous with the sum-total of psychic energy.

lie detector: apparatus for measuring physiological changes which are concomitants of affective disturbances, presumably some of the changes being related to guilt. Marston, an American psychologist, was a pioneer in this field (1912).

Liébault, Ambroise-August (1823–1904): French physician of Nancy who made use of hypnosis (*mesmerism*) in psychotherapy.

life force: according to Bergson, the idealistic tendency in the entire universe, including the human mind, to evolve into newer, and higher, emergents. He suggested this doctrine as a corrective for the tendency of psychologists to pre-occupy themselves with analyses of mental states.

life instinct: Freud's term for the drives which are said to culminate in self-preservation activities and sex gratification. These drives or instincts act in opposition to the "death instinct"; hence the Eros-Thanatos polarity was discussed by Freud (1910).

life style: Adler's term (1917) for the manner in which the individual in striving to reach the goals of life and to adjust to the problems of occupation, love, and community living. Life style is not fixed by heredity, but the family influences are the principal determinants during early life.

light adaptation: a term introduced by Lohman (1906) to designate the adjustment of the eye to continued stimulation by bright light.

light-waves: energy which stimulates the rods and the cones, and hence which elicits visual sensations. Light-waves are measured either from successive crest to crest (or trough to trough) or by height. They are either pure or mixed. Presumably (Titchener, 1897), mixed waves are concomitants of brightness differences; length, of hue. Titchener differentiated 32,280 separate color sensations or elements.

limen: threshold of awareness. A stimulus below or above the limen arouses no awareness or sensation. Thus, the determination of the limen for various sense modalities is a classical problem in psychophysics.

limit: the point beyond which further practice or training effects no improvement in a given function. The limit of achievement in simple neuromuscular activities (rate-of-manipulation tests and the like) and athletic performances is far more readily determined than is the limit for learning a complex function, though apparently there is a limit to all functions.

linear perspective: the diminished size or separation of distant objects. This illusion is employed by artists in obtaining the depth effect, and it is illustrated by the apparent convergence of railroad tracks in the distance.

lingam: the penis.

Linnaeus, Carolus (1717–1778): Swedish botanist who developed a classification of odors (1752): aromatic, fragrant, ambrosiac, alliaceous (fishy, like garlic), hircine (cheese-like), foul, and nauseous. This was the first of many attempts to classify the olfactory sensations.

Lipps, Theodor (1851–1914): German who did much to advance act psychology, and who introduced the concept of empathy.

literary psychology: the use of psychological theories (and fancies) in the delineation of characters, the explanation of motives, and the fabrication of plots.

Little's disease: congenital spastic cerebral paralysis; named

for William John Little (1810-1894), an English physician.

local sign: Lotze's term (1852) for the manner in which,
supposedly, the individual perceives spatial relations. A
number of different local signs are used as cues in the
interpretation of relationships among parts of the stimulus pattern. Thus, through experience (though the mind
has a natural tendency in this direction), space perceptions are developed.

localization of function: the doctrine that each function is
identified with a definite part of the brain. At the present
time, there is a tendency not to designate precise and
minute areas as the "centers" for detailed and specific
functions. Flourens (1824-1825) advanced the notion
(now given credence) that, though functions are broadly
located, there are not minute "centers" for diverse and
specific activities. Broca's discovery of a speech center
(1831) had led neurologists on the search for centers for
other precise functions.

Locke, John (1632-1704): British philosopher who upheld
empiricism (as opposed to nativism), differentiated between primary and secondary qualities (only the primary
qualities having an existence outside the mind), and, in
the *Essay*, anticipated the doctrine of the conditioned
response. He originated the phrase "association of ideas"
(1690).

locomotor ataxia: a condition resulting from lesions in the
posterior columns of the spinal cord, with such concomitants as intense pains, girdle-sensation, sensory abnormalities, loss of knee-jerk, and general incoördination of
muscular activity.

Loeb, Jacques (1859-1924): German (later American)
biologist who developed the theory of tropism and who

defended the materialistic (as opposed to the vitalistic) point of view in biology.

logical thinking: mental activity directed according to the canons of logic; hence subject to reality-testing, verification, experimental proof, and the like. Logical (or reflective) thinking is sometimes contrasted with creative thinking and autistic thinking. According to Dewey (1910), logical thinking is a trial-and-error process in which mental manipulation takes the place of overt random movements and in which the goal (solution of a difficulty) is constantly kept in mind.

logokophasia: a form of aphasia in which spoken language cannot be understood.

logology: Stumpf's term for the study of relationships among ideas.

logomania: ceaseless talk by psychotic or psychoneurotic individuals.

longoneurosis: a psychoneurotic condition characterized by a functional speech disorder.

logopathy: any form of dysfunction in motor speech.

logorrhea: incessant talking; usually in the sense that the speech is repetitious and full of circumlocutions but not incoherent.

logospasm: convulsive lip movements when speaking. Thus, the speech is enunciated in an explosive manner.

Lombroso, Cesare (1836–1909): Italian physician and criminologist who developed the opinion that criminals are characterized by morphological stigmata. He also defended the thesis that over-development of a capacity (art, literature, music, etc.) is accompanied by a tendency towards instability and degeneration, a view known as the degeneracy theory of genius.

Lotze, Rudolf Hermann (1817–1881): German philosopher

who developed an empirical theory of space perception. Strain in eye muscles, for instance, is the local sign for depth. Variations in thickness of skin tissues are the local signs for touch localizations. Opposing the teachings of Johannes Müller about innate signs, Lotze upheld the view that these cues are learned in experience. (See *empiricism, nativism.*)

loudness: the intensity of sound. (Not to be confused with *volume* or *pitch.*)

Lubbock, John (1834-1913): British naturalist who wrote about communal life among ants, bees, and wasps (1882) and used the concept of instinct to account for the complexities of their behavior; first to use the maze method.

lues: syphilis.

luminosity: brightness of colors.

Lunacy Act: an act passed by the English Parliament in 1890 consolidating previous legislation and protecting the rights of mentally ill persons. The Act was amended in 1891, and served as a model for enlightened and humanitarian care of the demented for many years.

lunatic: at one time, a popular term applied to the psychotic. Institutions for the care of mental patients were known as lunatic asylums. It was supposed that the moon exerted an abnormal influence upon them and caused their irrational behavior.

luster: as defined by Wundt (1873-1874), the visual experience when irregularities or reflections in the surface of an object cause it to appear somewhat indistinct.

lycanthropy: (1) the delusion that one has been transformed into an animal (such as a wolf); (2) the folk-belief that certain persons have the ability to turn themselves into animals. (This superstition about the werewolf is found all over the world.)

lypemania: profound melancholia together with total loss of desire to take nourishment. Esquirol introduced the term in 1838.

lypothymia: extreme melancholia caused by disappointment, grief, or organic pathology.

M: Rorschach's symbol (1922) for responses the content of which are human figures perceived in the inkblots of the Rorschach test.

M: symbol used by American (and other English-speaking Rorschach workers) to denote responses the determinant of which is perception of movement by human beings. (Rorschach Inkblot Test.)

m: Rorschach symbol introduced by Klopfer (1942), to designate responses to the Rorschach Inkblots, the determinant of which is perception of inanimate objects or forces in motion.

Macewen's sign: hollow sound when, in the neurological examination, the skull is explored by percussion. It is a possible indication of internal hydrocephaly.

Mach, Ernst (1838–1916): Austrian physicist, physiologist, and epistemologist who investigated the functions of the semi-circular canals and who formulated a type of structuralism as his systematic point of view in psychology.

machlaenomania: masochism (in a female); sexual perversion in which pleasure is afforded by pain.

machlosyne: nymphomaniac, a woman with inordinate sex desires.

macrocephaly: abnormally large head, with associated mental deficiency. In macrocephaly (as distinguished from hydrocephaly) the skull does not bulge in lateral aspects or forehead. The brain may weigh as much as 2800 grams.

macrocheilia: abnormally large lips, which are usually everted.

macrocosm: the universe as a whole; hence contrasted with the theory that man is the center of reference in all nature.

macrodactylism: abnormally large fingers and/or toes.

macroesthesia: a neurological disorder in which objects placed in the patient's hand are sensed as being abnormally large.

macroglossia: abnormally large tongue, which may impede clear speech. The condition occurs in mongoloid mental deficiency.

macrognathia: unusually large jaw. It is found in acromegaly.

macrographia: unusually large handwriting, as in the florid style of some types of psychoneuroses and psychoses.

macropodia: unusually large feet, about which the individual might be hypersensitive.

macropsia: a disorder of vision in which objects seem to be magnified.

macrosoma: unusually large or elongated trunk.

macrosplanchnic build: a bodily build in which the trunk is disproportionately large and the legs and arms are relatively short.

macula acusticae: endings of the portion of the auditory nerve extending to the utricle and the saccule.

macula lutea: the yellow spot on the retina, which is the point of clearest visual acuity.

macular fibers: nerve fibers forming the central core of the optic nerve.

Magendie, François (1783–1855) : French physiologist who discovered (1822) that anterior nerve-roots of the spinal cord are motor; the posterior, sensory. Bell, an English physiologist, had discovered this fact in 1807. Since there still remains some uncertainty about priority of the discovery, the reference is usually made to the Bell-Magendie law.

magic: belief in, or practice of, the accomplishment of certain outcomes which transcend the normal limits of human capabilities. It is the antithesis of scientific procedures or of valid reflective thinking.

magical use of language: the "Open-Sesame" type of speech behavior in which the individual implies a superstitious belief that language can affect the course of natural phenomena. Folklore about "rain-makers" and "pow-wow healers" implies a belief in the so-called magical powers of words.

Magnan, Valentin (1835-1916): French neurologist who studied the effects of addiction to cocaine.

Magnan's sign: the hallucination that ovoid bodies lie under the skin or that "cocaine bugs" are crawling on the body of the drug addict. It is a cutaneous paresthesia induced by pathological stimulation of the sensory nerve endings in the skin as a result of cocainism.

Magnan's tongue: spasmodic protrusions of the tongue in paresis.

magnetism, animal: Mesmer's term for a mysterious type of energy which he claimed to be able to use in healing illnesses. By 1766, knowledge of electricity, magnetism, and nerve impulses was beginning to attract popular interest; and Mesmer extended this popular knowledge to cover his allegedly supernormal endowment.

magnitude: a judgment regarding intensity differences between two or more sensations or perceptions. One of the classical experiments in psychophysics (Weber, 1834) deals with the determination of the least difference magnitude between pairs of weights.

Magnus, Heinrich Gustav (1802-1870): German physicist

who taught Helmholtz and whom Helmholtz succeeded at Berlin (1871).

maieusiomania: psychosis accompanying or immediately following childbirth.

maintenance functions: various bodily functions like respiration, digestion, elimination, and the like, which (Cannon, 1932) preserve a measure of physiological equilibrium in the living organism. Homeostasis, according to Cannon, subsumes all functions which pertain to the maintenance of relatively unchanging states of equilibrium in the body.

major psychosis: one of the serious mental disorders. The older textbooks in psychiatry list scores of psychoses under various diagnostic schemata. The modern trend is to emphasize the etiological and the therapeutic factors rather than nosological systems.

make-believe: the phantasies of young children. A make-believe playmate is not uncommon among bright children of pre-school age. Healy suggests that highly imaginative, improbable fiction and make-believe play of children may be related (1915).

maladjustment: any mild disturbance of the personality in which there is difficulty in securing a satisfactory adjustment to the environment, particularly to other persons. Maladjustments cause conflicts, which, most writers emphasize, nearly always have a social reference. Consequently, major maladjustments arise from impossible demands which society imposes upon the individual. The term is used in a paradoxical sense to cover all attempts to reduce tensions. Thus, whether a behavior pattern be adjustive or maladjustive depends upon the manner in which it is evaluated.

malaria therapy: treatment of certain disorders (especially paresis) by malaria fever. This form of therapy was introduced by Wagner-Jauregg in 1887 and first tried on a human patient in 1917.

Malebranch, Nicolas de (1638-1715): French philosopher who upheld the doctrine of occasionalism as the solution of the body-mind problem. Occasionalism is the theory that, although mind and body are completely different and independent, God occasionally intervenes to have them influence each other.

malformation: any type of abnormal growth or development in any part of the body.

malleus: the outermost ossicle of the middle ear. The handle is attached to the tympanum and the head is articulated with the incus. The bone gets its name from a fancied resemblance to a hammer.

malnutrition: a condition of insufficiency of energy-producing substances in the food, though the amount of in-take may surfeit hunger pangs. Pressey (1933) reports evidence to indicate that malnutrition has a deleterious effect upon the quality of school work. Patent medicine advertisements have made many people take a great interest in real or imagined dietary deficiencies.

Malpighi, Marcello (1628-1694): Italian anatomist and physiologist.

Malthus, Thomas Robert (1776-1834): English political economist who predicted that increases in population would always outstrip food supply. Darwin was greatly impressed by his discussion, and he based his principle of natural selection upon ideas gained from reading of Malthus.

mammalia: any vertebrates that suckle their young.

man-to-man scale: the first rating scale to be applied to large groups of persons. It was devised by W. D. Scott in 1917 for use in the United States Army. It was designed to obtain objective ratings of officers on the following traits: physical qualities, intelligence, leadership, personal qualities, and general value to the service. This scale was found to be cumbersome and unsatisfactory.

mana: Polynesian word connoting a vague, impersonal, quasi-mechanical force controlling destiny. Belief in luck, charms, and the like, are said to be the counterpart of Polynesian mana.

mania: psychosis in which frenzied excitement is the most obvious symptom. Aretaeus (*c.* 30–90) defined many of the manias, and he made the shrewd observation that spontaneous remissions are usually followed by relapses. The term was at one time used to cover many specific disorders, such as dipsomania (morbid craving for alcohol), monomania (obsessions or fixed ideas pertaining to one topic), arithmomania (obsessive counting), and so on.

manic-depressive psychosis: cyclic periods of elation and depression Kraepelin, 1899). Baillarger had previously defined the disorder (1851) as *folie à double form*. It is an affective disorder in which the following gradations have been defined: hypomania, acute mania, hyperacute mania, simple retardation, melancholia, and stuporous melancholia. In the manic type, excitement and flight of ideas are common symptoms; in the depressed form, despondency and retardation of movement. When the affects shift from one extreme to the other, it is referred to as the circular type. The nosological pattern includes various clinical pictures, such as unproductive mania, agitated depression, mixed types, and the like.

manipulation test: a set of materials to be assembled or arranged in a given pattern, the score being based on time and/or freedom from mistakes. The Minnesota Rate of

Manipulation Test (1930) is a widely known example of this type of measure.

mannerisms: (1) individualistic and differentiating patterns of behavior whereby one person's "style" is distinguished from another's; (2) stereotyped postures and gestures of catatonic schizophrenics.

Marbe, Karl (1869-   ): German psychologist of the Würzburg school who made experimental studies of judgment and of other higher mental processes.

Marey tambour: apparatus for recording sequential changes, whereby a stylus is moved on a smoked paper (*kymograph*) as a result of air puffs in the device.

Marie, Pierre (1853-1929): French physician who defined acromegaly. This is the result of a pituitary disorder and is characterized by abnormally large hands, feet, jaw, and trunk.

marihuana: widely used derivative of *cannabis indica* which, mixed with cigarette tobacco, soaked in various solutions, sprinkled with grains of nutmeg, or prepared in other ways, is smoked. Popularly called "reefers," the drug is said to distort judgments of temporal intervals, to lessen self-criticism and inhibitions, and (by some) to enhance sex potency.

Mariotte, Edme (1620-1684): French physicist who discovered the existence of the blind spot in the retina. This is the point where the optic nerve and the blood vessels emerge, and where there are no rods or cones. It is sometimes referred to as Mariotte's blind spot.

Maskelyne, Nevil (1739-1811): English astronomer who dismissed his assistant, Kinnebrook, in 1796 because of a difference in recording times. Bessel, a German astronomer, read an account of the dismissal, and then undertook research which led to the discovery of the personal equation in scientific work.

masking of odors: the cancellation of one odor by another. Thus, Peruvian balsam masks the odor of iodoform.

masochism: erotic gratification in being beaten. The term was taken (by Freud) from part of the name of Luther von Sacher-Masoch (1835–1895), an Austrian novelist who used this theme in his stories. Masochism may be actual (implying the use of whips or other means of inflicting physical pain) or symbolic (finding reasons to revel in self-pity).

mass action: Coghill's term (1929) to denote the behavior of larval *Amblystoma*, which, he observed, respond in unitary fashion. Thus, behavior is not built up additively, but specific patterns of response are emergents (by individuation) from the primitive mass actions of the organism.

Masson disk: a white disk upon which lines drawn from center to periphery appear darkest at the center and least dark at the periphery when it is rotated. The disk was designed by Masson for experiments on visual phenomena (1845) and used in experiments by Helmholtz (1860).

materialism: the doctrine that matter is the sole reality. Democritus (*c.* 460–370 B.C.) was one of the outstanding Greek materialists, and many philosophers in subsequent ages have defended, and amplified, this point of view. Psychological materialism denies the existence of mind and accounts for all psychological processes in terms of other natural sciences.

maze: apparatus consisting of pathways and blind-alleys through which the organism must discover a way to the goal. It is frequently used in studies of human and animal learning. The data from maze-learning experiments have been cited as evidence for the trial-and-error (Lloyd Morgan's term) theory of learning (especially by Thorndike, 1913–1914).

McDougall, William (1871–1938): English (later American) psychologist who wrote an influential treatise on social psychology (1908), developed a point of view which is called Hormic Psychology, vigorously opposed Behaviorism, and upheld certain animistic and vitalistic concepts in psychology. Hormic Psychology emphasizes the concept of purposive striving toward ends (teleology). He was one of the leading proponents of the doctrine of instincts (or propensities) in recent psychology.

McNaughton case: the record of a man who attempted to shoot Sir Robert Peel and who killed his secretary, the defense attorney offering a plea of insanity. The court gave a ruling that the accused must have been unaware of the difference between right and wrong and that he must not have known of the nature and quality of his act, if this plea were to be allowed. The ruling has been cited in many subsequent cases.

mean: the sum of the scores divided by the number of cases (arithmetic mean). It is one of the most commonly used measures of central tendency in a frequency distribution of scores.

meaning: the interpretation of sensory data (perception). Many factors (such as past experiences and mental sets) determine the meanings which are given to situations. Mentally disturbed persons are said to assign private meanings (those untested by reality) to situations confronting them.

measurement: the application of temporal or spatial units to psychological events or functions. Fechner (1860) was the most important pioneer in the application of techniques of physical measurement to stimulus magnitude. Since his day there has been an increasing emphasis upon measurement in psychology.

meatus: canal or passageway.

mechanical ability: proficiency in manipulating form-boards, various devices, work-samples, and the like. Tests of mechanical ability often include measures of speed of work, accuracy or precision, hand-eye coördinations, manual dexterity, and structural visualization.

mechanical aptitude: measurements, such as the Stenquist (1923) or the Minnesota tests (1930), which serve as a basis for predicting the degree of competence which a person is likely to attain following a course of training in mechanical work on the simpler levels.

mechanical intelligence: concrete, practical ability to deal with tangible materials, such as various articles to be assembled or with tools. By some psychologists, distinctions are drawn among mechanical, linguistic, and social intelligence.

mechanism: the habitual mode of response whereby a person achieves a measure of satisfaction for a thwarted motive. Compensation, direct or indirect; projection; rationalization; and condensation are examples of mechanisms.

median: the 50th %-ile, or the point on the frequency distribution of scores which divides them exactly in half.

medulla: (1) the central part of an organ, as distinguished from the cortex; (2) any tissues which (like fascia or marrow) fill certain cavities; (3) marrow.

medulla oblongata: that part of the brain stem which lies between the pons and the spinal cord. In appearance it resembles a truncated cone.

medullated nerve fibers: those which are covered with the white substance of Schwann, which is the sheath covering the bulk of peripheral nerves and the tracts in the cerebro-spinal axis. Fibers of the autonomic nervous system are not medullated or sheathed.

megalencephaly: large headedness.

megalomania: obsessive and unwarranted good opinion of one's self.

megalopsia: visual abnormality in which objects appear to be magnified.

Meinong, Alexius (1853–1920): Austrian philosopher-psychologist who was prominent in Act Psychology and who described form-qualities.

Meissner, Georg (1829–1903): German histologist who discovered receptor-corpuscles in the skin on the fingers, the palms, and the soles of the feet.

melancholia: depression of affects. According to the classical doctrine of humors (attributed to Galen, 130–200), this condition is the result of an excess amount of black bile. (Some attribute the doctrine to Hippocrates, 460–377? B.C.)

meliorative mental hygiene: the positive emphasis upon development of a wholesome personality, without the necessity for defining the ideal adjustment. Instead of centering attention upon prevention or correction of abnormalities, it is concerned with all measures which effect progressive and continuous improvements in the personality and in society.

memory: behavior appropriate to a situation not objectively present. Memory is described as the activity of bringing past experience to bear upon a present situation. Woodworth (1923) analyzed the function into the following: learning, retaining, recalling or recognizing.

memory, rote: reproduction of learned material in which the factor of meaning is disregarded.

memory, logical: the repetition of the meaningful substance of material that has been learned.

memory color: inexact perception of the color of an object because of some former experience, usually a recent one.

memory drum: apparatus devised (E. G. Müller and F. Schumann, 1894) whereby, on a revolving drum, material to be memorized can be exposed for brief intervals as it passes by a window in a screen.

memory span: the amount that can be reproduced accurately after one impression (Jacobs, 1887).

menarche: the age of the onset of menstruation.

Mendel, Gregor Johann (1822–1884): Austrian naturalist who discovered major facts about the mechanisms of inheritance. He presented his paper in 1865, but the import of his discoveries was not realized until De Vries, Correns, and Tschermak called them to the attention of the scientific world about sixteen years after his death.

meninges: membranes of brain and cord. The outermost covering is the dura; the middle, the pia; and the innermost, the arachnoid. The leptomeninx includes the pia and the arachnoid.

meningitis: inflammation of the membranes of brain or cord, sometimes with accompanying symptoms of mental impairment.

menopause: cessation of menstruation, sometimes accompanied by involution melancholia (defined by Kraepelin, 1899).

mens: mind. Mental; pertaining to the mind.

mental activity: any function pertaining to the mind, such as awareness, perception, imagination, reasoning, and the like. Act Psychology, as expounded by some writers (*e.g.*, Woodworth, 1923) treats the nouns of psychology as verbals and the adjectives as adverbials, thus emphasizing the dynamics of behavior.

mental age: (1) ability to acquire knowledge as readily as can other persons of the same chronological age (Esquirol, 1838); (2) mental development measured by comparisons with performances of average persons at various levels of chronological development. An American psychiatrist, testifying in a trial held in 1848, said that the accused "in point of knowledge is equal to a child of 3 years" and thereby introduced the concept into law. Binet (1905) established the concept in psychology.

mental chemistry: the term used by John Stuart Mill (1869) to denote the process whereby sensory elements are fused into unions which are more than the sum of the parts out of which they are built.

mental conflict: the simultaneous arousal of incompatible motives, drives, or wishes.

mental deficiency: inadequacy of intelligence or learning capacity. Esquirol (1838) presented one of the earliest definitions in terms of gradations: (a) those capable of merely uttering cries; (b) those who can utter monosyllables; (c) those using short phrases; (d) those who are normal. Many definitions and gradations have been proposed, most of them centering about one or more of the following criteria: capacity to learn the curriculum; economic status; obedience to laws; community adjustments; and moral responsibility. Psychometric and sociological definitions are not always in full agreement.

mental hygiene: measures which (a) serve to alleviate the conditon of persons with psychoses; (b) those which are designed to prevent the occurrence of mental disorders; and (c) the application of all principles which are thought to promote achievement and maintenance of a wholesome personality. Clifford Beers (1876–1943) organized the National Committee for Mental Hygiene in 1908.

mental image: Galton's term (1883) for "mental pictures that may be scrutinized with nearly as much ease and prolonged attention as if they were real objects." The term also refers to mental content appropriate to the result as if a sense organ were actually stimulated. Galton investigated the degrees of vividness of mental imagery in the visual modality.

mental set: (1) readiness (because of past experiences or present activities) to respond in a given manner to a stimulus; (2) according to the Washburn motor theory of consciousness (1916), implicit or subdued muscular adjustments which are in progress when the stimulus occurs, even though conscious, deliberate thought may be centered upon other responses. Mental set is a figurative term (as compared to the *set* of a sprinter on the mark) and it subsumes complex phenomena.

mentalism: the emphasis upon psychological events or states that are explored by introspection, as opposed to behaviorism.

Mesmer, Franz Anton (1734–1815): Austrian physician who claimed to have the ability to "magnetize" his patients and thus cure their afflictions. When he was in Paris, a committee reported (1784) that his cures were effected by "imagination." Charles Poyen, a Frenchman who had studied under Mesmer, gave demonstrations in the United States before the Civil War and aroused a great deal of popular interest in the phenomena of mesmerism.

mesocephalon: the large mass of nerve fibers which lie at the base of the brain in front of the medulla oblongata. The structure includes gray matter as well as fibers which are connected with the medulla, the cerebellum, and the cerebrum.

mesoderm: the middle layer of the embryo, from which the following tissues are developed: glands of generation, kidneys, and the skeletal and the vascular systems.

mesomorphy: Sheldon's term (1940) for the constitutional type in which connective tissues, bones, and muscles predominate over digestive viscera and nervous tissues. Sheldon believes that temperament and constitutional type are very closely related, and he states that the somatotonic temperament is found in an individual who is predominantly mesomorphic.

mesoretina: the layer of the retina which contains the rods and the cones.

Messer, August (1867–   ): German psychologist who conducted experimental investigations of thought and who developed a systematic point of view whereby the Act and the Content Psychologies were reconciled.

metapsychology: depth psychology as systematically formulated by psychoanalysts.

metazoon: any organism with two or more cells; hence all animals that are not protozoa.

Meumann, Ernst (1862–1915): German psychologist who made important experimental studies of memory.

Meyer, Adolf (1866–   ): American psychiatrist (born in Zurich) who introduced many concepts into the field and who developed a point of view called psychobiology. He is often called the dean of American psychiatry.

microcephaly: abnormally small head, with associated mental deficiency. The head has a cone-like appearance (oxycephalia), and the forehead and the chin have a marked recession. The brain is reported to weigh as little as 170 grams (the normal weight being 1375 for males and 1240 for females). Tredgold (1929) is among those who defined this condition.

micropsia: a visual pathology in which objects seem to be very small. Southard (1912–1913) is of the opinion that these phenomena are the artifacts of unintentional suggestions given by the examiner. Inman explains the condition in terms of psychoanalytic theory (1938).

Mill, James (1773–1836): Scotch philosopher and historian who (1829) wrote the culminating presentation of associationism, which he described, not as the result of forces or mental chemistry, but as the operation of mechanical principles. He carried out a system of education for his brilliant son.

Mill, John Stuart (1806–1873): the son of James Mill who developed the principles of associationism and introduced the concept of mental chemistry. He believed that sensory elements fuse or combine to form new patterns which are more than the substance of their parts. He was a precocious child, and is often cited as a remarkable case of extreme brilliance.

mind-body problem: the controversy about the nature of mind and/or body and their interrelationships. Materialism denies the existence of mind; subjective idealism upholds the view that mind is the only reality; dualistic theories assume the existence of both mind and body. Among the influential theories of dualism, the following have influenced the course of psychology: interactionism and psychophysical parallelism.

mind-twist hypothesis: Southard's arrestive term (1922) for the theory which states that psychogenic factors may cause more or less grave mental disorders. This is the psychogenic theory, as opposed to the somatogenic (brain-spot hypothesis) view, which states that all disorders are the result of organic pathologies.

Minkowski, Oscar (1858–1931): German physician who reported upon experimental studies of the human fetus.

mirror-writing: strephographia, a form of writing in which the characters are reversed and which can be read by holding the page before a mirror. It is assumed to be a neurological difficulty which indicates the need for special education before the habits become firmly established.

misanthropy: aversion to other persons as a result of unhappy experiences in making social adjustments.

Mises, Dr.: the pseudonym under which Gustav Fechner wrote articles dealing with philosophical and occult topics.

misopedia: neurotic dislike for one's own children, usually because they necessitate care or reveal the ages of their parents.

misopsychia: generalized disgust with life, but without accompanying thoughts of suicide.

Mitchell, Silas Weir (1830–1914): American psychiatrist who developed a type of psychotherapy in which the patient is placed in isolation and under complete silence.

mnemonic device: a scheme for facilitating the process of learning and recalling unrelated items by organizing them into an artificial relationship. The familiar device for recalling how many days there are in the various months of the year is an example.

mnemonics: the procedure (based upon false analogy) whereby the memory is strengthened by certain exercises (just as muscles are developed by exercise).

mode: the score or interval which in the frequency distribution has the highest frequency.

monaural: pertaining to a single ear. The opposite of binaural.

mongolism: a form of mental deficiency in which the eyes are slit-like and slope upwards; the tonge is large (macroglossia)and transversely fissured; the hair is sparse and dry (lanugo hair) ; and the skull small and rounded. The condition is thought by some to be attributable to defective ova, though other hypotheses have been proposed.

monoblepsia: capacity to sense but a single color.

monochromatism: same as monoblepsia.

monocular: pertaining to vision using a single eye; a disorder affecting but one eye.

monomania: Esquirol's term (1838) for a mental disorder in which one set of ideas or motives predominates over all others. Zilboorg (1941) states that Esquirol's monomanias were the forerunner of what today are called schizophrenic reactions.

monophasia: a type of speech pathology in which utterance is reduced to a single word or sound.

monoplegia: paralysis which affects a single group of muscles or a single limb.

monotonia: a pathology of the voice which results from paralysis of laryngeal muscles and in which inflections are consequently absent.

monism: the view that all reality is reducible to a single ultimate, such as matter or mind. Dualism and pluralism are differentiated from monism by the fact that they postulate two or more ultimate realities.

Moniz, Egas: the Portuguese neurosurgeon who introduced the technique of prefrontal leucotomy (lobectomy) for the treatment of certain mental disorders. He performed the first successful operation of this type in 1931. Fibers in the frontal lobes are cut, and as a result some psychotic symptoms disappear or improve.

moral defective: a concept introduced by J. C. Pritchard (1786-1848) to designate an individual with non-social, perverse inclinations and with a total disregard for the rights of others (1835). Moral imbecility and moral insanity were at one time standard concepts in psychiatry.

morale: zest for living; enthusiastic devotion to group endeavor. Positive or meliorative mental hygiene emphasizes measures which improve morale.

moralistic attitude: the attitude in counseling which results in condemnations of certain types of behavior and which is, therefore, out of harmony with the rationale of lay therapy. Understanding the causes for the symptoms is considered to be a preferable approach in psychotherapy.

Morel, B. A. (1809-1873): French psychiatrist who believed that mental disorders are the results of hereditary processes of degeneration and that the stigmata are clearly evident in the patient; described *démence précoce* (1860).

mores: Sumner's term (1907) for the ethical sanctions and taboos which are commonly enforced by religious or magical rituals and upon the observance of which group welfare is thought to depend. They are the moral code of the individual and of his group. Folkways are susceptible to change, and they do not pertain so closely to the code of morals.

Morgan, Conway Lloyd (1852-1936): British psychologist who was a pioneer in animal psychology, who developed the trial-and-error theory of learning, and who rejected the anecdotal method in studies of animal behavior.

Morgan's canon: C. Lloyd Morgan's axiom to the effect that the simplest explanation of all known facts is the best hypothesis or theory. It is a restatement of the principle expounded by William of Occam (*c.* 1325) and known as Occam's razor.

moron: the mental defective whose intelligence is above that of an imbecile but below that of borderline defective. The mental age of the moron is usually considered to lie between seven and twelve years of age.

mother-surrogate: a woman who represents the man's mother and who, therefore, revives the Oedipus situation. A social institution or one's country may serve as a mother-surrogate, and hence be the recipient of filial love, according to analysts.

motility: capacity to move freely.

motive: a goad to action; usually restricted to a more or less well-verbalized drive to behavior. The term is used in many senses, and theories of motivation are at wide variance with one another. A motive is not an observable entity, but an inference or hypothetical construct whereby to account for behavior.

motor nerve: a nerve fiber which transmits the nervous impulse to a muscle or gland. Charles Bell (1807) is usually given credit for having first discovered the distinction between motor and sensory nerves, though Magendie (1816) announced the same discovery.

motor theory of consciousness: the theory that consciousness (awareness) is the result of more or less implicit muscular activity, and not a psychic (non-physiological) function. M. F. Washburn published this view in 1926. The oldest objective theory upheld the view that consciousness is a concomitant of brain physiology, and the motor theory presents the view that peripheral factors are basic. Jacobson (1932) has reported on the electrophysiology of mental activities and offered supportive evidence for the theory.

Müller, Georg Elias (1850–1934): German experimentalist who developed the concept of perseveration tendencies and who directed one of the most important psychological laboratories (Göttingen). He is sometimes referred to as the first experimental psychologist (in the sense that experimental investigations were his sole concern, whereas Wundt was a systematist as well as an experimenter).

Müller, Johannes (1801–1858): German physiologist who developed the doctrine of the specific energy of nerve fibers and who made many contributions to physiological psychology, especially sensation and sense-physiology. The doctrine of specific energy of nerve fibers states that each nerve (or neuron) transmits a different form of nervous energy, and hence different sensations are thus explained.

Müller-Lyer illusion: the best known optical illusion (1889). Two straight lines appear to be unequal in length because of "arrow-heads" on the one and "arrow-feathers" on the other.

multiple causation: many diverse factors, not a single cause, lie at the basis of a psychoneurosis or a psychosis.

multiple correlation: a statistical technique whereby the relationships among three or more sets of variables may be determined. The elementary concepts underlying various statistical procedures in correlation were described by Galton (1885–1886).

multiple fiber theory: the view that intensity differences in sensation are the result of the number of nerve fibers which are stimulated. The greater the intensity of a sensation, the more fibers stimulated in the nerve (or nerves). The theory has been attributed to Volkmann (1863).

multiple personality: two or more diverse personalities in the same body. Ellicott (1815) published one of the first scientific accounts of a case, and Poe ("William Wilson") was the first to make literary use of the phenomenon. About 76 cases have been cited in the literature. The Beauchamp case, described by Morton Prince (1905), is one of the best known accounts.

Munsell system: a procedure for identifying colors by reference to standard tints and shades of various hues, thus objectifying color nomenclature.

Münsterberg, Hugo (1863–1916). German experimentalist brought by William James to Harvard (1892), where he is said to have founded applied psychology.

muscle-reading: the process of inferring what a person is thinking by sensing the slight movements of muscles in the subject's fore-arm. By this means, a skilled performer may be able to locate an object hidden from his knowledge when no other clues are available.

muscle sense: kinesthesis, a sense described by Sir Charles Bell (1826) and at one time referred to as the sixth sense. It is of interest to note that Sir William Hamilton has traced the history of its discovery (1846) as far back as 1557, but that Bell was the first to realize its importance. In 1863, Kühne described the receptors for the muscle sense.

mutism: inability, or want of desire, to speak. Many cases of organic and of functional (hysterical) mutism occur in the literature.

myasthenia: muscular weakness.

myatonia: pathological flaccidity (lack of tonus) in the muscles.

mydriasis: pathological enlargement of the pupil.

myelin: the white substance which covers the medullated

nerve fibers. This sheath was described by Schwann, a German anatomist; hence it is often called the substance of Schwann.

Myers, Frederick William Henry (1843–1901). English author who collected many data on occult phenomena, hallucinations (of normal persons), and abnormal states. Like James, he was deeply interested in topics which cannot be explored by the ordinary methods of laboratory experimentation, and he brought the erudition of an intelligent person to bear upon these fields.

myesthesia: sensitivity to muscular contractions.

myograph: apparatus for recording involuntary muscular movements or tremors. The automatograph (Jastrow, 1895) is a familiar piece of equipment used in psychological laboratories to demonstrate these movements.

mysophobia: irrational fear of dirt or contamination, often accompanied by incessant handwashing. The classic literary example of compulsive handwashing is found in *Macbeth*, Act V, Scene 1.

mythomania: pathological lying in which the informer actually believes the improbable tales which he relates.

myxedema: a condition thought to be due to thyroid pathologies which is accompanied by muscular weakness, tremors, dullness, slowness of reaction time, and general lethargy.

Nagel, Wilibad A. (1870–1910): German psychologist who contributed important research studies to various sense modalities, particularly to vision.

Nancy school: the physicians of Nancy, France, who, under the leadership of Hippolyte Bernheim, arrived at the conclusion that hypnotic phenomena are the result of suggestion. They collected data on about 10,000 hypnotic experiments, and thus were able to controvert the theories of the Salpêtrière school (led by Charcot).

nanism: a form of dwarfism in which the head is proportionately large and the rest of the body stunted. It is thought to be due to endocrine dysfunctions.

Napoleon: the Emperor of France, whose consultant physician was Pinel, the great psychiatrist, and who opposed the doctrines of phrenology.

narcissism (narcism): abnormal self-love; hence, according to Freudians, the inversion of the libido. Primary narcissism is the original, infantile direction of the libido upon the body before the object-love stage. A person with a defective capacity for object-love is said, by analysts, to be a narcissist.

narcolepsy: attacks of short intervals of deep sleep. It is associated with hysteria and some forms of epilepsy. Functional narcolepsy is said to represent an escape, through sleep, from intolerable reality and conflicts.

narcomania: morbid craving for sleep-producing drugs.

narcospasm: convulsion while in a condition of sleep induced by drugs or preceded by a grand mal attack of epilepsy.

nasopharyngeal: pertaining to the nose and the pharynx.

Nasse, O.: German physiologist who (1839) anticipated Waller's discovery that a nerve degenerates in its peripheral part only after it has been severed. Waller (1852) used this fact to assist him in tracing nerve tracts.

National Intelligence Tests: one of the most widely used measures of intelligence for public school purposes (now outmoded), modeled upon the Army Alpha, prepared by eminent American psychologists, and the first to contain practice tests or fore-exercises. It was published in 1920.

nationalism: the intense identification of the individual with the state. In extreme form, the spirit of nationalism requires the derogation of other national groups. It is said to mean that in-group barriers are erected against persons who belong to out-groups.

native: inborn or developed through maturation, as opposed to acquired or learned.

native character: a character (*e.g.*, hair color, Mendelian trait, and the like) which is inherited biologically.

native endowment: the sum total of all traits and characters which are biologically inherited.

natural method: the theory that nature is the best guide in the education of children, and, consequently, that adult interference should be held to a minimum. The theory is attributed to Rousseau (1712-1778).

natural philosophy: the traditional designation for such sciences as physics and chemistry. Before psychology was established as a science, it was taught in the department of philosophy as mental philosophy.

natural selection: Darwin's theory (1842) that favorable variations facilitate survival, and unfavorable variations cause death, hence extermination. Wallace developed the theory in 1858, and both men presented a joint paper on the subject in that year. Darwin published a full account of the theory in 1859. The theory takes cognizance of the facts of individual variations (not of what may cause them) and shows how some variations favor survival and others bring about extinction of individual organisms and of species.

natural scale: a musical scale that was developed by Didymos (*c.* 63 B.C. to 10 A.D.) to conform to mathematical requirements and which Newton endorsed.

nature-nurture controversy: the argument about the relative importance of heredity and environment.

nausea: visceral distress with tendency to regurgitate.

nauseous: one of the seven primary olfactory sensations in the classification of Linnaeus (1752) and included in Zwaardemaker's list (1895).

near point of convergence: the nearest point at which an object can be brought into focus by both eyes. It lies about three inches in front of the face.

necrosis: death of a group of cells surrounded by living tissues.

necrophilia: sex perversion in which the dead body of a member of the opposite sex excites lust.

Neftel, William Basil (1830–1906): American neurologist who defined a form of hysteria in which muscular control is lost when the patient attempts to rise from the bed.

need: a lack or imbalance in tissues which initiates behavior. Strictly, the term is limited to physio-chemical imbalances, such as dryness of the mouth, deficiency in diet (manifested by abnormal food cravings), pain, and the like. The term is also used in a wide sense to connote a condition of unsatisfied motives. In general, a need is anything which upsets the optimum equilibrium (Rignano, 1920).

negative adaptation: a term introduced by Smith and Guthrie (1921) as the complement of positive adaptation. Repeated stimulation by a weak stimulus raises the threshold, so that, even when the stimulus is intense, the response is not given. On the other hand, repetitions of responses are thought to lower the threshold, so that the stimuli may be weakened and still elicit a response.

negative afterimage: the reversal of a color which furnishes the stimulus, so that its complement is sensed after the removal of the stimulus. The effect is produced by looking at a small piece of colored paper and then shifting the gaze to a neutral gray background. Newton (1704) noted the existence of negative afterimages and terminal lags of sensations, and Johannes Müller described the phenomenon more fully (1838).

negative acceleration: a frequency curve which, after a sharp initial rise, gradually flattens. The classical learning curve and the intelligence curve illustrate negative acceleration.

negative practice: the Beta hypothesis in eliminating wrong habits (Dunlap, 1932), whereby conscious, deliberate practice is given in the wrong habit, the learner being aware of what is wrong and of what should be done.

negative response: abient or avoidant reaction to a stimulus.

negative transfer: the carry-over from one function to another function of skills, habits, or understandings which reduce efficiency. Thus, it is said that practice in literal translations, for example, has a negative-transfer effect upon spontaneity in the vernacular. Confusion is introduced, however, by the fact that educational psychologists speak of positive transfer with negative effect—as the carry-over of a cautious habit into a task which requires speed—and a negative transfer with a positive effect—as when a subject turns from a disagreeable task to a pleasant one. (Woodworth, 1938.)

negativism: tendency to do the opposite of what is expected or ordered. Primary negativism is said to appear in children about three years of age, when, by sulkiness or resistance, they express resentment of adult domination. Secondary (neurotic) negativism is said to be symptomatic of a weak ego. In catatonia and some types of hysteria, negativism takes the form of mutism, refusal to eat, spring resistance, and the like.

neologism: a word which is coined by the patient but which has no meaning for other persons. Normal children coin words, which are repeated again and again, and which sometimes form a part of the intimate family vocabulary (being meaningless to outsiders).

neonate: the infant from birth up to one month of age.

neopallium: the cerebrum exclusive of the olfactory lobes.

neophilia: excessive preference for novelty, change, newness, with corresponding lack of appreciation for anything considered to be traditional.

neophrania: Kahlbaum's term (1863) for a psychosis ("insanity") occurring in early childhood.

neoplasm: any new growth of tissues which serve no physiological function, such as cysts, tumors, and the like.

nerve: a number of axis-fibrillae which surround a central core (axis cylinder). The nerve fibers of the bulk of spinal and peripheral tracts are sheathed (substance of Schwann), and the autonomic fibers are unsheathed (non-medullated). Nerves are long, cord-like structures which transmit the nerve impulse from the point of stimulation (receptor) to the response mechanism (effector).

nerve cell: the structural element of the nervous system,

called the neuron(e). The functional unit consists (hypo-
thetically) of two neurons: sensory and motor, with a
functional connection (synapse) in the cord. The major
parts of the nerve cell are as follows: dendrite (receiving
end); cell-body, containing the nucleus; axon (or
neurite), which transmits the nervous impulse; and collaterals (side branches from the axon). Classified according to morphology, nerve cells are either bipolar (axon
and dendrite on opposite sides of the cell-body), or multi-
polar (with dendrites branching off at different angles).
Deiters (1865) was the first to describe the branchings
of nerve cells (collaterals, dendrites, and axons); His
was first to use the term *dendrite* (1904); and many of
the basic observations of the structure of the cell were
reported by R. Wagner (1865) and Remak (1854).

nerve (nervous) impulse: the change (electro-chemical)
which moves from the dendrite to the axon, and thence
(across the synapse) to the dendrite of the next cell or
to the tissues of the effector. The rate was measured first
by Helmholtz (1850), who reported it to be about 27
meters a second in the motor nerve of a frog; and 50 to
100 meters a second in the sensory nerve of a human
being. The rate is now set at about 120 meters a second
in the human being.

nervous energy: a loose term applied to a condition of hyperkinetic behavior of unsustained type. Excessive output of
energy is said to result in "nervous breakdown." Zealous
pursuit of unattainable goals causes mental conflict, with
a growing neglect of health regimen, and the patient has
to undergo rest.

nervous habits: functional tics, twistings, strained and awk-
ward postures, which indicate persistent conflicts, self-
consciousness, anxiety, and the like. They may indicate

health problems, such as excessive smoking, faulty diet, or graver conditions.

nervous system: the cerebrospinal and the autonomic systems taken together.

nervousness: heightened emotional tensions as the result of abnormal stimulation. Combat, questioning by police, final examinations, and the like, are conditions which might create nervousness. It should be differentiated from psychoneuroses, since even the well-adjusted person might encounter a situation which would cause nervousness.

Neumann, Heinrich (1814–1884) : German psychiatrist who, rebelling against the practice of classifying various mental disorders according to patterns of symptoms, advocated the use of *insanity* as the single label for all of them.

neuralgia: painful sensations which follow the course of a peripheral nerve-fiber.

neurasthenia: Beard's term (1875) for a condition of heightened fatigability lack of zest, various aches and pains, and minor epigastric disturbances. The term has been called a "dumping ground" for a diversity of psychoneurotic adjustments (Culpin, 1931).

neurobiotaxis: Kappers' term (1908) for the tendency of dendrites to grow in the direction of the cells which are active, and thus commence to form reflex arcs. Stimulogenous fibrillation (defined by Bok, 1915) offers a theory for the growth of axons.

neuroblast: the embryonic nerve cell.

neuroglia: the cells which form the supportive tissues of the nerve cells in the cerebrospinal system.

neurogram: Morton Prince's term (1905) for the trace

which, supposedly, is left in the nervous system and which is the basis of memory.

neurological examination: a study of various sensory and motor functions in order to ascertain whether lesions exist in the nervous system.

neuron: the nerve cell. Schwann (1839) reported that the existence of these cells was known as early as 1665, but not until Golgi developed a method of staining (1873) was it possible to study them thoroughly. Waldeyer (1891) established the theory that the neuron is the functional unit of the nervous system, basing his conclusions upon Cajal's accounts (1889) of the histology of the synapse. Waldeyer named this the "neuron theory." The archineuron responds to the stimulus; the teleneuron transmits the impulse to an effector (gland or muscle).

neuropathic trait: a characteristic which depends upon a pathology of the nervous system.

neuropsychology: the science which deals with the anatomical and the physiological characteristics of nervous tissues (connectors) which mediate stimulus-response mechanisms.

neurosis: a term used alternatively with *psychoneurosis* (preferred by Malamud, 1946) for functional disorders involving maladjustments. In psychoanalysis, it is a colloquialism for *psychoneurosis*; it is used in connection with experimental investigations of maladjustive behavior of laboratory animals (Pavlov, 1921). Pavlov accounted for experimental neuroses in terms of his theory of cortical balance between excitation and inhibition, in the neurotic animal this balance becoming disorganized as a result of stress.

neurotigenic factors: those which predispose an animal to become disorganized by an inescapable and unsolvable problem-situation. Heredity, drugs, diet, and general health are examples of factors which may predispose the animal to have an experimental neurosis. Other writers have expressed a preference for the term *audiogenic seizure* to denote the convulsive disorder induced in laboratory animals.

neurypnology: Braid's term (1843) for trance-like conditions induced by suggestions. He proposed this term to replace *mesmerism* and *animal magnetism*.

Newton, Isaac (1642–1727): British physicist who developed a theory of color-vision, stated two laws of color mixing, and identified the attribute of brightness of hues.

Nietzsche, Friedrich Wilhelm (1844–1900): German philosopher who emphasized the urge for power as the basic directive force in behavior, and who (1889) became psychotic. His disorder has been variously diagnosed, with *paresis* being frequently mentioned.

nihilism: the delusion that nothing really exists. It is mentioned as a symptom occurring in certain mental disorders, particularly in involutional melancholia.

nirvana phantasy: according to psychoanalysis, daydreams of a condition of total extinction, and hence an escape from tensions. Freud wrote of the *nirvana principle*, which is a compulsion of all living organisms to return to the inorganic state from which they first arose, and which is the opposite of the self-preservative (*eros*) principle.

noctambulism: sleep-walking.

noegenetic principles: those which are said to arise from the exercise of pure reason, and hence to be free from sensory elements. Hamilton (published posthumously, 1859)

introduced the concept into psychology to denote knowledge which supposedly, originates in the mind, and
which, therefore, is completely independent of sensation.

noise: unpleasant, non-periodic sound waves, and hence the
antithesis of tone. Helmholtz wrote a history of music
(1862) in which he mentioned that the noises of one age
may become the tones of the next. Titchener (1896) distinguished between explosive noises (pop, crackle, snap)
and continuative noises (hiss, sputter, rumble) ; and he
likened noise to sensations of light, which, compared to
sensations of hue, are dull and unstable.

nominal aphasia: Head's term (1920) for an inability to as-
sociate names with objects, as a result of a cerebral lesion.
The patient may be able to describe the object, but he
cannot think of the specific name for it.

nominalism: the doctrine that universals have no existence
and that, therefore, such a concept as the *group mind* is
nothing more than a name. It emphasizes the doctrine
that abstract and general concepts are built up out of
sensory impressions, and hence that they have no *a priori*
existence. The traditional philosophical argument between the realists and the nominalists has had some influence upon the theory of psychology.

nomothetic laws: principles which are discovered by scientific analysis and which are uniform elements throughout
the class of data to which they pertain. Windelband, who
introduced the term (1904), used it to denote those sciences which emphasize general laws; and he referred to
sciences which seek to understand the specific event (or
object or person) as ideographic. G. Allport (1937)
states that psychology, hitherto almost exclusively a
nomothetic science, should also find place for the ideographic approach.

non compos mentis: a legal term referring to an inability to manage one's affairs because of a mental disorder.

non-adjustive behavior: responses which do not serve to adjust the individual to the exigencies of any given situation, but which merely release some of the tension arising from frustration. Hamilton (1925) introduced this phrase to characterize behavior which, in spite of failure to effect an adjustment, is repeated over and over, often with mounting emotional tension as a result.

norm: a standard of reference in making judgments.

normal: the average, or that which lies within the limits of the first standard deviation in a frequency distribution.

normal distribution curve: the bell-shaped curve along which scores on a random-sampling are distributed.

normative science: one which sets the standards and the procedures for correct behavior, as a logic and ethics.

nosology: the study of symptoms, or the classification of mental disorders. The greatest nosographer in psychiatry was Kraepelin (1883), whose views have been incorporated into many textbooks.

nosomania: the obsession that one has a pattern of symptoms indicating the existence of some dire illness.

nosophobia: morbid dread of illness.

nostalgia: homesickness.

nucleus: the central element in the cell, which contains the chromosomes and which is differentiated from the cytoplasm.

nyctalopia: night blindness. It is often confused with day-blindness (*hemeralopia*).

nyctophobia: morbid fear of darkness.

nympholepsy: a trance-like state induced by erotic daydreams.

nymphomania: uncontrollable and insatiable sex desires in a woman. A similar condition in a man is known as *satyriasis*.

nystagmus: spasmodic oscillations of the eyeballs. The disorder occurs in albinos and color-blind persons frequently, and it is also found in individuals with certain types of organic pathologies.

O

O: the subject in a psychological experiment.

object: in psychoanalysis, a person or thing necessary for gratification of the libido. In object-cathexis, the libido is drained from its original sexual purpose into some other channel; in object-choice, it is directed into channels determined by experiences occurring before the genital stage is reached.

objective psychology: the systematization of psychological facts and principles from the empirical point of view. Bechterev (1913) first used the term.

objectivists: a term (usually) applied to German physiologists whose experiments on animal behavior were based upon the theory that mentalistic terms and concepts are outmoded (Beer, Bethe, and von Uexküll, 1899, being the proponents of psychological objectivism). The term also refers to behaviorists (Watson, 1913, *et al.*).

oblivescence: the gradual fading out of an impression.

obsession: a persisting, pathological drive, idea, or affect. Obsessions differ in degree, some being trivial (*e.g.*, a tune "running in the head"; others being disruptive and serious).

obstruction box: apparatus for measuring the strength of animal drives by determining the frequency with which the animal crosses an electric grid to reach the goal (Warden, 1926).

Occam, William (1280–1349): English Scholastic who stated that entities must not be multiplied beyond necessity, thus introducing the law of parsimony (C. Morgan, 1900).

occasionalism: a classical theory of body-mind relationship which states that the individual's intent to respond is merely the "occasional cause"; actually, God makes him respond. It also states that God is the real cause for the relationship between mental and physical events. This theory was expounded by Geulincx (1663) and Malebranche (1675).

occipital lobe: the posterior part of the cerebrum (in either hemisphere).

occupational therapy: originally, the use of diverting, interesting activities to help the patient pass the time in a hospital or institution; now, the use of activities which may be necessary adjuvants to the medical care (such as those which exercise certain muscles, afford release for tensions, prepare the patient for re-employment, for release, and so on).

ochlophobia: fear of crowds.

ocular dominance: the tendency of one eye to be used in such activities as sighting a rifle or threading a needle. One investigator has reported that about 30% of school children have a dominant left eye (Parsons, 1924). Preferential eyedness and handedness are assumed, by some psychologists, to be related, and each has a bearing upon causation of speech disorders (Travis, 1931).

ocular nystagmus: Bell's term (1808) for the spasmodic rotations of the eyeballs after an individual has been rotated.

oculomotor nerve: the third cranial nerve. It mediates the muscles of the eye, except the superior oblique and the external rectus.

od: Baron Reichenbach's term for an occult force supposedly emanating from magnets and from persons, which "sensitives" can see. Caspar Hauser (a "wild boy" of Nuremberg, 1828) was supposed to have convulsions when there was metal anywhere in his vicinity. Mesmerists claimed to work miracles with this force, even having subjects read mottoes enclosed in nutshells.

odorimetry: the measurement of the intensity of olfactory sensations (Zwaardemaker, 1888).

odors, classification of: organization of elementary olfactory sensations. Linnaeus (1752) organized seven classes: aromatic, ambrosiac, nauseous, fragrant, hircine, foul, alliaceous. Zwaardemaker's classification (1895) is as follows: aromatic, ambrosiac, alliaceous, empyreumatic, hircine, nauseous, foul, fragrant, ethereal. Henning, who developed the olfactory prism (1915), names six: ethereal, spicy, putrid, burned, resinous, fragrant.

Oedipus complex: according to psychoanalysis, a conscious or unconscious erotic attachment for the parent of the opposite sex, together with a jealous attitude towards the other parent. Normally, it occurs at about age five, and then infantile sexuality begins to be repressed and the child emulates the parent of the same sex (from six to about fourteen). In psychoneurotics, the Oedipus continues to exert great force.

oestrum (estrum): period of receptivity by the female animal.

oestromania (estromania): nymphomania.

Ohm, Georg Simon (1787–1854): German physicist who developed (with Helmholtz, 1863) the resonance theory of hearing. This theory states that complex tones are analyzed by the ear into simple components.

oikotropia: nostalgia.

olfaction: sense of smell.

olfactometer: apparatus (developed by Zwaardemaker, 1888) for stimulating the olfactory membrane by a stimulus of controlled intensity. Units of intensity are called *olfacties*.

olfactory lobe: the olfactory bulb, the olfactory tract, and the olfactory tubercle, considered as one.

oligophrenia: mental deficiency; feeble-mindedness.

onanism: coitus interruptus (Genesis 28:9); often (though incorrectly), masturbation.

oneirodynia: Cullen's term (1777) for a category of mental disorders (*vesanias*) which are characterized by somnambulism and nightmares.

oneirology: the study of dreams. Theories of dreams were expounded by Aristotle; Wundt investigated dream phenomena; and Freud's theory of dreams (1900) stimulated a great deal of study.

oniomania: a "buying spree." Paretics make extravagant purchases, and some hysterics lose all prudence when on a shopping tour.

onomatology: the science of finding, or of coining, the appropriate term to designate a psychological event or a psychiatric symptom.

onomatopoetic theory: one of the classical theories of the origin of speech, which states that primitive men imitated the sounds of nature in their first real use of communicative language.

ontogeny: the growth and development of the individual, as contrasted with *phylogeny*, the development of the species.

ontology: the study of the ultimate nature of reality. Wolff (1734) included rational psychology as one branch of ontology.

operationism: Bridgman's term (1928) for empirical standards which are consistent, definite, repeatable, intended to lead to concepts of greater validity, and linked to objective reality. Operational definitions do not pertain to absolute properties or values transcending the limits of any given experiment or group of experiments; they do include concepts which derive their meanings from the operations to which they are directed, and for which they are used, in an experiment. Hence operationism is said (Skinner, 1945) to mean that reports of psychological investigations should be limited to observations, procedures, and the steps which intervene between initial and final statements.

ophidiophobia: extreme fear of snakes.

Oppel, J. J.: German psychologist who reported studies of geometrical illusions (1855).

optical illusions: misperceptions of visual sensations. Necker (1832) described the reversible rhomboid, and Oppel (1855) dealt with many of the illusions. They are dependent upon (a) the configuration of stimuli, (b) the structure and the function of the eye, and (c) anticipatory set or expectation. Wertheimer (1912) introduced dynamic concepts into the field, with his report of the phi-phenomenon (illusion of movement).

ophthalmograph: apparatus for photographing the eye-movements in reading.

ophthalmoplegia: paralysis of muscles which move the eyeball. *Internal opthalmoplegia* is the paralysis of the muscles of the iris and the ciliary body.

ophthalmoscope: an instrument (invented by Helmholtz, 1851) for looking into the eyechamber and examining the fundus oculi.

ophthalmotonometer: apparatus for measuring the movements of the eyeballs, as in reading or surveying a scene.

Oppenheim, Hermann (1858-1919): German neurologist who described several conditions associated with sclerosis.

optic agnosia (aphasia): inability to recall the correct names of objects seen, as a result of cerebral lesions.

optic chiasm: the crossing of the optic nerves, just in front of the tuber cinereum.

optic disk: the small, round prominence where the optic nerve emerges into the eyeball.

optic nerve: the second cranial nerve, connecting the visual center in the occipital lobe and the retina.

optimum balance: homeostasis.

oral-erotic stage: the stage of pregenital development of libidinal cathexis in which the lips and the mouth are the principal erogenous zones. During the period of weaning, according to psychoanalysis, the infant becomes oral sadistic. The mouth is the first definite outlet for the libido, the anus and the genitalia being established as dominant areas in later successive stages of development.

orexia: appetite.

organ: any multicellular group of tissues with a definite physiological function.

organ of Corti: the receptor structure for hearing, which contains the dendrites of the auditory nerve. It was described by Corti in 1851.

organic sensations: a broad term referring to sensations arising from receptors within the body (*e.g.,* muscles, tendons, viscera, and so on). Bell (1826) established the existence of a muscle sense (*kinesthesis*); Weber (1846) described visceral sensations; hunger and thirst were mentioned by Haller (1747); and sensations of muscular innervation were described by Steinbuch (1811). Some writers include sensations from the semicircular canals under this heading, and Darwin's grandfather is mentioned as a pioneer in the field (1801).

organic psychosis: a mental disorder which is caused by a dysfunction of some organ or by a lesion in the brain or nervous system. Psychiatrists who emphasize somatogenic factors in psychoses are sometimes referred to as *organicists*, a term which differentiates them from those who defend the psychogenic (conflictual) point of view.

organismic: relating to the organism as a whole. The *organismic approach* to problems of behavior emphasizes the necessity for taking into account the whole situation and the entire organism, as opposed to the traditional methods of proceeding from analysis to synthesis. Fechner (1873) introduced this point of view into psychology.

orgasm: the height of genital excitation.

orientation: awareness of one's true relationship, spatial and temporal, in the environment. In routine examinations, the patient is asked about his name and identity, where he is, the date, time of day, and so on. In animal psychology, the term refers to the problem of determining by what methods the animal establishes a spatial position with reference to the energy field surrounding it. The classical work on this problem was done by Loeb (1890).

orthogenic class: a special class of children who require expert attention because of mental deficiencies or serious problems of maladjustment, with a teacher who is qualified to use palliative or remedial techniques of education.

orthopsychiatry: the branch of psychiatry which emphasizes a meliorative program for normal and near-normal individuals, and which utilizes the services of all persons who can assist in benefiting the individuals selected for treatment.

osmia: the sense of smell.

osphresiolagnia: the delusion that everything (or some things) has an unpleasant odor.

osphresiophilia: a type of perversion in which certain odors are associated with erotic stimulation.

ossicles: the bones of the middle ear—namely, malleus, incus, and stapes. Haller (1763) was among the first to give an accurate description of the middle ear.

otoliths: small calcareous particles in the endolymph of the utricle and the saccule, which, when the head position is changed, impinge against the nerve endings. Flourens (1828) reported the effects of destruction of the vestibular apparatus in pigeons.

overcompensation: Adler's term (1917) for a direct attack upon the situation responsible for the inferiority, which results in the removal of the obstacle and also in success in the very field which was hitherto a frustration for the individual.

over-determination: a psychoanalytic term referring to two or more dynamic elements, conscious or unconscious, which combine to bring about a symptom or to furnish the latent content for a dream.

over-protection: sheltering the individual against the effects of competition with others, making decisions for his welfare, and thus denying him the opportunity to achieve self-reliance.

overlearning: a term used by Ebbinghaus (1885) to denote any learning over and beyond that required for one correct reproduction of the material.

overtone: any of the partials, except for the fundamental, in a tone.

ovum: the female germ-cell.

P: symbol for a popular response to one of the figures of the Rorschach Inkblot Test.

p: Spearman's symbol (1925) for the tendency of mental functions to perseverate (or exhibit an inertia).

Pacinian corpuscles: small bodies lying along cutaneous nerves. They were described by Vater (1741), and Pacini amplified upon this account (1840); hence they are often referred to as Vater-Pacinian corpuscles. Rauber (1865) stated that their function is to mediate awareness of position of the limbs.

paidology (pedology): child study. At one time, G. S. Hall favored this term.

pain: an independent sense, the existence of which was established by von Frey (1895). Head (1905) described protopathic and deep pain. Experiments on adaptation to pain have shown equivocal results. In animal psychology, Hoge and Stocking (1912) were the first to demonstrate experimentally the efficacy of pain (electric shocks) in eliminating errors in maze-learning.

pain receptors: nociceptors. The work of von Frey (1895) established the pain sense as a separate modality, and Blix (1882) discovered pain spots in the skin. Sherrington (1906) used the label *nociceptor* for any sensory nerve-ending which mediates the sense of pain.

paired associates: words (or designs) which are learned in pairs, and then, when the first is presented, the second is to be recalled. This method of studying the memory functions was introduced by M. Calkins (1896).

paired comparisons: a method used in testing esthetic pref-

erences, the testee being asked to chose the better of two
pictures (colors, etc.).

paleoatavistic qualities: G. Hall's phrase (1904) for his
theory that psychological development recapitulates the
cultural history of the race, and that in childhood and
adolescence, there are examples of the stages of savagery,
barbarism, and so on. This doctrine is based upon
Haeckel's theory of recapitulation (1866).

paleopsychology: Jung's term for the study of the primordial
images which are supposed to lie deep within the mind.

paliphrasia: the purposeless repetition of certain words or
phrases in speech.

palikinesis: involuntary and stereotyped repetition of various
movements, as in catatonia. It is said to occur sometimes
in chronic epidemic encephalitis (Critchley, 1927).

palilalia: meaningless repetition of words and phrases, as in
catatonia.

pallesthesia (palmesthesia): sensitivity to vibrations.

palmistry: the pseudo-science which purports to interpret
mental traits from the lines and the prominences of the
palm. Hartlieb (1475) codified much of the ancient lore.
Chirognomy deals with the analysis of the personality
from the hand; *chiromancy* professes to read the past
and foretell the future.

palsy: paralysis.

panic: a condition of fear or anxiety together with a disorganization of behavior. Sidis (1898) made psychological
analyses of some panics.

panphobia: morbid fear of everything.

pantheism: the philosophical doctrine that everything, ani-
mate and inanimate, has no existence apart from God.
Spinozistic psychology introduced the concept into modern psychological theory.

papilla: a small eminence. The *papilla acoustica* is known as the organ of Corti in the human ear. The *lingual papillae* contain the taste buds. The *tactile papillae* contain sensory nerve-endings for cutaneous sensations.

para-: Greek prefix meaning "beyond," "distortion or perversion of."

Paracelsus (Theophrastus Bombastus von Hohenheim) (1493-1541): Swiss physician and celebrated alchemist who revolted against traditional theories of mental illnesses but had no consistent theory himself.

parachromopsia: inability to discriminate among certain colors.

paracusia: distorted sense of hearing.

paradoxia sexualis: Krafft-Ebing's term (1908) for strong sex drive in a young child or a very aged person.

paradoxical cold: the arousal of a sensation of cold as a result of stimulating cold spots by warm blunt-pointed rods (von Frey, 1896).

parageusia: distorted sense of taste.

paraleresis: a disturbance of speech during a fever delirium, the patient talking in a weak, incoherent fashion.

paralipophobia: dread of responsibilities because of real or fancied lack of ability.

parallelism, psychophysical: the metaphysical doctrine that mental and physical events accompany each other but are not causally related. Titchener (1896) accepted this doctrine for a working hypothesis in his systematization of the field of psychology.

paralogia: inability to reason clearly because of a pathological condition of the cortex of the cerebrum.

paralysis: loss of power to move (the whole body or a part may be involved) or an impairment of power to move. In *paralysis agitans*, the onset is often seen in involuntary tremors of the hand, and in advanced cases, the gait becomes an uncontrolled run (festination). In *Bell's paralysis,* immobility of the face is an obvious symptom. *Brown-Sequard's paralysis* is a motor involvement on one side of the body and a loss of sensation on the other side. *General paralysis* was described fully by Falret (1859), and its relation to syphilis was discovered by Krafft-Ebing (1897). Many other types of organic paralysis have been described, but the ones mentioned above are often found in the literature.

paralysis, hysterical: Charcot's term (1887) for hysterical symptoms closely resembling those caused by organic factors, which he found in some of the women patients under his care. Janet reported his extensive studies (1907) of hysterical paralyses and described the methods whereby the physician could differentiate them from organic disabilities. Essentially, he said, they do not conform to the patterns of nerve distribution but to geometrical areas.

paramimia: inability to correctly imitate gestures.

paramnesia: a distorted recollection of some past events.

paranoia: a term used by Hippocrates to designate states of mental disorder. Vogel (1794) used it to denote disorders of the thought processes, and Kraepelin (1883) defined it as a separate nosological entity. The term usually connotes the existence of systematized delusions without serious impairment of other mental functions. Under the head of *monomania,* Esquirol (1838) described the conditions of persecutory delusions.

paranoid: a condition resembling paranoia. In the paranoid form of schizophrenia (or dementia praecox) the delusional element is the uppermost and most obvious symptom.

paraphia: perverted tactile sensations.

paraphrenia: Kahlbaum's term (1882) for a disorder of the cognitive functions. Kraepelin (1912) adopted the term to denote those mental disorders which cannot be classified under dementia praecox or manic depressive because the patients retain their orientation to the environment and may continue to exhibit good emotional rapport.

paraplegia: paralysis of the lower half of the body.

parapsychology: the application of psychological techniques to the investigation of occult phenomena, such as extrasensory perception or the psychokinetic effect (Rhine, 1930 *et seq.*). In extra-sensory perception (E. S. P.), the investigator attempts to infer the design on cards(Zener pack) without the use of any known sense organs (clairvoyance) or to receive the impression from a person at a more or less remote distance (mental telepathy); in experiments on psychokinesis, the experimenter tries to influence (mentally) the fall of dice.

parasympathetic nervous system: the cranial and the sacral portions of the autonomic (vegetative) nervous system. Some writers prefer to divide the cranial portion into two parts: the ocular division (mediating the muscles which alter the size of the pupil and the shape of the lens), and the bulbar division (which is widely distributed). In general, the parasympathetic system is excitatory (*colinergic*) in its effect.

parathymia: a condition in which the moods are inappropriate to the situations.

parathyroid glands: small endocrine glands located near the thyroid. When they are removed from a dog, ataxia is an immediate effect, then muscular spasms, and finally (about ten days) death. In children, hypoparathyroidism is believed to be a cause of convulsions, which sometimes yield to treatment by soluble calcium salts.

Parchappe, J. B. M. (1800–1866): French psychiatrist who believed that all mental disorders are the result of brain lesions.

parergasia: Adolph Meyer's term (1915) for the behavior of schizophrenic patients.

paresis: a condition of mild paralysis as a result of syphilitic involvement of the nervous system.

paresthesia: perverted cutaneous sensations, such as those caused by certain drugs.

parietal lobe: the lobe of the cerebrum lying above the fissure of Sylvius.

Parkinson, James (1755–1824): English physician who described paralysis agitans. The *Parkinson syndrome* (or *facies*) is a mask-like, expressionless face which appears in epidemic encephalitis lethargica.

parorexia: perverted appetite; pica.

parosmia: distortion of the sense of smell.

parsimony, law of: Lloyd Morgan's statement (1900) that animal behavior should be described in the simplest possible terms. It is an application of Occam's razor to animal psychology. Occam (1280–1349) had said that entities must not be multiplied beyond necessity; and Morgan accepted this view, indicating that anecdotes, attribution of human mental activities to animals, and projection of introspections have no place in animal psychology.

partial correlation: a technique for indicating the ratio between two sets of variables when the linear effect of a third set of variables (or more) is held constant.

partial: any part of a compound tone. The lowest partial is called the fundamental, and the others are the upper partials. When they are discriminated separately, they are sensed as pure tones (Titchener, 1896). Helmholtz (1859) accounted for compound tones in terms of their partials.

patellar reflex: the forward jerk of the foot when the patellar tendon is struck, the leg being bent at the knee.

pathergasia: A. Meyer's term (1915) for a personality disorder caused by, or associated with, organic pathology.

pathetism: mesmerism.

pathogenesis: the origin and the course of development of a disorder.

pathognomy: the diagnosis of a disorder.

pathomimesis: deliberate feigning of the symptoms of disorders (malingering) or the use of symptoms by a patient with conversion hysteria in order to resolve some of the tensions arising from mental conflicts.

pathology: the science dealing with alterations in structure and function which occur in physical and mental disorders.

pathophobia: obsessive fear of contracting a disease.

Pavlov, Ivan Petrovitch (1849–1936): Russian physiologist who (1890) discovered the conditioned-reflex technique. Yerkes (1909) was among the first American psychologists to recognize its importance. Twitmeyer, an American psychologist, independently discovered the same type of response (1902).

pavor nocturnus: nightmare.

Pearson, Karl (1857–   ): English statistician and biologist who joined with Galton in establishing eugenics research (1904), and who developed the technique of the coefficient of correlation.

pederasty: intercourse *per anum*.

pedophilia: a sex perversion in which young children arouse erotic impulses in an adult (Krafft-Ebing, 1879).

penilingus: fellatio.

penis-envy: according to psychoanalysis, a stage through which many little girls go when they discover that they are unlike males, and hence they believe themselves handicapped and ill-treated.

peptic ulcer: a lesion in the stomach or the duodenum which is caused by erosion of the mucous membrane by gastric secretions. It is said to occur sometimes as a result of prolonged anxiety, and hence to necessitate psychosomatic treatment (Mittelmann, 1940).

percentile rank: the relative position of each score as arranged in a distribution of one hundred.

perception: awareness of sensory stimulation. Titchener (1896) defines perception as a complex of sensory and imaginal elements; Ehrenfels introduced the concept of form-quality (perception of relationships), which led to modern Gestalt theory. Whether spatial and temporal perceptual patterns are nativistic (Kant, 1781) or learned (the empiricism of Hobbes, 1651, and others) is one of the traditional problems in the history of psychology. The phenomenological view of the Gestaltists is allied to nativism; behavioristic psychology is strongly empirical.

performance test: a non-verbal measure of intelligence, usually in the form of blocks which are to be fitted into recessions. Séguin (1842) developed one of the first tests of this type (the Séguin form board). The Army Beta (1917) is the first group performance test to have wide use in measuring the intelligence of illiterates and non-English-speaking individuals.

perimeter: apparatus for locating the limits of various color zones on the retina (Aubert's experiment, 1857). Small colored objects are moved about the various quadrants of peripheral vision at various distances from the fovea, and thus the areas of maximal sensitivity for each hue are mapped on a chart.

peripheral nervous system: the nerves which join the brain and the cord with the receptors and the effectors.

peripheral vision: indirect vision, or that which is mediated by other areas of the retina than the fovea. It was first described by Young (1801), and Purkinje (1825) was the first to describe the differential sensitivity to colors in various peripheral areas of vision.

perseveration: the tendency of a mental activity to continue after the removal of the stimulus.

persona: Jung's term (1923) for the mask which conceals the deep components of personality, and which, therefore, meets the demands of everyday environment but hides the individual.

personal equation: variability among individuals who are assigned the task of recording the time of some event. It was discovered in 1820 by Bessel, the German astronomer, who reported an average difference of 1.041 seconds between his astronomical observations and those of Walbeck. Thus, he found that Maskelyne (Greenwich astronomer) had been unjust in his dismissal of Kinnebrook in 1796.

personalistic psychology: a systematic formulation of the principles of psychology around the concept of a Self or Person as the standard of reference. M. W. Calkins (1909) and Sterm (1923) are among those who have upheld this point of view.

personality: a broad, elusive term which has at least two diverse meanings: (a) the social-stimulus value of an individual, the sum of all traits which differentiate one individual from another, or the total behavior pattern of an individual; and (b) the inner organization or integration of conation, cognition, and affectivity. G. Allport (1937) lists fifty definitions of this ambiguous term.

personality trait: a distinctive and relatively permanent characteristic aspect of the behavior of an individual (*e.g.*, persistence, cheerfulness, etc.). There is a considerable amount of disagreement about the nature of traits and about the difference between individual and common traits. In the English language 17,953 words allude to traits (Allport and Odbert).

persuasive therapy: the method of appealing to the intellect of the patient, while skillfully making indirect suggestions, in order to gain the patient's coöperation in organic disorders or to remove hysterical symptoms (Paul Du-Bois, 1904).

Peterson, Joseph (1878–1935): American psychologist who investigated the learning process, acoustics, and individual differences.

petit mal: the minimal form of epilepsy; momentary loss of consciousness (*absence*), sometimes mild muscular movements, and often an automatic continuance of actions initiated before the seizure (*minor fugue*).

phagomania: pathologically insatiable appetite.

phenakistoscope: a device invented by Faraday (1831) for the study of apparent movement. It consists of disks with slits which revolve in opposite directions and which create the illusion of a stationary disk between them.

phenomenology: a doctrine introduced into psychology by Husserl (1900) which emphasizes the direct experience (as opposed to sensationalistic elementarism). Psychology is defined (essentially) as the science of the experiencing individual, and each experience has dimensions (Titchener, 1920) or Gestalt characteristics (Köhler, 1925).

phenotype: Lewin's term (1927) for similarities in the behavior of a number of individuals. It is to be distinguished from a *genotype*, which is the cause for the behavior and which, therefore, differs from individual to individual, though outward behavior may be similar.

phi-phenomenon: Wertheimer's term (1912) for the apparent movement which occurs when two stimuli are presented in a certain temporal and spatial order. This perception of movement is not reducible to the elements in the stiuation. Wertheimer's famous paper on this topic marked the beginning of Gestalt psychology.

philosophical psychology: the study of metaphysical questions (*e.g.*, the nature of consciousness, personality, the body-mind problem, and so on) which are related to the psychologist's frame of reference. Since the rise of experimental psychology (Wundt, 1879), philosophical questions have been under the "armchair taboo" (Scripture, 1895).

phobia: a morbid fear. Freud divides phobias into two general classes: (a) those which are exaggerations of emotional experiences common to normal persons (phobias concerned with impending doom, solitude, snakes, death, and so on); and (b) phobias which are peculiar to the individual (claustrophobia, agoraphobia, and the like).

phonautograph: apparatus for recording sound waves. Other instruments for recording sound waves in studies of acoustics are as follows: *phoneidoscope, phoneloscope, phonodeik,* and *phonscope.*

phonometer: apparatus for measuring auditory acuity (Wundt, 1893).

photism: a sensation of light caused by a change in the retina, not by stimulation by light-waves. Drugs, certain diseases, and the like, are said to be the causes of photisms, which may appear as small, bright lights or as an illumination of the entire visual field.

philoneism: obsessive interest in fads.

phlegm: one of the classical humors. According to the ancients, an excess produces the phlegmatic temperament (Hippocrates, 420 B.C.).

phrenasthenic: feeble-minded.

phrenology: the pseudo-science which determines mental status by the protrusions and recessions on the skull. The doctrine was announced by Gall (1796), and the term was coined by Spurzheim (1800).

phrictopathic: Head's term (1905) for a vaguely localized tingling sensation.

phylogeny: the evolution of the species, from the simplest protozoa to man. Haeckel (1866) stated that the individual goes through each stage that the race passed through in the process of evolution; hence that ontogeny recapitulates phylogeny.

physiogenic: disorders which are caused by organic pathologies.

physiognomy: the pseudo-science which purports to interpret mental characteristics from the morphology of the face. It was systematized by Gall in 1796.

physiological age: the status of an individual with reference to average persons of varying chronological ages, as judged on the basis of such factors as primary and secondary sex characteristics, endocrine status, and the like.

physiological limit: the ultimate achievement in speed, efficiency, or quality of performance which can be attained by practice.

physiological psychology: that division of psychology which deals with receptors, nervous system, and effectors. Wundt is usually regarded as the founder, since he wrote the first textbook bearing this title (1874).

pia mater: the innermost of the membranes which cover the brain and the cord.

piano theory: a popular term for the Helmholtz theory of hearing (1863), which states that the rods of Corti respond to vibrations like the strings of a piano or harp. It is also known as the resonance theory of hearing.

pica: perverted appetite.

Pick, Arnold (1851–1924): Austrian psychiatrist who described a presenile psychosis. Pick's disease occurs later than the Alzheimer psychosis but earlier than the usual type of senile dementia; and it is characterized by symptoms of cerebral-cortex atrophy, the principal symptoms being as follows: impaired judgment, blunted emotions, and loss of inhibitions.

Pinel, Philippe (1745–1826): French psychiatrist who removed the chains from patients (in the Bicêtre, 1793) and thus initiated the program of scientific, humane treatment of patients with mental disorders. He divided the field of mental disorders into mania, melancholia, dementia, and idiocy (1800).

pinna: the auricle, or outer portion of the ear.

pitch: the attribute of auditory sensations whereby they are judged to be relatively high, middle, or low. In absolute pitch, the stimulus is correctly placed on the scale; in relative pitch, the second stimulus is judged to be higher or lower than the first. The first experimental studies of pitch discrimination were made by Sauveur (1700).

pituitary: an endocrine gland in the base of the brain and contained in the sella turcica. Dwarfism, acromegaly, and gigantism are associated with pituitary dysfunction (anterior lobe). Tucker (1933) has reported psychotic disorders in connection with hypopituitarism.

placebo: a pill or a liquid given to humor the patient with a psychoneurotic disorder. Its therapeutic effects, if any, are psychological, not physiological.

planchette-writing: writing done automatically or in the hypnotic trance, the apparatus consisting of a freely moving platform on which the subject's fore-arm is placed. James described examples (1890) in support of his theory of simultaneously existing consciousness (co-conscious states or activities).

plantar reflex: flexion of the toes when the sole of the foot is scratched or stroked.

plasticity of the nervous system: James' doctrine (1890) which states that the nervous system is readily modified in youth but that it loses plasticity as the individual grows older (hence it is then more difficult to break old habits or to form new ones).

Plateau, Joseph Antoine Ferdinand (1801–1883): Belgian physicist who experimented with color mixing (1829) and stroboscopic effects (1833).

plateau: the period of no apparent improvement in learning a new function which occurs between the first ascent and the final ascent of the learning curve (Byran and Harter, 1896).

Plater, Felix (1536–1614): German psychiatrist who believed that certain mental disorders were caused by brain pathology, but that others were due to possession by the devil.

Plato (427–347): Greek philosopher who established the tradition of dualism, mentioned the integrative function of the mind, and recognized the existence of individual differences (in the *Republic*).

pleasure-principle: the psychoanalytic concept that physiological and mental tensions lead to immediate gratification unless they are controlled by the ego and/or the super-ego. Tensions serve as an inner stimulus to give impetus to behavior which will bring maximal pleasure and serve to minimize the suffering which arises from unresolved tensions. The id is governed solely by the pleasure-principle.

plethysmograph: apparatus for determining the blood-volume in a part of the body. The hand or a finger is immersed in water, with an air-tight collar; hence as the volume of blood changes, the water-level is altered. It is used in studies of emotion.

plexus: an intricate network of nerve fibers lying outside the central nervous system.

pneumogastric nerve: the tenth cranial nerve (which is also called the *vagus*).

pneumograph: apparatus for measuring inspiration-expiration movements of the chest. An elastic belt containing a double-headed tambour is strapped around the chest, and the record is made on a kymograph. Rehwoldt (1911) found that excitement increases respiration. Störring (1906) discovered that the inspiration-expiration ratio may be used in experimental studies of emotional behavior, and Benussi (1914) used this ratio in experiments on lie detection.

poikilothermic: cold-blood organisms.

polarities: the psychoanalytic concept that mental activities (instinctual tendencies) polarize about opposite extremes, and that there is a strong likelihood of a swing from one to the other of these extremes. The polarities which are said to be of great importance are the following: life-death; love-hate; self-object; activity-passivity. Jung emphasized the doctrine of polarities in his formulation of Analytical Psychology (1920).

polarity of neurones: the law of forward direction, which states that the impulse is transmitted from dendrite to axon.

polydactylism: supernumerary fingers and/or toes.

polydipsia: intense thirst.

polyesthesia: a cutaneous disorder in which a single touch is sensed as being two or more touches.

polygraph: apparatus for recording simultaneously a number of physiological activities, such as involuntary tremors, changes in blood volume, heart beat, inspiration-expiration ratio, and the like. It is used in investigations of emotion and in lie detection.

polylogia: a stream of incoherent talk by a patient in an excited phase of a mental disorder.

polymorphous-perverse: the psychoanalytic term to designate the characteristics of the young child's libido whereby a large number of outlets (even perversions) are possible. Normally, the libido finds outlets, successively, through the following stages of development: oral, anal, and genital.

polyphrasia: irrational, incessant talk by a mental patient.

polypnea: rapid breathing, as in hysteria. Sometimes, as a result of exhaustion of the CO_2 content of the blood, the hysteric goes into a cataleptic trance.

pons Varolii: a prominence consisting of transverse fibers lying in front of the medulla, beneath the cerebellum, and below the cerebrum.

poriomania: wanderlust.

position habit: a persistent mode of attempting to adjust to frustrations. In animal psychology, for instance, the rat is said to have a position habit when it repeatedly enters cul-de-sacs or, in the Lashley jumping apparatus, keeps jumping towards the left or right in spite of repeated punishment.

positive after-image: a continuance of retinal excitation after the removal of the stimulus, so that the image persists. After-images were described by Boyle (1663), and Newton (1691) wrote of his experience with positive after-images of the sun. The term *after-images* was introduced by Fechner (1838).

posthypnotic suggestion: a suggestion given during hypnosis, usually with amnesia also suggested, which is carried out by the subject after the operator has awakened him.

practice experiment: Aschaffenburg's method (1896), now traditional, of measuring the improvement in a task performed many times, when experimental conditions (new motivation, rewards, the test itself, and the like) are introduced. The method is usually applied to skills (*e.g.,* typesetting, mirror-drawing, telegraphy).

preconscious: in psychoanalysis, the conscious (that is, all that is not now in the foreconscious) and that part of the unconscious (if any) which are subject to voluntary recall.

pre-established harmony: the doctrine (Leibnitz, 1695) that God established a harmony between body and mind, so that, though they are unlike entities, they function simultaneously and in coördination.

pregenital stage: according to psychoanalysis, the polymorphous perverse, oral, and anal stages of libido attachment, which precede the direction of the libido to the genitalia. *Pregenital sexuality* denotes either the auto-erotic period which precedes object love or the unconscious desires of neurotic adults for auto-erotic satisfactions.

pregnance: Wertheimer's term (1922) for the tendency of every Gestalt to become as good as possible under the conditions permitted by the situation. Sander (1928) said that a poor figure or form is seen as if it were somewhat better than it is (the eidotropic principle or the law of pregnance).

prehension test: measure of immediate memory span, usually for digits but sometimes for sentences (Jacobs, 1887).

preparation: in creative thinking (as described by Wallas, 1926), the first stage, which is followed by *incubation, illumination,* and *verification.*

preparatory response: a set which facilitates the final or consummatory response.

pre-perception: a term introduced by McDougall (1923) to denote a preparatory set or conative tendency to select certain stimuli from a total situation and to ignore others. Illusions of recognition are cited as examples of pre-perception.

prepotent reflexes: Sherrington's term (1906) for the reflexes which take precedence over all others, such as withdrawal, struggle, hunger, and sex.

presbyophrenia: mental disorder caused by old-age deterioration.

presbyopia: a condition of inelasticity of the lens which occurs in later maturity, and which makes it difficult to see near objects clearly.

presenile psychosis: Alzheimer's or Pick's disease, or premature deterioration of the brain.

presentation: in psychoanalysis, the manner in which an instinctual drive expresses itself; in academic psychology, a sense perception.

pressure of thoughts: a descriptive term referring to the flight of ideas in mania, which apparently outrun the patient's ability to vocalize them.

pressure sense: the response to stimulation of spots lying on the hair follicles (von Frey, 1894), the device used to locate them being called a hair esthesiometer. The spots may be stimulated by wrinkling the skin, by brushing the hairs, and by any deformation of the surface of the skin.

Preyer, William (1842–1897): German psychologist who (1882) wrote one of the first systematic textbooks on child psychology.

priapism: a persistent erection of the penis due to a nervous lesion, not to erotic desires.

Pritchard, James Cowles (1786–1848): English psychiatrist who introduced the term "moral insanity" (1835), by which he meant a perversion of motives and affects without any impairment of intellectual functions. The term has been loosely employed by the courts to denote psychopathic behavior.

primary abilities: Thurstone's identification (by factor analysis) of nine basic traits measured by intelligence tests (1938): spatial relations (S); perceptual speed, visual (P); number calculations (N); verbal relations (V); word forms (W); immediate memory span (M); induction (I); deduction (D); and reasoning (R). Spearman (1904) had described the following: a general factor (g); group factors (found only in similar measures); and specific factors (occurring only in a single measure of ability).

primary attention: (Titchener, 1896) involuntary, spontaneous, passive; as contrasted with forced (secondary), and derived primary (acquired interest) attention.

primary dementia: Kraepelin's term (1883) for a major

category of mental disorders occurring in adolescence and differentiated from other disorders by a withdrawal from reality, fantasies, and inappropriate emotional behavior.

primary process: according to psychoanalysis, the tendency which leads to condensation (much represented by little) and displacement (shift of affect from one outlet to another).

primary qualities: Locke's term (1690) for solidity, extension, figure, and mobility—which inhere in the object; as contrasted with the secondary qualities (tastes, colors, sounds, odors, and the like)—which exist in the mind of the percipient.

Prince, Morton (1854–1929): American psychiatrist who described a famous case of multiple personality (1905), and who introduced Charcot's theories of dissociation of consciousness to Americans.

problem box: a device for experimental studies of animal learning (Thorndike, 1898) in which the animal must discover, by trial and error, how to escape from a box or cage. Other experimenters have devised boxes in which food is placed and which the animal must learn to open (*e.g.*, Sackett, 1913).

prodromal: that which warns of an impending disease or mental disorder.

profile: an arrangement of test scores (expressed in comparable units of measure, such as standard scores) which indicates the relative standing of an individual on various psychological measures (*e.g.*, linguistic intelligence, educational-achievement status, mechanical ability, and the like).

projection: Freud's term (1894) for the process of attributing to others the drives and complexes which belong to oneself. Ideas of reference and delusions of persecution are examples. In academic psychology, the term refers to the localization of sensations at the place of stimulation. *Visual projection* denotes the placement in space of the various stimuli in the visual field which arouse conscious responses.

projective technique: a method of appraising dynamic factors in the personality by having the individual interpret chance forms (inkblots), pictures (Thematic Apperception Test), use finger paints, supply omitted dialogue in cartoons, and so on. The purpose of these procedures is to obtain an insight into values, wishes, repressions, emotional organization, and so on, which the individual might be unwilling or unable to supply if the direct-question method were used. The Rorschach Inkblot Test (1922) is the oldest and best-known projective technique.

proprioceptor: a receptor located in a muscle, tendon, tendon sheath, or joint (also, the vestibular apparatus is sometimes included). Proprioceptive stimulation was once known as the "muscle sense" (described by Bichat, 1812). The term (proprioceptor) was coined by Sherrington (1905).

prosencephalon: the forebrain, which includes, in addition to the cerebral hemispheres, the following: optic bulbs and tracts, tuber cinereum, corporara mamillaria, and the posterior perforated spot.

protanopia: red-blindness.

protapathic sensibility: Head's term (1905) for a primitive cutaneous system which responds to pain and great changes in temperature. The individual finds difficulty in locating these sensations, but he reports that they are unpleasant and intense. Both *protopathic* and *epicritic* sensations are cutaneous (*deep* is subcutaneous). Head's theory was proposed to overcome some difficulties with the von Frey (1894) theory.

protoplasm: the essential substance of living cells, a jelly-like material consisting (usually) of *spongioplasm* (a network) and *hyaloplasm* (a fluid).

proximodistal axis: that which extends from the midline of the body to the uttermost extremities.

psellism: impairment of speech.

pseudo-angina pectoris: functional heart disorder induced by prolonged, intense anxiety.

pseudochromesthesia: the association of colors with sounds. Galton (1883) was the first to make a systematic investigation (by the questionnaire method) of the tendency for some people to experience a pseudo-sensation of colors when notes of varying pitches are played. This is a particular type of synesthesia.

pseudo-emotion: an affective change induced by a drama, a motion picture, a novel, and the like.

pseudolalia: meaningless, animal-like sounds made by mental defectives and psychotics.

pseudolalia fantastica: self-accusation of a crime which the individual did not commit, and which may never have occurred at all. It is sometimes found in schizophrenia.

pseudesthesia: a sensation which is referred to a part of the body which has been removed (*e.g.*, an amputated finger or arm).

pseudo-feeble-mindedness: Burnham's term (1924) for a superficial picture of mental deficiency caused by intense self-consciousness, lack of confidence, and a defeatist attitude, though the individual may actually have normal intelligence.

pseudophone: Thompson's term (1879) for a device which reverses the apparent direction of sounds, those actually coming from the front being deflected to the rear and thus being perceived as if they came from there. Young (1928) devised a technique for acoustical transposition of sound, that on the right being directed to the left ear (by crossed trumpets) and *vice versa*.

pseudoscope: mirrors or prisms which reverse the retinal images (Wheatstone, 1852).

psychasthenia: Janet's term (1889) for a psychoneurotic condition in which there is a loss of psychic tension, and in which such obsessive disorders as phobias, feelings of depersonalization, compulsions, tics, and morbid anxieties are the characteristic symptoms. Janet includes under this heading all those psychoneurotic symptoms which are not properly classified as hysteria.

psychataxia: inability to concentrate; mind-wandering.

psyche: the mind.

psychiatry: the branch of medicine which deals with the diagnosis and the treatment of mental disorders.

psychic: in occultism, the possession of a supernormal "faculty" or power to achieve knowledge hidden from ordinary persons.

psychic blindness: an outmoded term (once widely used) to denote impairment of visual functions as a result of lesion in the occipital lobe of the cerebrum.

psychic mechanics: Herbart's term (1816) for the systematization of knowledge about intensity differences among ideas in the mind. Strong ideas rise into the focus of consciousness; weak ones are pushed below the level of consciousness. The concept is of historical interest because it involves the first use of mathematical techniques in psychology.

psychic tension: Janet's term (1889) for a "mental tonus" comparable to muscular tonus. It is capable of becoming

weak; hence various mental elements become dissociated. This concept was introduced into America by
Prince (1905).

psychical research: the application of experimental techniques to the investigation of topics usually included in
the real of occultism. *Parapsychology* is the term preferred by many contemporary investigators.

psychoanalysis (psychanalysis): Freud's method for investigating the unconscious (1895). Through free association
and dream analysis, the patient is encouraged to overcome resistance and to verbalize all the conflictual material hitherto repressed into the unconscious. In 1903,
Freud began the task of systematizing and revising his
theories in the Viennese Psychoanalytic Association. In
1909, G. S. Hall invited Freud to present his theories to
the academic world (Clark University lectures). Sears
(1943) and others have investigated the theories from
the standpoint of experimental psychology and thus have
effected a closer relationship between Freud's views and
scientific psychology than existed during earlier decades.

psychobiology: a term used by Bernheim (1886) to emphasize the importance of dealing with mental as well as
with biological factors in diseases. In 1915, Meyer used
the term *objective psychobiology* to indicate the relationships which exist between the individual (both mentally and physically) and his environment.

psychodiagnostics: the exploration of the personality by the
Rorschach Inkblot Test (1922).

psychodometer: apparatus for measuring reaction time.

psychodrama: Moreno's technique (1938) for assisting the
patient to achieve mental catharsis by having him act
various roles with alter egos or soliloquize on the stage.

psychogalvanic reflex (P. G. R.): lowered resistance to conduction of an electrical current when the person is stimulated by a sensory or an ideational stimulus. Féré (1888) and Tarchanoff (1890) discovered (independently) that there is an alteration in electrical potential between points on the skin in strong emotion. In 1911, the method of measuring changes in resistance to a current was introduced (Wells and Forbes), and the term usually refers to this procedure.

psychogenic: a disorder which is of mental origin. The opposite of *somatogenic*.

psychography: the application of Freudian theories or psychoanalytic principles to a literary characterization of a well-known person.

psychological determinism: the psychoanalytic theory that every mental event has a cause, which is to be found either in the conscious or the unconscious mind.

psychology: the science of mental life, both of its phenomena and of their condition (according to the famous definition by James, 1890). Many short definitions have been proposed, the chief point of agreement among them being that psychology is an empirical science dealing with mental activities and objective behavior. Melanchthon is said to have used the term about forty years before it first appeared in the title of a printed book (by Gloeckel, 1590). Though the era of definitions in terms of the tenets of various schools of psychology has passed, there is still no acceptable single-sentence definition.

psychometrics: a term now restricted to mental testing, but once applied to measurement of reaction time, thresholds, and the like.

psychomotor: a term used by psychiatrists to denote the relationships between the ideational stimulus and the muscular response. Hence *psychomotor retardation* means that the patient delays making responses to his thoughts or to questions. The term also refers to voluntary (as distinct from reflex) responses to stimuli.

psychoneurosis: in psychoanalysis, the narcissistic and the transference neuroses, which arise from unconscious conflict and which affect the mental and social adjustments of the individual. They are distinguished from anxiety neurosis, hypochondriasis, and neurasthenia (which are the *actual neuroses*). In a more general sense, the term denotes psychogenic disorders which do not warrant institutionalization, but which impair the efficiency of the individual and cause him more or less anxiety.

psychopath: an egocentric, impulsive, asocial individual. The term is variously defined, and the category has been the occasion of much dispute, some writers referring to it as a "waste basket" into which patients who are neither psychoneurotic nor psychotic are placed.

psychopathia sexualis: Krafft-Ebing's term (1879) for all types of sex perversions.

psychopathology: the scientific study of mental disorders.

psychophysical parallelism: the solution of the body-mind problem which was proposed by Leibnitz (1695), and which states that mental and physical activities are unlike but function harmoniously in a parallel manner. This view was revised and adopted by Titchener (1896).

psychophysics: the science which determines the quantitative relationship between the stimulus and the sensation. The "father of psychophysics" was Fechner (1860), who defined the field as the "exact science of the functional relations or the relations of dependency between mind and body." The term is sometimes used synonymously with *experimental psychology.*

psychosomatic: pertaining to both mind and body.

psychosis: any grave mental disorder.

psychotechnology: the application of psychological facts and principles in practical affairs of business or industry. Münsterberg is often called the "father" of this science.

psychotherapy: the treatment of disorders by the use of persuasion, suggestion, educational techniques, occupational therapy, lay or religious counseling, psychoanalysis, and the like. Psychotherapeutic procedures may be used as adjuvant techniques in many disorders and as the principal mode of therapy in others.

psychro-esthesia: the illusion of feeling cold.

pubertas praecox: abnormally premature maturation of primary and secondary sex characteristics.

puberty: the stage of physiological development which marks the beginning of adolescence.

Purkinje, Johannes Evangelista (1787–1869): Bohemian physiologist who observed that the values of colors change in twilight (1825)—the *Purkinje phenomenon,* and who made extensive studies of vertigo.

purpose: a symbolically represented mode of eliminating a motive.

purposive accident: according to psychoanalysis, a slip of tongue or pen which reveals the unconscious.

purposive (hormic) psychology: McDougall's term for a formulation of psychological theories in terms of ends or goals (teleology) of which the individual may have no awareness, but which, nevertheless, are implicit in conation.

pursuit movements: coördinated movements in following a moving stimulus.

pygmalionism: erotic devotion to an object (*e.g.,* a painting or a machine) made by a patient with schizophrenia, paranoid type.

pyknic build: Kretschmer's term (1925) for a rounded physique, which is associated with a cyclothymic temperament. Cyclothymics tend to be gay, contented, friendly.

pyrolagnia: arousal of sexual excitement by fires.

pyromania: setting fires in order to achieve erotic gratifications. According to psychoanalysis, the pyromaniac has a urethral-erotic fixation, and, as a child, was an excessive bed-wetter (Ferenczi, 1926).

pyrophobia: morbid fear that one's residence will catch on fire.

Q: symbol for quartile deviation.

quadrigemina, corpora: four small, rounded protuberances in the dorsal or superior part of the midbrain.

quadriplegia: paralysis of both legs and both arms.

qualitative data: statistics of attributes. Examples of qualitative data are as follows: good, accurate, moderate speed, fairly intelligent, and so on. See *quantitative data*.

quality: the unique attribute which differentiates each sensation from every other sensation (Titchener, 1896). Warm, bitter, loud, red, and the like, are examples of qualities.

quantitative data: statistics of variables. Numbers or other mathematical symbols are examples of quantitative data. In psychological research, the investigator is faced by the problem of quantifying data in order that it may be manipulated by statistical procedures.

quantity objection: James' (1890) term for his objection to the opinion that sensory elements have magnitude (*e.g.*, that "pink is a portion of our sensation of scarlet").

quartile: one of three points on the abscissa of a frequency distribution curve whereby the scores are divided into four equal parts.

quartile deviation: one-half the range between the first and the third quartiles. In the Gaussian curve, the quartile deviation equals the probable error.

querulant paranoia: systematized delusions of persecution which take the form of incessant complaints about alleged mistreatment, lack of appreciation.

questionnaire: Galton's (1883) method for gathering data about mental imagery, whereby he circularized many contemporary Englishmen to ascertain facts regarding individual differences in images. Hall adopted the method for use in his studies in child and adolescent psychology; Münsterburg derided it.

questionnaire, attitude: a list of planned questions or statements designed to measure attitudes towards a given situation (Thurstone and Chave, 1929).

questionnaire, personality: a list of questions, such as a psychiatrist or a psychological counselor would ask in a face-to-face interview, which is printed and which the subject reads to himself and indicates his answers by checking or encircling his likes, preferences, symptoms, dislikes, and so on. Woodworth (1917) developed the first personality questionnaire.

Quetelet, Lambert Adolphe Jacques (1796–1874): Belgian mathematician who is called the "father of statistics" and who discovered that certain variables are distributed in a curve of theoretical probability. He established the belief that the average man represents the ideal of nature, and hence that deviations are more or less undesirable. See *normative concept*.

Quincke, Heinrich Ireneaus (1842–1922): German physician who discovered that cerebrospinal fluid could be obtained by lumbar puncture, thus facilitating the development of knowledge about the identity between syphilis and general paresis.

Quincke's tubes: a set of whistles for demonstrating different tones.

quintile: one of four points on the abscissa of a distribution curve whereby the frequencies are divided into five equal groups.

quotient, achievement: the measured accomplishment of a

person divided by mental age. The accomplishment is ascertained by a standardized test which gives an achievement age, and the mental age is obtained by means of an intelligence test. When a battery of tests is used to measure general achievement in all subjects within the curriculum, the score may be converted into *educational age*, and the quotient obtained by dividing this age by the mental age is called the *educational quotient*.

quotient, intelligence: mental age divided by chronological age (usually multiplied by 100 to clear of decimals). Esquirol (1828) first used the concept of mental age. Stern (1900) and Terman (1916) introduced the concept of IQ into intelligence measurement.

R

R: response; in psychophysics, stimulus (*Reiz*).

r: Pearson product-movement coefficient of correlation.

Rank, Otto (1884–1939): an early disciple of Freud's who developed many theories of his own, particularly the theory of the *birth trauma* (1923). This theory states that neurotics are individuals who never get over the anxiety produced by the birth experience.

range of consciousness: an introspective term referring to the rhythmical grouping of clicks. Dietz (1885) reported that the range is approximately ten seconds. Other introspectionists have reported the *conscious present* as a single second. Herbart (1816) attempted to work out the problem mathematically.

rapport: an attitude of confidence and trust on the part of a client (counselee or patient) towards the counselor (or psychiatrist). Some psychoanalysts prefer to use the word *transference* to denote the patient's esteem and respect for the analyst.

race psychology: a study of likenesses and differences among various races in such psychological topics as interests and preferences, intelligence-test scores, reaction times, feelings and emotions, aptitudes, sensory acuities, and the like. The first experimental study was made by Woodworth (1904). Many of the early studies were made on Negroes (*e.g.*, Ferguson, 1916) and Indians (*e.g.*, Garth, 1921).

radical: a person who adheres to extreme opinions or unusual views, and who, according to some psychologists, may be compensating thereby for an attitude of inferiority. An extreme radical is said to be unaware of the nature of his motivations and defense mechanisms and to rate low in insight. Like the extreme conservative, he makes extensive use of rationalizations.

rating scale: a technique for objectifying judgments of the order of merit on several traits of personality so that one individual may be compared with others. Heymans and Wiersma (1906) made the first thorough attempt to rate individuals on personality traits, and the Man-to-Man Scale used in the United States Army (W. D. Scott, 1917) is the first major use of a rating scale for practical purposes.

rational psychology: Wolff's term (1734) for a study of the soul and its faculties.

rational type: Jung's term for individuals whose functions are predominately thinking and feeling (as distinct from the irrational type, in whom sensation and intuition are the principal functions).

rationalization: a term introduced by E. Jones (1908) to denote the method of self-justification whereby acceptable, not real, reasons are given for past behavior. It is also used to denote an intellectualized attempt to account for an unconsciously motivated thought or act.

raw score: a score which has not been subjected to statistical treatment.

Ray, Isaac (1807-1881): American physician who developed an eclectic system of psychiatry.

Raynaud, A. G. Maurice (1834-1881): French physician who described a disorder (*Raynaud's disease*) once thought to be psychoneurotic when found in women; the symptoms include circulatory changes in extremities, paresthesias, and astereognosis. It is now considered to be somatogenic, whether occurring in men or in women.

reaction: an integrated pattern of responses to a situation. It differs from a response in that it is more complex, though some writers use the two terms synonymously.

reaction apparatus: a device for measuring the time interval between a stimulus and a response. Studies of this type are often referred to as *reaction experiments.* Helmholtz (1850) was a pioneer in this work.

reaction-formation: a term used in psychoanalysis to denote the psychoneurotic's defense against infantile urges by the adoption of the opposite tendency in conscious behavior.

reaction time: the interval between stimulus and response. The experiments on this important topic were initiated by Helmholtz (1850), Donders (1868), and (particularly) by Wundt (1874).

reaction-type: A. Meyer's term (1915) which includes the following specific psychiatric syndromes: affective, delirious, deteriorated, organic, paranoid, and substitutive.

reaction psychosis: a serious mental disorder precipitated by environmental factors, such as imprisonment or a profound disappointment (Bleuler, 1930).

readiness, law of: Thorndike's principle (1914) which states that when a stimulus-response bond is ready to conduct, for it to do so is satisfying; when it is not ready to conduct, for it to do so is annoying.

reality-principle: according to psychoanalysis, the function of the mature, normal ego in protecting the individual against immediate gratification of a libidinal desire lest there be a painful outcome.

reasoning: the act of thinking in conformity with the principles of logic. Ability to reason is appraised by tests involving syllogisms, verbal analogies, problems in arithmetic, and common-sense judgments. Thorndike (1898) was one of the first to offer experimental proof for the argument that animals are unable to reason (thus advancing the theory of radical behaviorism). Ruger (1910) concluded that human beings also think by trial and error, and hence that no reasoning occurs. Binet, however, was firmly convinced that reasoning ability is the essence of intelligence (1886, 1905).

reassurance: a technique of psychotherapy in which the patient's self-confidence is restored, and constructive activities are initiated, by a directive type of counseling in which suggestion (direct and indirect) has a large part.

recall: the revival of a past experience. The term is sometimes used to denote the revival of a past experience when a cue or surrogate for the original situation is presented. In a *recall test*, the testee is required to fill in missing words, phrases, or numbers.

receptor: the ending of the sensory nerve which is stimulated by some form of energy (light-waves, sound-waves, thermal, and so on). Each receptor has a low threshold for one particular type of energy and a high threshold for all other types. Histologically, the receptor is the dendrite of an afferent nerve cell.

recessive character: an inherited character which does not develop when balanced by a dominant character, but which may be transmitted through heredity (Mendel, 1866).

recidivism: a return for treatment in a mental hospital or a second conviction after having served a sentence in a penal institution. A *recidivist* is a person who has had two or more returns to the hospital or commitments to prison.

reciprocal innervation: Sherrington's term (1906) for the relaxation in one member of a pair of antagonistic muscles when the other member is contracted.

recognition: the feeling of familiarity when a previously encountered situation is present. In a *recognition test*, the testee is required to choose among the various items those which have been presented in lectures or stated in the textbook (usually by indicating *true* or *false*, as the case may be).

recollection: a broad term denoting revival of memory images.

reconditioning: the process of disestablishing a conditioned response, thus reinstating the original response. M. C. Jones (1924) used two methods in reconditioning: (a) experimental extinction (repetition of the substitute stimulus without reinforcement), and (b) associating the stimulus with an antagonistic response.

recurrent images: perseverative visual images which are experienced when the individual is influenced by powerful emotions.

red: the response to light-waves 670–760 millimicrons in length.

red-green blindness: dichromatism.

redintegration: Hamilton's term (published posthumously, 1859) to denote the tendency of each impression to revive in consciousness the whole situation of which it was originally a part. A cue or a surrogate for a broad situation can serve to revive the total response once made to the situation. Thus, he sought to correct the schematized theories of contemporary associationists by emphasizing the factor of total experience.

reduced cues: a theory of learning which states that, as learning progresses, a cue or surrogate acquires potency to elicit a response once attached to a total situation. Finally, an ideational stimulus may redintegrate a complex response pattern.

re-education: the method of restoring a lost function or integration, as in the case of a multiple personality (Prince, 1905), aphasics (Franz, 1907), or victims of bodily injuries.

referred pain: the localization of a pain in some other area than that which is actually involved.

reflective thinking: according to pragmatists, the logically patterned mental activity which proceeds as follows: a difficulty, definitions, hypotheses, testing the hypotheses and rejecting those which are illogical; and verification (Dewey, 1914).

reflex: an immediate, unlearned response to a specific stimulus. The *reflex arc* includes at least the afferent neuron, a synaptic connection in cord or brain, and a motor neuron. The theory of reflex action was proposed by Descartes (1650); Marshall Hall (1833) and Cabanis (1802) were among the first to relate the concept to the nervous system. Pavlov's work on reflex-action (1890 *et seq.*) has become a standard topic in psychology.

reflex-circle: Bok's term (1915) denoting the tendency for proprioceptors to be stimulated when muscles are contracted, and hence for the response to be a stimulus for another response, and so on. Holt (1931) used the concept and gave it special meaning.

reformism: a paranoidal zeal in advancing one's own views which are compensatory for frustrations and feelings of inferiority, and which are intended to enhance one's own prestige, not to advance the social welfare.

refractory disorders: myopia, hyperopia, aniseikonia, presbyopia, and other ocular defects which are the result of imperfections in the eyeball.

refractory period: the interval during which a neuron or muscle cell does not respond to stimulation. Immediately after excitation there is an *absolute refractory period,* which is followed by a *relative refractory period*. This phenomenon was described by Gotch and Burch (1899).

regression: according to psychoanalysis, unconscious displacement of libido-outlets to those which were established at an earlier period of normal development. The libido retreats to an infantile or childish localization or love-object in order to escape from frustrations in the present situation of the individual.

regression, filial: Galton's principle (1869) which states that offspring tend to regress towards the average level of the family. For example, the offspring of tall parents tend to be less tall; their offspring, still less tall; and so on, until the average height of the family stock is established. Galton stated this principle as a law of heredity.

Reid, Thomas (1710–1796): Scotch philosopher who taught that there is a "faculty of common sense," through which man knows that both external reality and his own mind exist. He objected to the theory that consciousness is built up by accretions of sensations, and he advocated the theory that consciousness is the primary datum in psychology (1764).

Reil, Johann Christian (1759–1813): Dutch anatomist who investigated the topography of the brain. The *island of Reil (gyri operti)* consists of from three to five gyri at the base of the fissure of Sylvius.

reinforcement: the facilitative influence of one neural pattern upon another, the excitation of the one increasing the intensity or efficiency of excitation in the other.

Reissner, Ernst (1824–1878): German histologist who described the structure of the cochlea. *Reissner's membrane* separates the scala media from the scala vestibuli.

rejection: deprivation of affection. This causes a condition known as *affect hunger* (Levy, 1937).

relapse: the return of a disorder shortly after the period of convalescence or readjustment.

relational thinking: the process of discovering interrelationships among ideas, or the isolation of the essential characteristic which exists among otherwise discrete ideas.

relative pitch: ability to judge differences between successive pitches.

relaxation therapy: E. Jacobson's technique of progressive relaxation (1929), which consists of teaching patients how to relax skeletal muscles and the incipient motor responses found in essential hypertension, the anxieties, stuttering, tics, insomnia, and the like.

release therapy: a technique of psychotherapy in which the child works off anxiety-tensions through the use of play materials (blocks, finger paints, sand box, and the like).

reliability: the consistency or accuracy with which a given test measures a function, or the dependability of the sampling which has been chosen to represent the totality from which it has been drawn. In the study of the individual, the term is applied to the dependability of observations, memory, and the like (*e.g.,* Münsterberg's pioneer studies on the reliability of witnesses).

religious psychology: a branch of psychology (founded by G. S. Hall, 1895) which investigates psychological aspects of conversion experiences (Starbuck, 1897), the psychological basis of belief (Leuba, 1896), revivals (Davenport, 1905), and the like. The first journal in the field was established in 1904; and the founders of religious psychology were often called the *Clark School.*

remembering: the activity of reviving memory images.

reminiscence: as defined by Ballard (1913), the rise in the curve of retention in the first two or three days after partial learning of a poem (or other material). According to Ballard, the rise is not due to review, though many other investigators have attributed the phenomenon to voluntary or involuntary rehearsal during the interim between two tests.

remission: the abatement of the symptoms of a disorder, or the temporary amelioration of an affliction.

repetition-compulsion: according to psychoanalysis, the unconscious tendency to repeat infantile patterns of behavior, even when these repetitions violate the pleasure principle.

replacement: the substitution of psychoneurotic or psychotic ideational trends by wholesome associations stimulated by occupational therapy, recreational activities, non-directive counseling, and the like.

repression: Freud's term (1900) for the unconscious tendency to exclude from consciousness unpleasant or painful ideas. It is a concept of major importance in psychoanalysis; and Freud made a notable alteration in his theory of anxiety, which he first believed to be due to repression, but which he later (1932) believed to be the cause for repression.

reproduction, method of: oral or written restatement of material learned or perceived, the purpose being that of measuring the individual's retention. Philippe (1897) was the first to develop a technique for using reproduction as a measure of the quality and the quantity of retention.

resistance: in psychoanalysis, opposition to revealing the unconscious. The ego and the super-ego, which effected the repressions, seek to keep them in the unconscious; hence there is resistance against any attempt to bring them into consciousness.

resonance theory: Helmholtz's explanation of hearing

(1863), which states that complex sound waves are analyzed in the cochlea. He designated the rods of Corti as the receptors or resonators, some of which vibrate when stimulated by waves of low frequency; others, of middle frequency; and some, of high frequency.

response: glandular, ideational, or muscular reaction to a stimulus. Sometimes, the term is restricted to the motor activity elicited by a stimulus; and *reaction* is used in referring to a complex pattern of responses.

retained members, method of: the measurement of retention by determining the percentage or the number of items which can be correctly reproduced.

retardation: a slight degree of mental deficiency.

retention: the after-effects of a response or an excitation, which may alter subsequent responses or excitations. One of the most important experimental studies of loss of retention was made by Ebbinghaus (1885).

retifism: foot and/or shoe fetichism; the term is derived from the name of a French pervert (Retif de la Bretonne, *c.* 1775).

retina: the innermost membrane of the eyeball which contains (among other structures) the rods and the cones. Kölliker (1854) was one of the first to describe the histology of the retina.

retinal rivalry: Helmholtz's term (1863) for the simultaneous stimulation of the retinas by two different colors or by designs which cannot be fused. The impression is unstable and fluctuating.

retroactive inhibition: inability to recall a list of nonsense materials or rote items when the list exceeds the span or when other learning is interpolated between the end-test and the re-test. G. Müller and Pilzecker (1900) were the first to define it.

retrogression: adjustment to difficulties by reverting to childish or infantile modes of behavior. The term is preferred by some because it does not have the psychoanalytic connotation of *regression*.

retrospective falsification: unintentional distortions and inaccuracies in the reproduction of past experiences. Henderson (1903) investigated the phenomenon and reported the existence of tendencies to symplify, generalize, and distort; and many subsequent investigators have amplified his conclusions.

reversal-formation: the adoption of conscious behavior and affective trends which are the opposite of the unconscious (repressed) impulses, thereby lessening the tensions and anxieties, aggressions and hostilities, or infantile sex wishes.

reversible figure: a perceptual experience in which the same figure is seen in two successive, incompatible perspectives (Necker, 1832). The oldest example is the Necker rhomboid. Lange (1888) was the first to record the times for reversals. Koffka (1930) developed a theory of tridimensional dynamics or fluctuations.

reward: the incentive used to motivate animal and human subjects in experiments on learning. It is used in studies of improvement of human efficiency.

Rhazes (860–930): Arabian physician who was interested in advancing the methods used in treating mental disorders.

rhinencephalon: the olfactory lobe of the brain.

rhinolalia (rhinophonia): a nasal voice.

rho: the symbol for a rank-difference coefficient of correlation.

Ribot, Theodule A. (1839–1916): pioneer experimental psychologist in France (1885). *Ribot's law of regression* states that in mental deterioration, memory for recent events goes first, and finally only the primitive emotions and childhood memories remain.

ritualistic behavior: stereotyped actions which serve as a defense against anxiety by preserving the fiction of security.

rivalry: competition for dominance status. In sibling rivalry, there is competition for primacy in parental affections, school marks, and the like.

Rivers, William Halse R. (1864-1922): British psychiatrist and anthropologist who (1899) participated in a pioneer psychometric study of primitive people, and who wrote extensively upon the characteristics of the primitive mentality.

rods: a receptor for vision, located in the retina. They were first differentiated by Kölliker (1854), and the theory that they respond to light-waves giving rise to achromatic sensations was stated by von Kries. Rods contain visual purple, which (Parinaud, 1881) is believed to be essential for dark adaptation.

Rolando, Louis (1773-1831): Italian anatomist who described one of the major fissures in the brain (*fissure of Rolando*), which separates the frontal from the parietal lobe.

Romanes, George John (1848-1894): English naturalist who (1882) wrote the first book on comparative psychology (having coined the phrase), and who introduced the anecdotal method into animal psychology.

Romberg, Moritz Heinrich (1795-1873): German physician who noted that victims of locomotor ataxia tend to sway when standing with heels together and eyes closed (*Romberg sign*).

Rorschach, Hermann (1884-1922): Swiss psychiatrist who developed a projective technique (1922) for appraising

personality by a study of the individual's responses to a
standard series of inkblots.

rotation: a method of exploring vestibular sensitivity by turning the individual rapidly around (Purkinje, 1820).
Mach (1873) devised a revolving chair for these studies,
and Goltz (1870) was the first to note that the after-
effects of rotation depend upon the semicircular canals
(not upon a motion of the brain itself, as Purkinje believed).

Rousseau, Jean Jacques (1712–1778): French philosopher
who taught that educational procedures should be based
upon the natural impulses of the child.

Royce, Josiah (1855–1916): American philosopher who
wrote a text on psychology (1903) from the standpoint
of idealism.

Rubin, Edgar: German psychologist who (1912) commenced a study of figure-ground relationships in visual
perception. His theories have been incorporated into Gestalt psychology.

Rush, Benjamin (1745–1813): American physician who is
said to have founded psychiatry in this country (1812).
Not until 1844, however, was there an organization of
physicians specializing in mental disorders or a journal
in this field. Rush developed methods of calming excited
patients by ducking them or by whirling them rapidly.

S: (a) the subject; (b) the stimulus.

s: Spearman's symbol (1904) for an individual's special abilities (as distinguished from general ability or *g*).

saccadic movement: the rapid jump of the eyes from one fixation point to another (described by J. Müller, 1826).

saccule (sacculus): a membranous sac in the inner ear, which (together with the utricle) is thought to contain receptors for static equilibrium.

"sacred disease": grand mal epilepsy. Hippocrates is said to have objected to the connotation of this label.

saddle nose: a flattened root of the nose occurring in congenital syphilis.

sadism: a form of sex perversion in which cruelty, ill-treatment, and suffering are inflicted upon the love-object. The earliest form is said to be oral sadism (biting) and both anal and urethral sadism may develop during toilet training. The term has been extended to include any type of pleasure achieved through the infliction of pain upon another. Freud coined the word from the name of the Marquis de Sade (1740–1814), a French novelist.

saggital axis: that which extends from front to back; the dorsoventral axis.

Saint Vitus' dance: chorea.

Salpêtrière: a hospital in Paris where Pinel served as chief physician (1809–1826), and where Charcot (1893) developed his theories of hypnosis and of hysteria. The *Salpêtrière school* (Charcot's theories) taught that hysteria arises from a physical pathology. The *Nancy school* (Bernheim) opposed this opinion, and taught that hysteria is psychogenic and that hypnosis is nothing more than the result of suggestion.

saltatory growth: growth by sudden spurts, as contrasted with progressive maturation.

saltatory spasm: clonic muscular spasms which make the patient jump when he attempts to stand erect.

Salzburg meeting: the first scientific gathering at which Freud had an opportunity to present his theories to Bleuler and Jung (1908). Two years later they joined in establishing the International Psychoanalytic Association (1910).

sampling: the choice of representatives of the totality to be used in a survey, psychological experiment, or investigation. What is true of the sampling is (if the *sampling error* be avoided) likely to be true of the totality. The sampling error occurs when the sample is not truly representative of the group. The reliability of the sampling is usually expressed in terms of probable error or standard error, and it is generally related inversely to the square root of the number of samples chosen to represent the totality.

Sanford, Edmund Clark (1859-1924): American experimental psychologist who prepared the first laboratory manual in the field (1898).

sapphism: Lesbianism, or female homosexuality.

satisfier: Thorndike's term (1914) for the gratifying outcome of a stimulus-response connection which favors a repetition of the bond.

saturation: a hue produced by a single light-wave; the attribute of chroma at a maximum (Titchener, 1896).

satyriasis: excessive sex desire in a male.

Sauvages, Boissier de (1706-1767): French psychiatrist who specialized in nosology.

Savart's wheel: a device for locating the lower and the upper thresholds for auditory sensitivity (1830). The limits were found to lie between about 8 and 24,000 cycles per second by this method.

saving method: Ebbinghaus's term (1885) for a method of measuring retention. After he had learned some material, he allowed a standard time-interval to elapse, and then recorded the amount of time required to relearn the same material (nonsense syllables).

scala media (cochlear duct): the smallest of the three membranous sacs in the inner ear. It is filled with endolymph, and it contains the organ of Corti.

scala tympani: a membranous sac in the inner ear which communicates with the scala vestibuli at the helicotrema. It is filled with perilymph.

scape-goating: a device used by propagandists in which an individual, group, or race is cited as the reason for the frustrations of those to whom the propaganda is addressed.

scatter diagram: a two-way table (or bivariate frequency arrangement) in which scores on two psychological tests or measures are arrayed. The first use of this device was made by Galton (1885) in his essay on the stature of midparents, and from this technique Pearson and others have developed the method of correlation.

Schäfer, Edward Albert (1850–1935): English physiologist whose schematic illustrations of the histology of the nervous system (1877) frequently appear in textbooks, and who (1900) edited a textbook on physiology containing material on sensory functions.

schema: a frame of reference for the orderly presentation of facts and principles of psychology or any psychological topic. The term is also used to refer to the drawing of a young child (under five or six) in which habits, not the model, determine the form; hence the model and the drawing appear to be more or less disconnected.

schemograph: apparatus for tracing the outlines of the visual field.

Schilder, Paul (1886–1940): psychiatrist (Austria, later America) who planned to systematize the work of Freud.

schizoid: nonsocial and introverted.

schizophrasia: an incoherent jumble of words, often called a "word-hash," which sometimes occurs in cases of schizophrenia.

schizophrenia: Bleuler's term (1911) to describe a mental disorder characterized by autistic thinking. The term was quickly adopted in America as being more appropriate than dementia praecox (Kraepelin, 1883). The clinical symptoms are varied, but the following are often mentioned: loss of emotional rapport with the environment; negativism or automatic obedience; individual logic in thought processes; and hallucinations. The types often mentioned are: dementia simplex (simple type); catatonia; paranoid; and hebephrenia. This disorder has been explained in various ways. Freud (1911) stated that it is the result of unconscious homosexual trends; Boisen (1936) said that it is based upon conflicts pertaining to an intolerable loss of self-respect; many writers object to the psychogenic theories and uphold the view that it has an organic pathology.

schizothymia: Kretschmer's term (1918) for a condition which in some particulars resembles schizophrenia, but in which the trends are kept within normal limits. The individual is strongly introverted, prefers his own company, engages in daydreaming, and lacks emotional rapport with the environment; but there are no organic pathologies, hallucinations, or other symptoms of psychosis. The schizothymic has an asthenic (leptosome) build.

Schlemm, Friedrich (1795–1858): German anatomist who described a canal in the eyeball (*Schlemm's canal*) through which the aqueous humor is supplied.

Schneider, Conrad Victor (1614–1680): German anatomist who described the membrane in the nose (*Schneiderian membrane*) containing the receptors for smell.

Scholastics: the philosophers of the 11th century who, by deduction, formulated systems of rational psychology and developed many of the abstract concepts which influenced the history of pre-scientific psychology (before 1879).

"schools": a loose term referring to various and divergent frames of reference in psychology. The term was popularized by the publication of books on conflicting theories (1920, 1930), and particularly by the debate between J. B. Watson and McDougall (1923–1924). At one time, the term "new school" was applied to those who, like Wundt, sought to introduce into psychology the methods of scientific experimentation.

Schopenhauer, Arthur (1788–1860): German philosopher who taught that will is the unconscious driving-force in human nature. Freud adopted some of his teachings.

Schreber case: the record of a German attorney who developed a paranoid psychosis and exhibited strong homosexual interests. Freud studied the case and developed the theory that in the paranoid form of schizophrenia the principal etiology is the repression of homosexuality (1911).

Schrenck-Notzing (1862–1929): German psychiatrist.

Schumann, Friedrich (1863–   ) : German psychologist
whose studies on visual space-perception contributed a
great deal to Gestalt psychology, especially his illustrations of the manner in which dots are grouped.

Schwann, Theodor (1810–1882) : German anatomist who
described the medullary sheath (*substance of Schwann*)
which surrounds most peripheral and cerebrospinal
nerve fibers. The thin membrane on the outside is known
as the *primitive substance of Schwann* (or the *neuri-
lemma*); the myelin (white, fatty cells) is known as the
white substance of Schwann (or the *medullary sheath*).
These substances are not found on autonomic fibers.

scientific management: application of psychological techniques to the increase in output in industry. Frederick
Winslow Taylor was the first to apply the method (Bethlehem, Pennsylvania, 1881), when he increased the output of pig-iron handlers about 400%. This was once
known as *Taylorism.*

sclera: the outermost covering of the eyeball. The *sclerotic
coat* is tough and opaque; the cornea is continuous with
the sclera and covers about one-sixth of the surface, the
sclera including the remaining five-sixths.

sclerosis: hardening of nervous tissues, or a thickening of the
walls of the arteries. In *multiple sclerosis,* the hardening
process occurs in various parts of the nervous system; and
the principal symptoms are as follows: nystagmus, weakness, slurred or monotonous talk, spastic gait, and in-
tention tremors (tremors when voluntary actions are
attempted).

scotoma: a dark spot in the visual field, usually due to a
lesion in the retina. *Scotomata* may be sensed as a ring
around the macula lutea, flashes of light, sparks, dimness,
and total absence of visual sensitivity in a certain part of

the field. Their location and extent are mapped by a *scotometer.*

scotopic adaptation: darkness adaptation (Aubert, 1865).

scrabbling: running movements (while in one place) by the rat having an audiogenic seizure (Maier, 1939). It is a part of the running attack which follows the air blasts (Hall and Martin, 1941).

screen-memory: a protective or defensive memory which serves as a concealment for a repressed memory. According to psychoanalysis, this is the reason why recollections of childhood are fragmentary, deal with trivial episodes, and appear in highly condensed form.

screening test: a method of appraisal by psychological tests and measures in order to discover those individuals who should be given a more searching, individual study.

Scripture, Edgar Wheeler (1864-   ): American experimental psychologist who opposed the traditional philosophical psychology (Ladd and others), and who developed laboratory psychology (the "new psychology") at Yale.

scrying: crystal gazing.

seclusiveness: (not to be confused with *introversion*) nonsocial behavior; schizoid.

secondary qualities: Locke's term (1690) for the changeable, subjective qualities which constitute sensation (*e.g.,* tastes, colors, tones and noises, and so on). These qualities exist in the mind of the percipient, not in the stimuli (which have primary qualities—motion, number, size, and the like).

security: according to W. I. Thomas (1918), one of the fundamental wishes, and the origin of mankind's conservatism. Mental hygienists sometimes state that the pivot of mental health is a feeling of emotional security in interpersonal relationships.

Seguin, Edouard (1812–1880): French psychologist and physician who (1842) established the first specialized curriculum for mentally defective children, and who constructed the first form-board for the appraisal of intelligence. He came to America to establish schools for the training of subnormal children.

selective learning: the process of "stamping in" satisfying responses, and "stamping out" unsatisfactory responses, in the trial-and-error sequence (Thorndike, 1898). The curve of learning represents the process of "learning by varied reaction through selection of the successful variants" (Thorndike).

selective perception: a tautological term (Pillsbury, 1908) denoting the fact that every perceptual activity emphasizes one aspect of a situation to the neglect of others. Some phase of the total situation is in the focus of consciousness; others are on the periphery of consciousness or not perceived at all.

self: the sum-total of all that the individual can call his, including both physical and mental data; and having the following constituents: the material, and social, and the spiritual selves; and pure ego (James, 1890). The term is used to denote the feeling of self-awareness or of personal identity. The pure self is sometimes defined as the soul or the judging thought (James). Calkins (1917) wrote that the self "*is* a mind and *has* a body." The doctrine has no place in objective psychology; but it is a basic topic in *Geisteswissenschaft*, personalistic, rational, and *Verstehende* psychologies.

self-abuse: a popular term for masturbation, which was once believed to be the cause for serious mental disorders.

self-accusation: pathological self-incrimination for minor faults or for fancied crimes, which may occur in anxiety hysteria or in manic-depressive psychosis, depressed type. In *involution melancholia*, the patient may accuse herself of having committed the unpardonable sin; an individual with a strong guilt-complex may talk of his own unworthiness and sins.

self-consciousness: (technically) the awareness of one's own identity as a more or less persisting entity. Popularly, the term refers to embarrassment or lack of self-confidence.

self-deception: the use of various mechanisms (*e.g.*, rationalization) as defenses against self-disparagement. The practice is said by mental hygienists to be harmful and to indicate resistance (*e.g.*, Klein, 1944).

self-observation: a loose term used as a synonym for *introspection*.

self-psychology: a frame of reference which emphasizes the primacy of the *self*, and which states that all mental activities are the manifestations of a *self* (Calkins, 1910).

selenogamia: sleep-walking (so named because it was once believed to be caused by the influence of the moon, *selene*).

semantic aphasia: Head's term (1920) for loss of ability to understand the meanings of words, a condition which results from an organic pathology in the brain.

semicircular canals: three osseous canals, containing membranous sacs, lying at right angles to one another in the inner ear. They are named as follows: *anterior* or *superior* canal; *posterior* or *vertical* canal; and *lateral* or *horizontal* canal. The enlargement of each canal as it leaves the vestibule is called the *ampulla*. They mediate the sense of equilibrium (Flourens, 1824), or the *static sense* (a concept introduced by J. Breuer, 1875). Crum

Brown (1874) did most of the pioneer work on the functions of the semicircular canals in the human ear.

semi-interquartile range: one-half of the difference between the 75 %-ile and the 25 %-ile.

semiotic (semeiotic): pertaining to symptoms.

senescence: old age. G. S. Hall was the first to write on the psychology of senescence (1922).

senile psychosis: shrinking of the brain due to breakdown of neuroglia and atrophy of nerve cells, with such accompanying psychological symptoms as the following: loss of memory for recent occurrences; depression; poor judgment; confusional states; emotional poverty; delusions; and/or analogous disorders. Esquirol (c. 1830) and Prichard (1842) were the first writers in the modern period to describe the symptoms. In *melancholia vera*, the principal feature is delusions of sinfulness; in *anxietas senilis*, a great sense of insecurity; and in *depressio apathetica*, a loss of interest in the environment. Shakespeare's *King Lear* is said to present many of the psychological aspects of this disorder.

senium: enfeeblement in old age.

sensation: the state of awareness which results when a sense organ is stimulated, and which cannot be analyzed into any elements (Titchener, 1896). In psychophysics, a sensation is the awareness which accompanies the excitation of the brain (Fechner, 1860), and which, though unmeasurable itself, can be approached indirectly by measuring the differences between stimuli and the strength of any given stimulus correlated with any sensation.

sensation-type: one of Jung's four function-types (1923), in which responsiveness to sensory stimuli predominates. When the sensation and the intuitive functions are strong, the individual is said to belong to the *irrational* function-types.

sense experience: awareness which results from direct stimulation of sense organs. In educational psychology, the term denotes the type of education for young children which Froebel introduced in 1826 (*sense realism*) to replace or supplement the traditional emphasis upon ideational experience.

sense organ: the receptor and the accessory apparatus considered as one (*e.g.*, the eye or the ear).

sense perception: immediate interpretation or recognition of data present to sense.

sense unit: Fechner's term (1860) for each noticeable difference in stimulus intensities.

sensitivity: responsiveness to stimulation. The term is sometimes used to denote the degree of sensory acuity in the various modalities, and it most often appears in these forms: *vestibular sensitivity* (sense of equilibrium) and *visceral sensitivity* (responsiveness to vague stimuli from the digestive tract).

sensorium: those parts of the cerebral cortex which mediate awareness of direct stimulation of sense organs, and the integrity of which is explored in a neurological examination. Occasionally, psychiatrists use the term to connote the patient's degree of orientation to the immediate environment.

sensory acuity: threshold of responsiveness to various stimuli.

sensory nerve: a nerve fiber which connects a receptor to the brain or the spinal cord.

sensory threshold: the strength at which a stimulus, increased or decreased by constant increments, is just strong enough to elicit a conscious response. The lower limit is RL-l (*Reiz*, stimulus; L, *limen*; l, lower); the upper limit is

RL-u (*u*, upper). Weber (1831) was the first to report systematic measurements of sensory thresholds.

sentiment: McDougall's term (1923) for an organized, more or less permanent tendency to experience certain emotions and desires with reference to some particular situation. Hatred, contempt, love, respect, and self-regard are examples of sentiments (in McDougall's psychology).

sequelae: after-effects of a physical or mental disorder.

set: a temporary condition which favors the selection of certain stimuli or facilitates a particular type of response.

sex character: any trait, mental or physical, which differentiates the sexes. Primary sex characters are those which are directly involved in reproduction; secondary sex characters are those which have no direct bearing upon reproductive functions but which differentiate the sexes.

sex differences: those which are found in psychological tests and measures to differentiate the sexes, the traditional debate being whether or not measured deviations in mental tests indicate the existence of inherent differences.

s-factors: Spearman's designation (1904), in the two-factor theory of intelligence, of psychoneural elements which account for success in variable special abilities, and which are differentiated from the *g-factor*, a general factor common and basic to all correlated abilities in the same individual.

shade: any color which lies below mid-gray in brilliance.

"shell-shock": a loose term designating emotional disorganization as a result of prolonged overstimulation in combat (1915). Since analogous conditions were found to exist among non-combatants and civilians, the term was discarded as inappropriate.

Sherrington, Charles S. (1857–   ): English physiologist who contributed to physiological psychology, and who

described the integrative action of the nervous system
(1906).

shock therapy: the use of convulsant drugs and electric
shocks as palliative or therapeutic measures in some
severe psychoneuroses and in certain psychotic conditions. Meduna (1928) started the use of convulsants
(metrazol), Sakel (1936) has reported the use of insulin
shock, and Berkwitz (1940) initiated the use of electric
shock.

sibling: brother or sister, not a twin, of the same parentage.

Sidis, Boris (1876–1923): American psychiatrist who wrote
on the psychology of suggestion and allied phenomena.
His son was a child prodigy often referred to in the literature on gifted children.

sigma: the standard deviation; also, in psychophysics, one
one-thousandth of a second.

sign: a stimulus which serves to elicit a response originally
evoked by another stimulus. The term connotes a great
reduction of the original stimulus, so that a small part or
a surrogate will suffice to redintegrate the response (as in
learning to read).

similarity: the characteristic of a group of stimuli which
gives them potency to elicit the same, or approximately
the same, response.

sinistrality: left-handedness.

sitomania: pathologically strong appetite; bulimia.

situation: a complex pattern of stimuli; every factor which
determines the behavior of an individual at any given
moment.

skeletal musculature: the striated (striped) muscle fibers attached to the bones and controlled by the central nervous
system.

skewness: asymmetrical frequency distribution or frequency curve.

skill: a rapid, efficient performance, mental or physical, which has been learned (*e.g.*, mental arithmetic, golf, and so on).

skin eroticism: according to psychoanalysis, sexual gratification by rubbing or scratching the skin, particularly the erotogenous zones.

skopophobia: paranoidal fear of spies, foreign agents, Bolsheviki, and the like. When not the result of propaganda effects, it may indicate hysteria, schizophrenia, and other disorders.

smooth muscle: unstriated muscle fibers controlled by the autonomic system.

social climate: folkways and mores of a community, state, or nation, particularly those which are not objectively measurable, but which impress the social scientist as constituting the Gestalt of the group.

social facilitation: (A. Mayer, 1903) the mild degree of rivalry which increases the output of an individual in the group; (Allport, 1923) the sight and the sounds of other persons at work, which increase the quality and the quantity of the performance of the individual.

social intelligence: ability to deal with, and adjust to, other persons. Traits considered to be measurable aspects of social intelligence are the following: sense of humor, memory for names and faces, common sense in social relations, recognition of the mental state of the speaker, and common observation of social behavior (Moss, 1927).

social mind: Durkheim's term (1912) for a collective religious consciousness, which, in his studies of Australian aborigines, he considered to be the basis of religious experiences.

social psychology: study of individual behavior which stimulates, and is stimulated by, other persons, together with a description of such conscious experience as depends upon other persons (Allport, 1923); the study of all those processes which make a socialized being out of the human animal (LaPierre and Farnsworth, 1936).

socialization: the process of becoming habituated (or conditioned) to symbolic action.

sodomy: sexual relations between human beings and animals (Genesis XVIII–XIX). *Bestiality* is a preferable term.

somatic: pertaining to the body.

somatogenic disorder: one which has an organic etiology.

somatopsychic: pertaining to both body and mind.

somesthesia: the vague pattern of cutaneous sensations.

somesthetic area: that part of the cortex of the cerebrum which is transversed by the fissure of Rolando and which extends for some distance back in the parietal lobe. The area was first described by Munk (1881). Campbell (1905) would limit it to the postcentral gyrus.

somnambulism: sleep-walking. In *monoideic somnambulism* (Janet, 1889), the same ritual is carried out night after night; in *polyideic somnambulism*, various conflicts produce varied behavior. Janet considered hysterical somnambulism to be an example of dissociation.

somniloquism: talking in sleep.

sophomania: delusions of omniscience.

sound cage: apparatus for charting the ability to locate the source of auditory stimuli (Matsumoto, 1897). Preyer (1887) was the first to explore the problem of tridimensional localization of sound by using a series of wire pointers attached to the head of the subject and serving as points for the presentation of stimuli.

sour: established as one of the primary taste qualities by Stich (1857), but omitted from the earlier lists.

Spallanzani, Lazaro (1729–1799): Italian physiologist who studied the regenerative capacity of cells.

spasm: sudden contraction of muscles.

spasmodyspnea: spasms of the muscles involved in respiration, as in stuttering, hysterical asthma, and organic disorders.

spastic movements: those characterized by sudden, intense contractions of muscles.

Spearman, Charles Edward (1863–194): English psychologist who developed the two-factor theory of intelligence. He taught that a general factor, g, is revealed by the hierarchy of correlations and accounts for a part of the individual's achievement in each test; and that a number of special abilities, *s-factors*, are revealed by the inequalities which are found when the individual takes a series of tests of diverse functions. He identified a *p-factor* (mental inertia), which makes it an effort to shift from one task to a different one; and a *w-factor*, which may be identified as the tendency to act upon the dictates of reflective thinking, not impulse.

specific energies of nerves: J. Muller's doctrine (1826), anticipated by Bell (1811), that each sensory neuron is identified with one, and only one, type of sensation, no matter what the stimulus may be; consequently, that each sensory nerve fiber mediates only one sensory process and quality (*e.g.*, the optic nerve, vision; the auditory nerve, hearing; etc.).

specificity: the established relationship between a response and a conditioned stimulus, no other stimulus being potent to elicit that given response. The conditioned response is in a state of *irradiation* at first, many stimuli being potent to elicit it; after training, however, it is elicited only by the conditioned stimulus (Pavlov, 1890).

specious present: James's term (1890) for the duration (protensity) of a single conscious experience.

spectral scale: the 150 (Titchener, 1896) discriminable hues around the base of the color pyramid, arranged according to just noticeable differences when brilliance is not taken into account.

spectrocolorimeter: apparatus for measuring color sensitivity to isolated spectral hues.

speech disorders: according to the White House Conference data (1931), the following (in order of frequency): oral inactivity; structural disorders in articulation; stuttering; sound substitution; functional disorders of the voice; dilectal; structural disorders of the voice; articulatory disorders resulting from paralysis; aphasia; "hard of hearing" speech; and disorders of the voice resulting from paralysis.

speech center: usually denoting Broca's area (1861).

sphincter control: control of defecation and urination (normally established by the 42nd month).

sphygmomanometer: apparatus for measuring blood-pressure, as in studies of the physiology of emotion (Marston, 1917).

spinal cord: the long, cylindrical column in the vertical canal. The principal ascending fibers are the following: spinothalamic; column of Goll; column of Burdach; direct cerebellar tract; and the tract of Gowers. The chief descending tracts are: the direct pyramidal; the crossed pyramidal; and the extra-pyramidal tracts. Cross-section reveals an H-shaped gray matter. The cord mediates certain reflexes, and it is the great path of conduction from and to higher centers.

spinal nerves: (in man) the thirty-one pairs of nerves attached to the spinal cord and named (from the area of emergence) as follows: cervical (8); thoracic (12); lumbar (5); sacral (5); and coccygeal (1). Charles Bell (1807) discovered that the anterior nerve-roots of the spinal cord are motor; the posterior nerve-roots, sensory.

Spinoza, Baruch (1632–1677): Dutch philosopher who developed the *double-aspect theory* (1665), the view that mind and body complement each other (like the concave and convex portions of a curved line). He also taught the doctrine of determinism.

spiritism: the belief in a materialistic survival after death, and hence that spirits can appear, at the behest of mediums, at seances, where they blow trumpets, leave fingerprints, and so on. Modern American spiritism began with the allegedly occult phenomena produced by Kathie and Margaret Fox (1851 *et seq.*). The British Society for Psychical Research was founded in 1882 for the investigation of spiritistic phenomena.

spirograph: apparatus for measuring inspiration-expiration.

Spitzka, Edward Charles (1852–1914): American neurologist who located some major nerve-tracts.

splanchnic: visceral.

Spranger types: Eduard Spranger's ideal fundamental types of individuality (1909); theoretical; economic; aesthetic; social; religious; and political.

spurious correlation: a relationship between two sets of variables which is the result of other factors than those mistakenly assumed to be the same.

Spurzheim, Johann Caspar (1776–1832): an Austrian who developed Gall's craniology (which he named *phren-*

ology), and who (1834) professed to be able to judge the "powers" of the mind by feeling of the "organs" of the mind (*i.e.*, protrusions and recessions in the skull).

staircase illusion: Schröder's reversible-perspective illusion (1858) in which a line drawing of a flight of stairs may be viewed as if seen either from above or below.

standard deviation (sigma): the square root of the mean of the deviations from the mean squared. It is used both as a measure of variability and as a basis for higher operations in psychological statistical work.

Stanford Revision of the Binet-Simon Tests: an individual test of intelligence which Terman and associates developed (1916) from the Binet-Simon Scales (1905, 1908, 1911). It contains ninety items (thirty-six more than the Binet-Simon), and it was standardized on about 2,300 subjects. In 1937 Terman, Merrill, and associates published another revision. Two scores are obtained from these revisions: *mental age* and *intelligence quotient*.

static sense: Flourens' term (1875) for sensations which accompany the stimulation of the semicircular canals, and later applied to the sense of balance.

statistics: the application of mathematical techniques to the manipulation of variables (test scores and the like) as a propaedeutic for induction and inference in an investigation. Galton (1869) was the first to make serious use of methods for quantifying data in psychological research, and then using statistical techniques in classifying them.

Stein, Stanislav Alexander von (1855–   ): Russian otologist who explored the problem of vestibular sensitivity.

stereognosis: recognition of objects from handling (not seeing) them. *Astereognosis* is indicative of a lesion in the parietal lobe, and hence exploration of this sensory

process is a routine part of a neurological examination
(Grinker, 1941).

stereoscope: apparatus for the fusion of disparate drawings
or pictures so that they are sensed as tridimensional
(Wheatstone, 1838). O. W. Holmes devised the familiar
hand stereoscope (1861). It is used in studies of visual
depth perception (*stereoscopy*).

stereotype: an emotionalized concept of a race, an individual,
a scale of values, and so on, which is not changed by
attempts to demonstrate its absurdity or falsity.

stereotypy: purposeless repetition of words and/or actions,
as in catatonia.

sterilization: an operation (on human beings) which involves
cutting the vas deferens (in males) and cutting or ex-
cising the fallopian tubes (in females), and which has
been advocated by eugenicists as a means of combatting
the "rising tide of the biologically unfit." In 1934 an
American Neurological Association committee, appointed
to study the matter objectively, brought a somewhat adverse report.

Stern, Ludwig Wilhelm (1871–1938): German (later American) psychologist who developed the concept of the
intelligence quotient (1912), and who applied the philosophy of personalism to the theory of psychology
(1938).

stigmata: gross physical abnormalities associated with (or
said to be associated with) abnormal behavior. Lombroso
(1876) developed the theory that criminal types can be
identified by *atavisms* (recrudescence of morphological
characteristics normally found only in savages); Rosanoff
(1905) referred to the following as the stigmata of ar-
rested development: microcephaly, macrocephaly, sca-
phocephaly (keel-like projection from front to back of

skull); and both extreme brachycephaly and extreme dolichocephaly. Charcot (1893) described the stigmata of anesthetic areas and the like, which he believed to occur only in *grande hystérie*.

Stiller, Berthold (1837-1922): Austrian physician who believed that a floating tenth rib is a stigma of neurasthenia and of an intestinal displacement.

Stilling, Benedict (1810-1879): German anatomist who made a study of the structure of the spinal cord.

stimulogenous fibrillation: Bok's term (1915) for the manner in which axons develop from the neuroblasts of chick embryos. An axon grows in the direction of a positive electrical discharge.

stimulus: any form of energy which elicits a response. In psychophysics, the letter R (*Reiz*, stimulus) is frequently used as an abbreviation.

stocking anesthesia: Janet's term (1889) for a type of hysterical insensitivity which does not conform to neurological pattern, but which is the result of a process of dissociation.

strabismus: cross-eyedness.

Stratton experiment: reversal of the visual field by a system of lenses (first done by G. M. Stratton, 1896, and repeated by Ewert, 1930), the purpose being that of ascertaining the extent to which bodily orientation furnishes the context for visual perceptions.

strephosymbolia: a rare disorder in which printed material is read as if reversed. When the writing is reversed, the condition is known as *strephographia* or *mirror-writing*.

striatum: the caudate and the lenticular nuclei, which are masses of gray matter at the base of the cerebrum extending into the lateral ventricles.

striped muscles: the skeletal muscles, which under microscopic examinations are observed to have a *striated*, or striped, appearance, and which are involved in adjustments to the external environment.

stroboscope: a device for creating two visual illusions: rapidly moving objects may appear to slow down or to be at rest; successive scenes, differing only slightly from one another, may appear to be in motion. Faraday (1831) and Plateau (1833) were among the first to devise methods of rotating disks in opposite directions or viewing them through rotating slits. It is now used in studies of perception of movement (*phi-phenomenon*).

Strong Vocational Interest Blank: 420 items to be marked *like, indifferent, dislike,* which, when scored according to weights established for various occupations, discover whether a person's interests resemble those of a given occupational group (Strong, 1927). It has been extensively used in research studies and in counseling.

structuralism: the point of view which considers the chief task of psychology that of analyzing the *contents* (Wundt, 1873) or the *structure* (Titchener, 1896) of consciousness. It is the antithesis of *act psychology* or *functionalism*. Mental states are composed of sensations, images, and feelings; and all complex mental organizations can be reduced to certain basic elements.

Strümpfell, Adolph (1853-1925): German physician who taught that hysteria has an organic basis (1892).

Stumpf, Karl (1848-1936): German psychologist who contributed a great deal to the psychology of music (1883), and who was influential in introducing phenomenology into systematic psychology.

stuttering: a disorganization in the rhythm of speech accompanied by tonic spasm of the larynx, abdominal expiration and thoracic inspiration, tremors, prolongation of certain sounds, and repetition of other sounds. The term is often used to include *stammering* (speech blocking). Many theories have been proposed to account for this disorder, and many diverse therapeutic procedures have been tried.

subconscious: either mental activities which occur on the periphery of awareness or which lie below the threshold of consciousness. The term was popularized by Herbart (1816) and James (1890).

subjective data: those which are not directly accessible to other investigators, and which cannot readily be quantified.

subliminal stimuli: those which are not sufficiently potent to elicit a response.

sublimation: Freud's term (1900) for the achievement of a socially acceptable outlet for a drive. Desexualized, aim-inhibited interests and motives are examples of the sublimation of the infantile libido.

substitutive psychoneurosis: Meyer's term (1915) for a disorder in which conflicts, repressed into the unconscious, manifest themselves in disguised manner.

suggestion: influencing the beliefs or the actions of another person without resort to direct orders (McDougall, 1923). The procedure in suggestion is essentially that of presenting stimuli which build up attitudes, release them, or augment the release of incipient responses, with a minimum of reflective thinking on the part of the individual to whom the suggestions are given (F. Allport, 1923).

sulcus: furrow or groove. The sulci of the cortex of the cerebrum are often used as convenient points for mapping various areas.

Sully, James (1842-1923): English psychologist who

founded a British society for child study (1895), and who
wrote some influential textbooks.

summation of stimuli: the cumulative effect of repeated stimulation of a given receptor. In the psychology of adver-
tising, the term denotes the continuous presentation of a
slogan or an appeal (*e.g.*, "Eventually, why not now?").
If a single presentation of a stimulus be inadequate to
elicit a response, a repetition of the stimulus may have a
summation effect, and thus evoke the response.

supraliminal: above the threshold.

sweet: one of the elementary taste sensations (Bravo, 1592).
Cohn (1914) coined the term *glucogenes* to denote the
stimuli for this sensation.

Sweetser, William (1797–1875): American physician who
was the first to use the term *mental hygiene* as the title of
a book published in this country (1843).

Sydenham, Thomas (1624–1689): English physician who
investigated chorea. *Sydenham's chorea* is an infectious
disorder with the following symptoms: irritability, involuntary tremors, spasmodic movements, disturbances
of emotion, loss of memory, hallucinations, and delirium.

symbol: any stimulus (*e.g.*, object, spoken word, ideational
element) which elicits a response originally attached to
another stimulus. The term often denotes the redintegration of a response-pattern when a cue or surrogate of
the original situation is the stimulus. In psychoanalysis,
symbolization is the unconscious process in which emotional values are displaced from one object to another, so
that repressed wishes may achieve a measure of disguised
satisfaction; but the conscious mind is entirely ignorant
of the fact that symbols have been employed.

sympathetic nervous system: the thoracicolumbar portion of
the autonomic nervous system, which consists of a paired

chain of ganglia and efferent fibers innervating the visceral organs, duct and ductless glands, muscle walls of blood vessels, and so on. Cannon has demonstrated (1929) that when the sympathetic portion is dominant over the craniosacral (*parasympathetic*) portion the following physiological changes occur: inhibition of salivation, acceleration of heart beat, constriction of small blood vessels, acceleration of adrenal outflow, and the like. In short, the body is prepared for an emergency reaction.

symptomatic act: according to psychoanalysis, a slip of the tongue, misplacing objects, lapse of memory, and the like, which represent an unconscious determinant; hence any *purposive accident*. The individual regards these acts as mere chance or explains them as being due to inattention, but actually they are unconsciously determined.

symptomatology: the study of symptoms. Many of the discussions of personality types make use of the terminology of psychiatric symptomatology (*e.g.*, schizoid, cyclothymic, paranoid trends, and so on).

synapse: the functional junction of the axon and the dendrite of nerve cells (Cajal, 1889), the term itself having been introduced by Sherrington (1906).

syncope: a fainting spell.

syncretism: a characteristic of the thinking of young children (Piaget, 1922) in which the demands of objective reality (from the standpoint of the adult) have no relationship to the cause-and-effect, temporal, or spatial relationships which are established.

syndactylism: web fingers or toes (a Mendelian trait).

syndrome: a pattern of symptoms indicating a given disorder; a symptom complex (Kahlbaum, 1874).

synergy: the coördination of motor activities into a unified response pattern.

synesthesia: a phenomenon discovered by Galton (1869) in which the individual has a vivid sensory image when another sensation is aroused (*e.g.*, color imagery when tones are sounded).

syntactical aphasia: Head's term (1920) for a speech disorder (somatogenic) in which the grammatical relationships among words is incorrect and more or less unintelligible.

syphilis: a venereal disease caused by *Spirochæta pallida* or *Treponema pallidum*, which is related, in a way not fully explained, to *locomotor ataxia* and *paretic dementia*.

syringomelia: a lesion of the spinal cord which involves loss of pain and of temperature sensitivity.

systematic psychology: that branch of psychology which deals with the philosophical implications, the postulates, and the unification of psychological facts and techniques.

systematized delusion: an unfounded belief which is made plausible, coherent, and relatively permanent, but which rests upon premises palpably fallacious from the standpoint of the well-adjusted, intelligent person.

systemic sense: the response to interoceptive (visceral) receptors.

systole: the contraction of the heart.

T

T: Rorschach's symbol for responses to the inkblots in terms of animal content.

t: ratio of a score to its standard error.

tabacosis: toxic conditions resulting from excessive use of tobacco, sometimes having concomitant mental symptoms of disorientation.

tabasheer: name of an aphrodisiac.

tabes: pathological condition marked by progressive degeneration of tissues.

tabes dorsalis: locomotor ataxia (disorder of syphilitic origin) due to sclerosis of posterior columns of spinal cord. A mental disorder characterized by hallucinations, delusions of persecution, and general anxiety is a frequent accompaniment of tabes dorsalis.

tabula rasa: term attributed to John Locke (1632–1704) to denote the idea that all knowledge is derived from experience. Although he did not actually use this term in his writings, he did oppose the current beliefs in nativism and he did emphasize the doctrine of empiricism.

tachistoscope: device for rapid exposure of material. A. W. Volkman, German physiologist, described the principles and first used the term in 1859.

tachy-: Greek word meaning "rapid."

tachycardia: rapid heart, as in states of excitement or organic ailments.

tachylogia: unusually rapid talk, as in states of nervousness or in mania.

tachyphagia: rapid eating and swallowing, as in some psychotic states.

tachyphrasia: extremely voluble speech. (Mr. Jingle in Charles Dickens' *Pickwick Papers* would be called a tachyphrasic.)

tactile: pertaining to the sense of touch. Touch is a popular term for the four cutaneous sensations: pressure, cold, warmth, pain.

tactometer: apparatus for measuring sensitivity to pressure on a minute point of the skin.

Talbot-Plateau Law: light-waves from two disks being rotated (beyond point of flicker) fuse into an intensity the same as that which would be sensed if light-waves corresponding to this intensity were directed upon the disks. (Named for William Henry Fox Talbot, 1800–1877, an Englishman who is mentioned as one of the inventors of photography; and Jean Plateau, who (1853) reported investigations on mixtures of light-waves.)

talent: unusual proficiency in some field, such as music, creative writing, or art. Since the ability of a talented individual exceeds that of the average, the assumption is that, if others had an equal opportunity and failed to make comparable achievements, talent depends upon inherent capacity.

talion principle: according to psychoanalysts, the exaction, by the unconscious (or id), of retribution because of repressions enforced by ego and/or super-ego.

talipes: deformed or club foot.

tambour: drum-like apparatus which moves a stylus as puffs of air cause a diaphragm to rise or fall.

tantrum: violent rage.

taphephobia: morbid fear of being buried alive. The fear is thought to be a survival, in folklore, of premature burials which took place during the plagues of the Middle Ages.

tapping test: a simple measure of speed of movement in

which the testee taps a metallic plate with a stylus, the number of taps per minute being recorded by a counter. It is often used as one of the tests in studies of effects of caffeine, tobacco, alcohol, sleep deprivation, and the like.

tapping test, Knox's: a measure of attention or memory span in which four cubes are touched in various orders of difficulty (*e.g.*, 1-4-3-2; 1-3-2-4-3-), the testee to repeat immediately the pattern given. The test was developed by H. A. Knox as a nonlanguage test for use at Ellis Island (*c.* 1914).

Tarde, Gabriel (1843–1904) : French sociologist and criminologist who wrote *Laws of Imitation* (1890), a book which led early workers in social psychology to emphasize the so-called instinct of imitation as the basic principle in social life.

Tartini, Giuseppe (1692–1770) : Italian musician who discovered the difference tone. If two notes are sounded continuously and intensely, a third note is heard, the vibration frequency of which is the difference between the frequencies of the two notes sounded. This phenomenon is known as *Tartini's tone* or the *difference tone*.

taste: the sense of gustation, the receptors for this sensation having been discovered by Schwalbe and Loven (1867). Taste is generally considered to be a chemical sense; hence the receptors have been called *chemoreceptors*. Sir Charles Bell (1774–1842) described the papillae (1803) and W. Horn observed that diverse sensations arise from stimulation of different papillae (1825).

taste adaptation: gradual loss of taste discrimination as a result of continued stimulation of the papillae by a given substance.

taste tetrahedron: Henning's graphic representation (1921) of the theory that there are four salient tastes: sweet, sour, bitter, salty. Between each of any two of these, there are other salient tastes, the basic four merely being the "corners" of the tetrahedron.

tarantism: in the seventeenth century, thought to be a mental disorder caused by the bite of the tarantula. *Tarantism* was possibly a manic condition or hysterical excitement, and the psychiatrists of that time were concerned to define a specific cause for each mental disorder, tarantula bite having been chosen as the etiological factor in these conditions. The Italian anatomist Baglivi (1668–1707) is said to have coined the term.

tau-effect: judgments of the distance between two lines exposed successively for short intervals depend upon the length of the time lapse.

taxis: Verworn's term to denote simple responses to simple situations, as among lower animals.

Taylor, Frederick Winslow: pioneer in applying the principles of efficiency to industrial operations. His demonstration at the Bethlehem Steel Plant, in which he increased the output of a pig-iron handler by about 400%, is mentioned as the first application of scientific management-techniques in industry (1885).

Tay-Sachs' disease: amaurotic family idiocy, which is an inherited condition of partial or complete blindness together with extreme mental deficiency.

Td: Rorschach's symbol for responses the content of which is animal detail (*Ad*).

technical term: that which is employed in a restricted denotation in a science, whereas in general usage it has a wider connotation; or that which does not occur in general usage at all, the term being restricted entirely to a given field of science. "Touch," for example, is a term which has no place in scientific psychology, as E. B.

Titchener has pointed out; but it has a wide usage in popular speech. "Talent" is a term which has a more restricted denotation in psychology than it has in daily speech. "Telencephalization" is a term which would scarcely ever be heard in ordinary discourse, but it has a technical denotation in one phase of psychology.

technique: the procedure for carrying out a psychological experiment or investigation. It includes the selection and use of appropriate apparatus, the selection of a random sample of cases, the manipulation of the data by statistical procedures, drawing conclusions, verifying the results, and preparing the summary or report.

techtorial membrane: the thick membrane which overlies the organ of Corti (in the inner ear).

teichopsia: temporary dullness of vision (such as that occurring in excessive use of tobacco), often with accompanying visual images of subjective origin.

telekinesis: according to occultists, the mysterious power whereby objects at a distance are moved, allegedly without the interposition of any connivance or deceit.

telencephalization: Tilney's designation of the theory that the brain structure last to appear in evolution dominates the functions localized in brain structures which were of earlier phylogenetic origin. The doctrine also implies that the latest part of the brain to be developed in evolution has an unstable control over functions which are based in lower centers.

teleologic hallucinations: Bleuler's term for hallucinations which warn the patient of ill to befall or which give helpful advice. Such hallucinations are said to reveal the fact that sometimes the "voices" have a relationship to other mental content, such as persistent difficulties or problems of adjustment.

teleology: the doctrine that all nature shows a progressive adaptation towards the achievement of higher ends and purposes. In psychology, this doctrine was upheld by William McDougall (1871–1938), who vigorously opposed the mechanistic emphasis of American psychologists and who upheld the theory of purposive causation.

teleostereoscope: apparatus consisting of a series of mirrors which produce an effect as if the eyes were set farther apart. Objects then appear in relief and at close range. It is an adaptation of the stereoscope, invented by Wheatstone (1838).

telepathic experiments: the studies of extra-sensory perception carried out by J. B. Rhine since about 1927 (also known as the Duke University experiments). The experimenter looks at a card, and the subject attempts to "sense" what the card is. In the pack of 25 cards, five designs are used; hence "hits" consistently above chance expectations are said to indicate a paranormal situation.

telepathy: transmitting thoughts from one person to another without any known sensory capacities being involved. William James was greatly interested in telepathy, but he never gave it his full endorsement. Much of the literature on this topic consists of anecdotes and hearsay evidence; consequently, many psychologists include telepathy under the heading of vagaries of belief.

telephone theory of hearing: colloquial term referring to the theory advanced by Rutherford (1886–1887) that the impulses initiated in the ear by sound waves are analyzed in the brain. It was advanced to overcome some of the difficulties present in the "piano theory" of Helmholtz.

telepsychic: a term used among occultists to designate an alleged capacity for knowing future events or for being able to predict outcomes of present events.

telesthesia: allegedly paranormal capacity for responding to stimuli which are below the threshold for normal persons. Some occultists claim to have "x-ray eyes" or to make use of "electrical waves."

telic: pertaining to the accomplishment of ends or purposes.

telodendron: the arborization of the axon of the neurons.

temperament: the more or less stable effective pattern characteristic of an individual. It is revealed by one's susceptibility to emotional stimulation, by reaction time, by strength of responses, by quality and intensity of moods, and by all that is subsumed under "emotional nature"; and it is very largely a matter of inheritance (G. W. Allport, 1937). According to Hippocrates (*c.* 400 B.C.), there are four basic temperaments, with corresponding humors; choleric (yellow bile), melancholic (black bile), phlegmatic (phlegm), and sanguine (blood).

temperature illusion: the experience occurring after one hand has been immersed in hot water and the other in cold water, and then both hands are placed in tepid water, the illusion being a reversal of judgment. The water feels cold to the hand that was in hot water, and hot to the other hand. John Locke (1632–1704) described this illusion.

temperature sense: referring to "cold spots" and "warmth spots" located on the surface of the skin. Charles Bell (1803) commented briefly upon them, and Blix (1882) and Goldscheider (1884) experimented by applying blunt-pointed rods to minute areas of the skin, thus locating areas of sensitivity to warmth and cold.

temporal lobe: the portion of the cerebral hemisphere which lies below the fissure of Sylvius and in front of the exoccipital fissures.

temporal sign: an episode which can be recalled and hence which facilitates recall of other events occurring closely before or after that time. Temporal signs are used in hypnotic studies of regression, the subject being told to revive a recollection of a known episode and thus to recall other (apparently forgotten) experiences which took place near that time.

tendinous sensation: awareness of tensions in the tendons.

teniophobia: morbid fear of tapeworms. (*Tæniphobia.*)

Tenon's capsule: the socket within which the eyeball is set. It is named for Jacques René Tenon (1724–1816), French anatomist.

tension: a general term denoting upsets in complacency or optimum balance, an emotional upheaval being the principal characteristic of hypertensions. Anxiety, irritability, incoördination, and hyperactivity are common symptoms of upsets. The basis of tension lies in the activity of the sympathetic portion (*thoracico-lumbar*) of the autonomic nervous system (Cannon, 1929; Kempf, 1918). Physiological and psychological tensions are said to be the results of such conditions as unsolved problems, continued frustrations, sudden and intense stimulations, and prolonged worry. According to psychosomatic medicine, unresolved tensions may have a deleterious effect upon health.

tension-relaxation: Wundt's term for one of three dimensions of feeling. Tension rises as an event is about to happen; it relaxes after the event has occurred.

terminal inhibition: cessation of a muscular response when the antagonistic muscle is stimulated.

Terman, Lewis Madison (1877–   ): American psychologist best known for revisions of the Binet-Simon Scale (1916, 1937); director of a study of genius.

terrors: intense fears caused by relatively minor external stimuli. Night terror (*parvor nocturna*) may signify intense mental conflicts or a health problem.

test: any procedure whereby a score is obtained for a performance, mental or physical. Tests are classified in diverse ways, such as form or pattern of items, purpose, content, and manner of construction. Essay-type tests are the traditional devices for measuring achievement in various branches of the curriculum. New-type tests are objective, impartially constructed, easily scored measures of achievement. J. M. Rice (*c.* 1895), an American schoolman, was one of the first to objectify the achievement test. Intelligence tests (Binet, 1905) measure capacity to learn. Literally, thousands of tests of various psychological traits have been published in America, especially since 1918.

testes: two glands in the scrotum which secrete spermatozoa.

tetanus: a disease causing convulsive seizures, muscular spasms, and heightening of reflexes.

tetanoid-type: Walther Jaensch's term for a psychoconstitutional make-up which, though not pathological, resembles in a superficial way the victim of tetanus.

tetrachromatism: normal color vision from the standpoint of the Hering theory; hence the capacity to distinguish red, green, yellow, and blue. See *trichromatism.*

tetrad differences: the earliest method of factor analysis, which was developed by Carl Spearman (1912) in his studies of the two-factor theory of intelligence. The method is of importance because it represents the pioneer investigation into the nature of intelligence by statistical procedures and because it opened up a field of research in which American psychologists have made many contributions.

thalamus: the ovoid mass at the base of the cerebrum. Injury to the ganglia on the ventral side beneath the thalamus (hypothalamus) has long been recognized as an etiological factor in pathologies of emotion. When the hypothalamus is impaired (as by a tumor), the individual is apathetic. When the hypothalamus is intact but when the thalamus is impaired, the individual is very excitable. Cannon (1929) advanced the hypothesis that it is the "center" of control in emotions, and Masserman (1943) has reported experiments on animals which seem to offer support for this view.

thanatos instinct: according to psychoanalysis, the urge to destroy or to injure one's self. It is the antithesis of the *eros instinct* (life), and is one of the most important polarities in the psyche. Self-mutilation, the talion principle, and suicide are said to illustrate the workings of the thanatos instinct.

thanatomania: neurotic obsession for attending funerals, visiting cemeteries, or reading obituaries.

thanatophobia: morbid dread of death. A thanatophobic, for instance, might not permit anyone to mention the subject of death in his hearing.

thaumatrope: apparatus consisting of figures on opposite sides of a rotating plaform which blend into one figure. When the rotation ceases, the figures may continue to appear to be blended, thus furnishing an index to the persistence of the terminal lag of the sensation.

theelin: hormone from the ovary.

theism: any belief in the existence of God or a deity. According to some psychologists, philosophical and theological concepts have hampered the development of the science (*e.g.*, J. B. Watson, 1919). Others would draw a line between metaphysical issues (*axiological propositions*) and scientific descriptions (*existential propositions*), thus avoiding arguments about theism. Rational psychology (stemming from Thomistic philosophy) would keep theistic views as a central problem in psychology.

theomania: morbid concern about religious cults and emotionalized modes of worship. In extreme form, a deluded person may believe that he is God or that he has been selected as the founder of a "true" religion.

theopathia: belief that medications and surgery are of no value, but that prayer alone will effect cures.

Theophrastus (*c.* 300 B.C.): Greek philosopher who described, in crisp style, thirty "types" of personality. He is said to have been the "father of literary characterology."

theory: a statement of the relationships among observed data which is tentatively accepted but not finally demonstrated.

therapeutics: the division of medicine which deals with the treatment of disease. Psychotherapeutics deal with clinical techniques for treating mental difficulties, and the principles are usually subsumed by the term *mental hygiene*. Techniques of changing attitudes, of inducing relaxation, of engrossing tasks, of directive or nondirective counsel, psychoanalysis, persuasive methods, or seeking to alter the environment are a few of the procedures used in psychotherapeutics.

thermal sensitivity: response to stimuli which induce awareness of warmth or cold. Max von Frey (1895) discovered "warmth" and "cold" spots in minute areas of the skin. Altruz (1896) found that "hot" is the result of stimulation for warmth, cold, and pain.

thermalgesia: painful response to stimuli for extreme warmth or heat.

thermesthesiometer: apparatus for measuring sensitivity to warmth and heat. Thunberg (1896) was the first to devise a grid for congruent stimulation of warmth and cold areas on the skin surface.

thermohyperesthesia: abnormal sensitivity to fluctuations in temperature.

thermohypesthesia: abnormal insensitivity to changes in temperature.

thigmesthesia: sensitivity to pressure stimuli. "Touch" sensitivity is most acute on the "windward" side of hairs. Research has failed to identify a specific type of nerve cell which is the receptor for thigmesthesia.

thigmohyperesthesia: neurotic or organic disorder in which one symptom is a complaint about the weight of clothing or about the bed covers.

thinking: (1) problem-solving behavior, involving a delayed response until after various possible courses of action have been considered; (2) implicit speech behavior; (3) the process of generalization from specific experiences; (4) phantasy-making, or daydreaming; (5) the reorganization of past experiences into novel combinations, whereby new and untried possibilities for behavior are explored. The term is used in a great variety of connotations and implies a frame of reference in the theory of psychology. In general, it subsumes three distinct types of mental activity: free associations (stream of consciousness); reflective (logical) thinking; and creative thinking.

thirst: awareness of dryness in mouth or throat, resulting from tissue lacks. A. von Haller (1747) was one of the first to analyze this sensation.

Thorndike, Edward Lee (1874–   ): one of the pioneer American students of animal psychology and a leading contributor to the field of educational psychology.

thought-reading: according to occultists, the power of apprehending, without the use of known sense organs, the contents of the mind of another person. It also refers to the ability to judge what a person is thinking of by noting subdued muscular activity (*muscle-reading*).

thought-transference: according to occultists, the ability to communicate with another person by use of supernormal powers.

threshold (limen): term first used by Herbart (1816) to denote the point at which ideas rise into consciousness. Fechner gave the term its modern denotation by applying Herbart's concept to measurements of the magnitude of stimuli which elicit sensations (1860).

threshold, absolute: Fechner's term for the magnitude of a stimulus which is necessary to elicit a sensation. Sound waves of 10 double-vibrations per second, for example, are below the absolute threshold for audition.

threshold, differential: Fechner's term for the magnitude of difference between two stimuli necessary to give a sensation of twoness. See *Weber-Fechner law*.

thymia: the general sphere of feelings and emotions, moods, and temperament. The following terms are rarely used: *agriothymia:* savage or uncontrolled affects; *athymia:* lacking in all warmth of emotional response; *barythymia:* crudity of affects; *parathymia:* warped or distorted affects. The following are frequently used: *cyclothymia, hypothmia,* and *schizothymia.*

thymus gland: an endocrine gland lying in the upper part of the thorax and the throat which gradually atrophies about the time of puberty. Its function is uncertain, and it is often referred to as "the gland of childhood."

thyroid gland: an endocrine named from its fancied resemblance to a shield (Greek) which lies anterior to the trachea. Hypofunctioning of the thyroid gland leads to cretinism and myxedema; hypertrophy of this gland leads to or is associated with a disorder known as *exophthalmic goiter.*

tic: (1) an involuntary jerking of a small group of muscles; (2) habit-spasms, such as blowing upon the fingers, facial grimaces, or clearing the throat. Tics may be due to organic factors, such as extreme fatigue, drugs, and the like. They are often due to psychogenic factors, such as purposeless, unintentional jerks, twitches, and the like, which are in no way adjustive to the situation confronting the individual.

timbre: the qualitative characteristics whereby different voices and musical instruments are differentiated, even when the same fundamental tone is used. The accompanying sound-waves (overtones) and the adventitious sounds (rasping noises) make up timbre.

time sense: referring to one of the classical controversies of 18th and 19th centuries regarding *a priori* vs. *a posteriori* perception. Kant, for example, upheld the doctrine of nativistic time-sense; whereas Locke advocated the empirical concept. At one time, the nativistic-empirical controversy was a central issue in discussions of time and space perceptions.

tinnitus aurium: subjective noises in the ear, such as those caused by air-pressure differences between the middle and the outer ear, impacted cerumen, changes in the endolymph of the inner ear, and the like.

tint: the result of an admixture of white with a primary or an intermediate hue. See *color pyramid.*

Titchener, Edward Bradford (1867–1927): American psychologist (born in England) who systematically worked out, by experimental analysis, the elements of consciousness and who sought to make psychology as exact a science as physics. In 1915 he revised his point of view regarding the primacy of elements of consciousness ("sensationistic elementarism").

tobaccoism: toxic condition resulting from excessive use of tobacco.

tolerance: the amount of a given stimulus which can be endured without pain or without a withdrawal response. The term also refers to the amount of drug (caffeine, alcohol, etc.) which can be ingested without appreciably affecting physiological or psychological functions.

tonal islands: areas within the field of auditory stimuli which do not elicit a sensation. Inacuities may exist in a limited range of sound-waves, but the ear may function normally in other ranges. (Helmholtz, 1862).

tonal pencil: Titchener's diagrammatic representation of a spatial aspect of tone, designed to illustrate the fact that deep tones seem to be large; middle tones, more or less the same size; and high tones, thin (1896).

tonaphasia: loss of ability to carry a tune, as a result of cerebral lesion.

tone: periodic vibrations of sound waves evoking an auditory sensation with more or less well-defined attributes. The distinction between tones and noises is not wholly within the realm of physics, however, since Helmholtz pointed out that the noises of one generation may be the tones of the next in the history of music. Titchener (1915) differentiated three attributes of tones: pitch, volume, and octave similarity; other psychologists have described other attributes.

tone-deafness: inability to judge differences among the sequential pitches of tones; hence inability to enjoy music. Once considered to be the result of organic disability, it is now believed, in certain cases, to be caused by lack of training or indifference.

tonic spasm: sudden, intense contraction of a muscle or group of muscles.

tontriphobia: intense fear of thunder.

tonus: muscular tension. The opposite of tonus is *flaccidity*.

topoalgia: neurotic localization of pain, as in a region where no organic cause for the discomfort can be found or where the distribution of the sensory nerves does not justify the complaints.

topography, mental: the psychoanalytic description of regions of the psyche, whereby the conscious and the unconscious minds are delimited and whereby the id, the ego and the superego are separated. These concepts are said by their proponents to be useful metaphors.

topological psychology: Lewin's point of view in which concepts of geometry and vectors are used to describe the individual in his environment. Negative and positive forces repel or attract the individual within a given life-space; hence diagrammatic representations may be used to describe any individual at any time.

topothermesthesiometer: apparatus for measuring the degree of sensitivity of various areas on the skin surface to stimuli for warmth.

torpor, initial: the warming-up period necessary before undertaking a task. Presumably the reduced output at the commencement of a task is attributable to such factors as persistence of interrupted activities, different mental sets, and the like.

torsion: a twisting movement.

torso: the trunk.

torticollis: a twisted neck, as in a catatonic posture, an organic disorder, or a neurotic pose.

totem: the animal regarded by savage tribes as the carrier of the spirits of the deceased. Freud (1904) traced survivals of totem-worship in modern times and described a similarity between primitive culture and practices of neurotic or psychotic adults.

touch: a popular name for the cutaneous sensations of cold, warmth, pain, and, especially, pressure. Titchener refers to three degrees: contact, pressure, and granular pressure (1896).

toxanemia: anemia resulting from poisonous substances in the body; hence a condition which would lower efficiency in mental or physical work.

toxicomania: frenzied determination to commit suicide by taking poisons.

toxiphobia: morbid fear that enemies are trying to poison the individual.

trace reflex: Pavlov's term for a conditioned reaction produced when the substitute stimulus is given some time before the adequate stimulus in the training, and hence when the substitute stimulus is followed, after a pause, by a weak response. Pavlov reports that he was able to establish delays as long as five minutes in dogs (1927).

tracheophyma: goiter.

tract: a more or less well-defined group of tissues, such as the columns of the spinal cord or a nerve.

trade test: a series of brief questions or a relatively simple task designed to indicate whether an applicant possesses the knowledge or skill which he claims to possess. Trade tests were introduced by the United States Army in 1917.

trait: a distinctive pattern of behavior which is more or less permanent; hence a group of habits, such as persistence, introversion, accuracy, and the like.

trance: a sleep-like condition induced by drugs or hypnosis.

transfer of training: the improvement in an unpracticed function which is supposed to result from practice in another function. Thus, the study of Latin is said to have a *transfer effect* upon ability to speak and write the vernacular. Thorndike and Woodworth (1901) emphasize the factor of identical elements as the cause for what appears to be a transfer automatically taking place; Judd (1902) found evidence for mentioning the factor of *generalization* in transfer.

transference: displacement of the libido from an infantile love-object to some other object or person, especially the psychoanalyst during the course of treatment.

transference, negative: displacement of resentment against some one, especially the parents, towards the psychoanalyst during the course of treatment.

transmute: the process of converting raw scores into meaningful equivalents by reference to a table of norms.

transnormal: according to occultists, the capacity for gaining knowledge or for performing acts which transcend the abilities of normal persons.

transplantation experiments: the transposition of tissues, as in the newborn animal, from one part of the body to another, the object being to observe whether the transplanted tissue develops into the same type of tissues as already exist in this region.

transposability of Gestalten: the exchange of one *Gestalt* for another.

transposition: the exchange of one letter or word for another. Dunlap (1932) describes the technique of *negative practice* for overcoming a habit of transposition.

transvestism: the adoption of clothing and mannerisms of the opposite sex.

trauma: a wound or injury. The term is extended to include mental shocks, severe disappointments, and tragedies as well as bodily injuries.

traumatic experience: one which has a more or less permanent and devastating effect upon one's self-confidence or self-esteem.

traumatic delusion: one which is developed as the after-effect of a head injury.

traumatic psychosis: a severe mental disorder which ensues from an injury to the brain.

tremor: very slight convulsions in the striated muscles; shaking movements.

tremograph: apparatus devised by Jastrow to record the involuntary trembling which accompanies certain forms of stimulation. The usual form of the apparatus consists of a glass plate mounted on bearings, the subject's arm being placed on the plate.

Trendelenberg, A. F.: German professor of philosophy who (c. 1860) interested Brentano in the teachings of Aristotle and thus exercised an indirect influence upon modern psychology.

triakaidekaphobia: fear of the number 13. Sometimes this term is cited as a humorous example of the older custom of building up a long list of phobias by using various Greek prefixes.

tribadism: production of the orgasm by friction without the insertion of the penis into the vagina. Also, friction between two females.

trichoesthesia: awareness in response to the touching of a hair.

trichoesthesiometer: apparatus for determining the threshold for sensation when a hair is touched.

trichotillomania: frenzied tearing of the hair, as in certain types of psychoses or conditions of hysteria.

trigeminal nerve: the fifth (and largest) of the cranial nerves, containing both sensory and motor fibers.

tristemania: depressed moods. (*Tristimania*).

tritanopia: a condition of color-blindness marked by inability to sense light-waves for violet. According to Helmholtz (1852), there are three types of cones in the retina which are especially responsive to red, green, and blue (violet), respectively; hence *tritanopia* refers to an absence or malfunctioning of the third type of cones.

trochlear nerve: the fourth cranial nerve.

trophic functions: those which are concerned with assimilation, digestion, and nutrition.

tropism: Loeb's (1918) term for forced movements induced in the cell by stimulation. This concept was offered as a mechanistic explanation of behavior; hence as a means of avoiding anthropomorphism. The stimulus (some form of energy) induces chemical reactions in the protoplasm of the cell, and thus approach-avoidance behavior ensues. (De Condolle, 1835, introduced the term.)

tropometer: apparatus for measuring the rotations of the eyes.

T-scale: McCall's (1922) arrangement of test scores on a 100-unit scale, each unit being 0.1 sigma of the distribution and the mean of the distribution being set at 50, with a standard deviation of 10.

T-type: Walther Jaensch's term for a personality type which, supposedly, resembles the effects of parathyroid dysfunction.

tubercle, Darwinian: a rounded or pointed eminence on the upper part of the outer ear which, theoretically, resembles the quadriped ear; hence it was once taken to be a sign of atavism or "throw-back" to an earlier stage of evolution of the human species.

tumor: a mass of tissues having no physiological function but often disrupting the functions of normal tissues. Intracranial tumors are causative factors in many disruptions of mental activities. In the diagnosis of certain types of brain tumors, electroencephalography is used.

Twitmeyer, Edwin Burket (1873–1943) : American psychologist who (1902) reported the conditioned knee jerk (independently of the work of Pavlov).

tympanic membrane: the drum-like membrane separating the outer from the middle ear.

types of personality: the doctrine that personalities differ qualitatively as well as quantitatively, and that individuals tend to fall into more or less well-differentiated categories. Many doctrines of types have been expounded by theorists. Following the early work on mental tests, it was an accepted dogma of psychology that all differences among people are quantitative; but, with the rise of Gestalt psychology, the dogma of qualitative differences has been revived.

typology: the point of view that individuals fit into more or less well-defined biosocial categories. Kraepelin's (1899) classification of psychoses established the practice of using psychiatric symptomatology in delineations of non-psychiatric expositions of personality types; hence terms like *cycloid, schizoid* and *paranoid* have a wide vogue. The rise of an intense enthusiasm for a nationalistic psychology in Germany (1933 *et seq.*) popularized the doctrine of racial types in certain quarters.

Ucs: commonly used by psychoanalysts as the shortened form of *unconscious mind.*

Uexküll, J. von: German psychologist who, with Th. Beer and A. Bethe, proposed (1899) that psychology dispense with mentalistic terminology.

ulnar muscle: muscle on inner side of forearm, frequently used as an area for experiments in touch localization.

ulnar reflex: response when tendon of bent forearm is struck; hence not strictly a reflex.

ululation: animal-like groans and cries of some mental defectives, hysterical persons, and psychotics.

Umweg: roundabout or circuitous.

uncinate hallucinations: taste and smell hallucinations, usually unpleasant, caused by pathological condition in the uncinate gyrus of the hippocampal convolution of the temporal lobe.

uncinate seizures: convulsions caused by organic disease in the uncinate gyrus.

unconditioned stimulus: in the Pavlovian experiments, that which "naturally" elicits the response. Food in the mouth of a hungry dog, for example, is the unconditioned stimulus for the parotid reflex. The sound of the buzzer or the bell is the unconditioned stimulus for an auditory response.

unconscious: a loose term connoting activities which proceed without concomitant awareness, such as digestion, pupilary reflexes, or heart beats. In the older discussions of habit, references were made to the automaticity of well-established habits, no conscious control being considered necessary to maintain them. The adjective has a mentalistic connotation; hence it is not used by objectivists.

unconscious mind: a troublesome and controversial term used, metaphorically, by psychoanalysts to subsume the basic drives, repressed ideas, and unwelcome impulses; it is the part of the psyche in which the id reigns supreme and which is dominated by the pleasure principle. Free associations and dream analyses are said, by psychoanalysts, to be the royal road into the unconscious mind. The doctrine of the unconscious mind was advanced by Sigmund Freud (1856–1939) in his early writings, especially in *The Interpretation of Dreams (Die Traumdeutung)*, 1900. Among the philosophers who anticipated this doctrine was Eduard von Hartmann (1842–1906). Objective psychologists either omit reference to the unconscious mind or account for it in terms of implicit speech behavior or unverbalized behavior.

undoing: the process whereby, according to psychoanalysts, the unconscious mind seeks to wipe out painful thoughts and memories.

unicellular organisms: those which have but a single cell. *Protozoa.*

unilateral: affecting or pertaining to one side. Opposite of *bilateral.*

unimodal: a frequency curve with a single mode or peak.

unintentional act: according to psychoanalysts, an act which, though consciously unintended, really expresses an unconscious wish.

unintentional humor: psychoanalytic theory which holds that amusing slips of tongue are releases for unconscious, repressed tensions. The humor, usually having double meaning, resolves or reveals thwarted sex trends. Condensation and displacement occur in unintentional humor, just as they do in dreams.

unproductive mania: excitement and hyperactivity without the flight of ideas which usually accompanies mania.

unstriated muscles: smooth muscles; often called the involuntary muscles.

upset: loss of complacency. According to Eugenio Rignano (1870–1930), the drive to action is an upset in the optimum balance; the end or goal of behavior is the drive to maintain or regain balance.

uranism: homosexuality. Karl Heinrichs coined the term in 1862, denoting the male homosexual *uraning* and the female *urinde*.

urethral eroticism: sexual pleasure by the male in urination. According to psychoanalysts, the male can experience greater pleasure from the act because the urethra is about 8 to 9 inches long in the male; in the female, it is only about 1½ inches long.

urolagnia: type of sex perversion in which pleasure is derived by urination or by watching others urinate.

uterine theory: a point of view attributed to Hippocrates (460–359?) which states that the uterus wanders about the body of the female, hence causing mental and physical difficulties which do not occur in males. For a long time, it was believed that hysteria is exclusively a female disorder (the term being derived from the Greek for *womb*).

urticaria: blotches or raised spots on the skin which come suddenly and disappear in a short time. They are of interest because they are often concomitants of emotional conditions and because they are supposed to be corrected by psychoanalytic or psychotherapeutic techniques.

utricle: membranous sac in the vestibular apparatus of the inner ear.

V

V: Rorschach's symbol for the popular response to the ink-blots.

vagina: canal from vulvar opening to cervix of uterus in the female. One of the controversies in contemporary psychoanalytic theory pertains to the effect of the discovery of the vagina, the discovery of the clitoris usually having preceded it. Desire for vaginal receptivity, is, according to Freud, developed only after the onset of puberty.

vaginismus: reflex spasms of the vagina. In hysteria, it is supposed to be a concomitant of extreme distaste for coitus.

vagus nerve: tenth cranial nerve (*pneumogastric nerve*). See *cerebral nerves.*

valence: Kurt Lewin's terms for the attracting-repelling characteristics of a stimulus (which is postulated to exist in a field of forces). Valences are either positive or negative. The Lewinian concept is said to be more dynamic that the older theory of approach-avoidance mechanisms, and even to be more useful than the *adient-abient* drives described by Edwin Bissel Holt (1931).

value: (1) brilliance of a color; (2) judgment about the worth of an entity or concept. Judgments of values are axiological propositions; statements of fact are existential propositions.

vas deferens: excretory duct of testes.

vascular: pertaining to blood vessels.

vasoconstriction: increased tension of muscle walls of blood vessels, such as, for example, occurs when one turns pale.

vasodilation: decrease of tension in muscle walls of blood vessels, such as, for example, occurs in blushing.

vasomotor: pertaining to tonus in muscle walls of veins and arteries.

vasomotor paresis: syphilitic involvement of vasomotor nerves.

Vater, Abraham (1684–1751): German anatomist who discovered nerve endings in deep layers of the skin which were once thought to be the receptors for touch.

vecordia: obsolete term for mental diseases.

vector: force, the qualities of which are strength, direction, and point of application. Strength and direction may be represented by a vector.

vector psychology: the application, in a general way, of some of the principles of vector physics; but the concepts are used as operational principles. Life is considered from the standpoint of space, and "forces" of varying magnitudes and distributions act upon the individual at any given moment. The life spaces may be extremely fluid, relatively stable, or quite fixed. "Space" includes the internal condition of the individual as well as the objective environment. The theory has been expounded by Kurt Lewin (1890–   ), a German psychologist now an American.

vegetative nervous system: the autonomic nervous system.

velocity of nervous impulse: said by Helmholtz (1850) to be 90 feet a second in the motor nerve of a frog and about 150 meters a second in a sensory nerve of man. Some would assign credit for the discovery to Albrecht van Haller (1776), who recorded the time required to articulate *r* and concluded that the impulse travelled at a velocity of about 45 meters a second. Modern physiologists state that the velocity of the nervous impulse in human beings is about 123 meters a second.

ventral: forward aspect of an organ or structure; the anterior portion.

verbal amnesia: unusual difficulty in finding the suitable work to convey an idea. The organic type is said, by Adolph Meyer (1908), to indicate a lesion in Wernicke's area. In the functional type it is said to be symptomatic of self-consciousness; absurd phrases like "what-do-you-call-it" are used to fill in the gaps. Some careful writers would prefer to restrict *aphasia* to speech disturbances based upon organic pathology.

verbal aphasia: impairment of ability to articulate and enunciate words, as a result of lesions. Difficulty with *l* (paralambdacism) and with *r* (pararhoticism) are relatively common forms of verbal aphasia.

verbigeration: Kahlbaum's terms for stereotyped, meaningless repetition of words, phrases, and sentences by demented persons.

verbomania: torrent of words, spoken with compulsive force, by demented persons. Loosely, an excessive preoccupation with words, as by a pedant.

Vernes' test: blood test for syphilis.

vernier chronoscope: apparatus, consisting of pendulums which swing at different intervals, used in measuring reaction times. Devised by Pierre Vernier (1580–1637), a French physicist; and adapted by Edmund Clark Sanford (1859–1924), American psychologist, as a standard piece of simple apparatus for the psychological laboratory.

veronal addiction: one of the most common forms of drug addiction, the dosage varying from seven to thirty grains of diethylmalonylurea, a hypnotic. Veronal is sometimes used by dipsomaniacs to assist in recuperation from a spree. Stupor, blurred speech, and disorientation are concomitants of excessive use of veronal.

vertigo: dizziness or fainting spells.

Verworn, Max: German biologist who anticipated the theory of tropisms (about 1890) and who would rid psychology of all mentalistic concepts and biology of all vitalistic concepts. All responses, he believed, could be adequately explained by full descriptions of the mechanical forces which initiate and sustain them.

Vesalius, Andreas (1514–1564): Italian anatomist (though born in Belgium) known as "the father of anatomy."

vesania: Kahlbaum's inclusive term for all mental disorders.

vestibular apparatus: the portion of the inner ear lying between the cochlea and the semicircular canals. It contains the utricle and the saccule, two membranous sacs filled with liquid. On the ventral wall of each sac there are hair cells in which the dendrites of the vestibular nerve are distributed and in contact with which are otoliths. This apparatus contributes to maintenance of posture and balance.

vibration: formerly believed to be a sense modality. Max von Frey reported (1894–1895) that the "vibration sense" involves merely a stimulation of receptors for pressure.

vibration doctrine: David Hartley's theory (about 1750) that stimuli initiate vibrations of minute particles in the nerves, and that these vibrations are transmitted to the brain. States of consciousness are concomitants of the vibrations set up at the nerve endings in the sense organs and transmitted at a diminishing frequency along the pathways of the nervous system.

vibratiuncles: the minute vibration of particles in the brain, according to David Hartley, English physician and philosopher, which accompany consciousness.

vicious circle: the idea that worry, anxiety, fear, and the like, initiate bodily tensions, and that these tensions heighten the mental state. As usually stated, the idea implies acceptance of interactionism (q.v.).

vicious habits: expressive, colloquial phrase used by Adolph Meyer (1866–   ) to denote persistent nonadjustive habits which produce or resemble the so-called functional psychoses.

Vierordt, Karl (1818–1844): German physiologist who made substantial contributions to knowledge of vision.

Vintschgau, Max von: German physiologist who isolated the four elementary taste sensations (1880).

violet: visual sensation resulting from light-waves about 430 millimicrons in length; obtained by mixing light waves for red and blue.

Virchow, Rudolph (1821–1902): German pathologist who investigated craniometry.

virilism: result of hyperactivity of adrenal cortex in women. Sex functions are inhibited, voice deepens, and hair grows profusely on face and body.

vis a tergo: force from the rear; the goad to action; extrinsic motivating factors.

viscera: smooth-muscle organs encased in the abdominal cavity and innervated by the autonomic nervous system. The diffuse pattern of sensation from the viscera is called *coenesthesis*, and it contributes to feeling of malaise, well-being, sloth, energy, and the like.

viscerotonia: one of the temperaments delineated by W. H. Sheldon (1942) associated with endomorphy. Viscerotonics are relaxed, slow to act, comfort-loving, uninhibited in emotional expressions, companionable, and easy-going.

vista: term used by F. L. Wells to symbolize tridimensional percepts of the Rorschach inkblots.

visual purple: chemical alteration in the retina during dark adaptation, the rods of the dark-adapted eye becoming purplish in hue. Visual purple quickly disappears when the eye is stimulated by light. F. Boll and W. Kühne, German physiologists, are mentioned as the discoverers (about 1880).

vitalism: doctrine in biology that many important topics cannot be adequately explained in mechanistic terms; hence concepts of purpose, teleology, supernormal guidance, and the like, must be introduced. The theory of inherited motives and instincts is sometimes criticized as being vitalistic. William McDougall (1871–1938), British psychologist who taught in America, and Hans Driesch (1867–1941), German biologist, are often said to be leading modern proponents of vitalism.

vitreous humor: jelly-like substance filling the posterior chamber of the eyeball.

vividness, law of: the principle which holds that the more vivid an impression is, the better it is retained.

vorbeireden: talking past the point; excessive talk, as in certain mental disorders, which never comes to the point.

vocational guidance: the application of psychological and educational techniques for appraisal of fitness for various occupations, information about occupations, training, help in securing a job, and counsel regarding post-school training opportunities. The National Vocational Guidance Association was founded in 1915.

vocational psychology: application of psychological principles to various occupations. It may include such topics

as job specifications and analyses; techniques of employ-
ing, training, and promoting personnel; labor management, and the like.

Vogt, Karl (1817–1895): German philosopher who upheld
the materialistic point of view in psychology.

Volkmann, A. W.: brother-in-law of Gustav Fechner and
assistant in many of the major experiments in the early
days of psychophysics; contributed some important
studies on vision (1836).

Volkmann, W. F.: author of an important textbook on psychology (1856); disciple of Herbart.

volley theory of hearing: view that the neurones discharge
at differential rates but synchronously with the sound
wave; hence the volley of the impulses reproduces the
sound frequency. This theory was propounded by Wever
and Bray (1930), American psychologists, to effect a
compromise between the theories of Helmholtz and
Rutherford.

volt: force sufficient to cause an electrical current of one
ampere to pass the resistance of one ohm.

Volta, Alessandro (1745–1827): Italian physicist. Rolando,
the anatomist, used a piece of apparatus he devised in the
famous experiments on direct stimulation of the cerebrum (1800).

Voltaire, François Marie Arouet de (1694–1778): ac-
claimed for attacks upon superstitions; upheld the doctrine of determinism (in his later life).

voluntary control: a controversial, mentalistic term connoting behavior which is initiated, sustained, and terminated
by choice. Striated muscles are said to be under direct
voluntary control. Some objectivists (who uphold the
motor theory of consciousness) regard voluntary behavior

as merely the conditioned responses to implicit speech or
nonverbal motor activity.

volume: the spatial characteristic of a tone. Low notes are
often perceived as if massive; high notes, as if small and
thin. Titchener objected to the notion that volume is a
primary attribute of auditory sensation, and he constructed the tonal pencil to show that volume is a concomitant of pitch. (Volume is not to be confused with
loudness.)

Vorstellung: idea.

voyeur: one who achieves erotic gratification by watching a
member of the opposite sex undress. In symbolic voyeur-
ism, erotic impulses are stimulated by reading pornographic literature, viewing lewd pictures, and the like.
Voyeurs find gratification in watching coitus.

vulva: external parts of female genitalia.

W: Rorschach symbol for response to the entire blot.

w: a factor, defined by statistical analysis of test data, tentatively labeled "will" by Carl Spearman.

Wagner-Jauregg, Julius: Austrian neurologist awarded Nobel prize, 1927, for malaria-fever treatment of paresis.

Wahnsinn: German term embracing the whole field of mental disorders.

Wagner, E: German physiologist who (1854) studied the effects of fear-provoking stimuli on the rabbit's heart, and who was one of the earliest to study nerve cells.

Waldeyer, W.: German physiologist who (1891) reported that nerve cells are joined together functionally but not anatomically, and who was the first to use the term "neurone." He is called "the father of the neurone theory."

Wallas, Graham: English psychologist who analyzed the stages in creative thinking (1926). Four distinct stages are described: preparation, incubation, illumination, and verification.

Waller, Augustus: English physiologist who (1852) discovered that when a nerve cell is cut the portion dissevered from the cell body atrophies. This discovery paved the way for histological investigations of nerve tracts, and it is known as the Wallerian theory of degeneration. He also made studies of the catabolic effects of repeated stimulation of nerves.

wandering impulse: the tendency of senile dements and some other types of psychotics to wander, often in a condition of disorientation. In hysteria, the wandering impulse is called a *fugue*, the individual often going to a strange place and assuming a new identity, presumably to escape from mental conflicts.

wandering speech: failure to keep to the point, as in certain types of mental disorders, irrelevant topics and chance associations upsetting the unity and the coherence of the exposition.

Ward, James (1843–1925): outstanding figure at the end of the non-experimental period of psychology. He developed the ideas of Brentano and disseminated them among English philosopher-psychologists. The basic axiom in psychology is mind.

warming-up period: loose term denoting a time of initial torpor in beginning a new task, particularly after the preceding one has been interrupted.

warmth: sensation experienced when the stimulus is above the normal temperature of the body or of skin surface. Exploration of the surface of the skin (M. Blix and A. Goldscheider, 1884) reveals "warmth spots." Histological-psychological research has failed to locate separate receptors for the sense of warmth.

war neuroses: loose term subsuming effects of battle fatigue, fear, mental conflicts, and the like. "Shell shock," a loose term used during and after World War I, has been abandoned as inappropriate.

Warren, Howard Crosby (1876–1934): American psychologist who wrote an authoritative history of associationism; one of the pioneer experimental psychologists.

Washburne, Margaret Floy (1871–1939): author of one of the most important books on animal psychology; discredited the anecdotal method.

Wasserman, August (1866–1925): German bacteriologist who developed a test for syphilis.

Watson, John Broaddus (1878–   ): founder of radical behaviorism; author (1907) of one of the most important studies of behavior of the white rat.

Watt, Henry J. (1879–1925): English psychologist who contributed to the theory of imageless thought and who wrote an important book on memory (1909).

wave-length: distance from crest to crest, or trough to trough, of light waves. The visible portion of the spectrum extends from about 400 millimicrons to 700 millimicrons. Wave-length is said to be associated with hue or chroma.

waxy flexibility: condition occurring in catatonic form of schizophrenia, the patient offering little resistance to alterations of posture or positions of arms and legs. Also called *cerea flexibilitas*.

Weber, Ernst Heinrich (1795–1878): first to measure the awareness of differences between pairs of stimuli. German physiologist who began his studies with measurements of least noticeable differences, judged by 4 of his medical students, and who perfected the esthesiometer, apparatus consisting of blunt points for measuring the "sense of twoness."

Weber-Fechner law: statement by the German physicist Fechner (1860) that as the physical intensity is increased or decreased by a constant ratio, the magnitudes of sensations increase or decrease by equal increments. The law is also stated as follows: sensation of difference is proportional to the logarithm of the stimulus.

weight-lifting experiment: (first reported by Weber, 1834) discriminations of differences of weights may be expressed by a constant ratio—about 1/40—of the total weight. E. B. Titchener referred to this experiment as one of the classical investigations of quantitative psychology.

Weiss, Albert Paul (1879–1931) : protagonist of radical behaviorism in America.

Weltanschauung: world view; total frame of reference.

Weltschmerz: prevailing mood of sadness and despair.

Wernicke, Carl (1848–1905) : German neurologist who defined some of the aphasias.

Wernicke's area: region in the temporal lobes, a lesion in which is thought to be the etiologic factor in sensory aphasia. Identified by Carl Wernicke (1874).

Wertheimer, Max (1880–1934) : German psychologist (later on, American) whose paper on perceived movement (1912) laid the basis for Gestalt psychology. He reported that perception of movement is not analyzable into discrete sensations or elements but that it is a unique experience—a *phi-phenomenon*.

werewolf: old superstition that, by demon-possession, human beings may be transformed into wolves or other animals. In certain parts of the world, mentally disturbed persons were fearfully regarded as "werewolves."

Westphal, Karl Friedrich Otto (1833–1890) : German neurologist.

Westphal's sign: functional disorder having a superficial resemblance to multiple sclerosis, the principal symptoms being weakness and tremors (defined by Karl Westphal.)

Westphal symptoms: (1) the symptoms which differentiate tabes dorsalis and general paresis, Westphal (1871) having demonstrated that the knee jerk is absent in tabes; (2) obsessional thoughts. (Karl Westphal.)

Wever-Bray effect: the reproduction in the auditory nerve of an electrical phenomenon which duplicates the stimulating sound waves (1930).

whistle, Galton's: apparatus (devised by Sir Frances Galton, about 1880) for measuring the upper limits of auditory sensation. The Galton whistle was perfected by Edelmann, and is now a piece of standard equipment for research in acoustics.

white: (1) in the Hering theory, one of the six primaries and the complement of black; (2) in the Young-Helmholtz theory, the result of the admixture of all light waves.

White, William A. (1870–1937): American psychiatrist; author of major works on neurology and psychiatry; protagonist of psychoanalysis.

white matter: referring to the whitish appearance of the myelin sheath of medullated nerve fibers. The anatomical difference between gray matter and white matter of nervous tissues was described by Theodor Schwann (1810–1882), a German histologist.

whole-part learning: referring to two procedures for learning. In the whole method, the material is studied in its entirety; in the part method, it is broken up into convenient units for mastery. Lottie Steffens (1900), an American psychologist, reported that the whole method is preferable. Many investigators have undertaken to check upon her findings, and the reports are somewhat ambiguous.

Whytt, Robert (1714–1766): English psychiatrist.

will: a controversial term of ambiguous connotation. In rational psychology, will is a central concept; in radical behaviorism, it is a label for the triumph of the strongest stimulus; in philosophical psychology, it is a mental faculty. Many contemporary psychologists consider the matter to lie outside the province of psychology, though there is a strong implication of determinism in modern psychology.

will-to-power: Alfred Adler's term for the dominant human motive. Adler (1870–1937) is thought to have been influenced by youthful readings of Nietzsche (1844–1900). Frustrations of the will-to-power lead either to compensatory reactions or to an attitude of inferiority.

Williamsburg Asylum: the first public-supported institution in America for the care and treatment of mental patients. It was opened under this name in 1773, and has been renamed the Eastern (Virginia) State Hospital.

wish: symbolically represented mode of attaining satisfaction for an unfulfilled motive. Most writers restrict the term to conscious, verbalized expressions of that which, if attained, would bring satisfaction. According to Freud, wishes may be unconscious as well as conscious. W. I. Thomas (1918) defined four basic wishes: new experience, recognition, response, and security.

wish-fulfillment: vicarious satisfaction, through dreams and phantasies, of frustrated desires. Every dream, no matter how distasteful it may appear when superficially examined, is the fulfillment of an unconscious wish (Freud).

wit: according to Freud that which (1) has no other end than to afford pleasure and which (2) serves to release repressions.

Witasek, Stephan (1870–1915): Leader in the Austrian school of act psychology and a disciple of Brentano and Meinong.

witchcraft: term (often limited by psychologists) referring to the outburst of fanaticism in Salem Village, Massachusetts, in 1691–1692. Ten young girls, having learned folklore superstitions from a slave woman, accused her and two other old women of bewitching them. The mass hysteria which resulted from their accusation brought about the arrest of several hundred persons, the deaths by hanging of 19 and by weights of one. When the Governor took legal action, the delusion died out as quickly as it had sprung up.

Witmer, Lightner (1867-1946) : American psychologist who opened the first psychological clinic (1896) for "the study and remedial treatment of mentally or morally retarded children, and of children suffering from physical defects which result in slow development or prevent normal progress."

Wolff, Christian von (1679-1754) : German university professor, who, reputedly, was the first to use *psychology* in the title of a printed book (*Psychologia Empirica*, 1734) ; because of his systematization of current views regarding mental faculties, called "the father of faculty psychology"; regarded psychology as a branch of metaphysics. Much of the terminology of faculty psychology continues into modern times, but the concept of mental faculties has been abandoned.

womb-phantasy: according to psychoanalysts, the unconscious wish to return to the peaceful security of the womb. Otto Rank expressed the view that birth is a traumatic experience, and hence that it is a disruption of the Nirvana-like prenatal existence, which remains as the unconscious ideal.

Woodworth, Robert Sessions (1869–) : a leader in American psychology.

working-over: the psychoanalysts' technique for getting to the deepest unconscious roots of symbolisms.

worry: undue concern about past behavior or about anticipated dangers in future behavior. The term is usually restricted to anxiety over specific situations, not to vague apprehensions or anxieties.

Wündt, Wilhelm (1832-1920) : sometimes called "the great man in psychology," founder of the first important psychological laboratory in the world (Leipzig, 1879); "the father of physiological psychology"; founder (1882) of the first journal devoted exclusively to publishing reports of psychological research; teacher of many eminent American psychologists (especially between 1880 and 1900); often called "the father of experimental psychology."

Würzburg school: German psychologists who, under Oswald Külpe (1862–1915), improved methods of introspective study of higher mental processes and who developed the theory of imageless thought. The imageless-thought theory was criticized by E. B. Titchener and supported by R. S. Woodworth when it first came to the attention of American psychologists.

xanthrocyanopsia: insensitivity to light-waves for red (by some writers, for green as well).

xanthropsia: condition in which objects are sensed as having a yellowish hue, as in jaundice.

xenoglossia: (1) speaking in unknown tongues (Acts: 2: 4-13); (2) unintelligible talk by persons who are in a condition of religious ecstasy or excitement; (3) according to occultists, the power of a person to speak or to understand languages while in a trance which would be incomprehensible while the person is in a normal state.

xenomania: morbid preference for foreign words, customs, or dress. It is said to indicate a wish to attract attention or to maintain prestige-status by an individual who has an inferiority feeling.

xenophobia: great fear of foreigners or of foreign practices. It is said to indicate an over-identification with the in-group on the part of an insecure personality.

Y

Y: S. J. Beck's symbol (1944) for responses to Rorschach inkblots determined by surface shading.

yellow: response to wave-lengths of about 585 millimicrons and (Hering and Ladd-Franklin theories of color vision) one of the "primaries."

yellow-blindness: the most uncommon form of color-blindness.

yellow spot: a small area (also known as *macula flava* or *macula lutea*) which lies in the central posterior section of the retina. The small depression in the "yellow spot" is known as the *fovea centralis*.

Yoga: (1) formalized techniques of abstract contemplation by Indian philosophers; (2) system of practices including formalized postures of body, breathing exercises, and diets, which are said to facilitate self-hypnosis and trances.

York Retreat: one of the earliest institutions to be established for humane treatment of patients with mental disorders. William Tuke, Englishman and member of the Society of Friends, worked for the establishment of an institution in York, England, which would show by contrast with the York Asylum the advantages of enlightened methods. The York Retreat was opened in 1796, and the success of its methods led to the appointment of an investigating committee of the House of Commons (1814), which reported need for drastic reforms in mental hospitals.

Young, Thomas (1773-1839): British physiologist whose theory of color vision (1807) was developed by Helmholtz (1860). Young observed that visual acuity is greatest at the *fovea centralis*.

Young-Helmholtz theory of color vision: a theory which postulates the existence of three types of receptors (or nerve fibers) responding, respectively, to wave-lengths for red, green, and violet. All other color sensations are analyzable into combinations of these fundamentals. This theory has gained wide acceptance among physicists. It was first proposed by Thomas Young (1807), an English physiologist, and developed by Herman von Helmholtz (1860), German physicist and physiologist.

youth: usually defined as the period between childhood and maturity. The American Youth Commission (1935) defined youth as the period between 15 and 24 years of age.

Z: symbol used by S. J. Beck and M. R. Hertz to denote capacity for organizing Rorschach inkblots into meaningful patterns (*Assoziationsbetrieb*).

zero, psychological: (1) the point at which, theoretically, psychological behavior just barely commences to function; (2) the theoretical point at which mental age is 0; (3) the temperature of the surface of the skin (normally about 85–90 degrees Fahrenheit), which is the point of reference in judgments of coldness or warmth of objects (though the temperature shifts from time to time).

Zeigarnik effect: the relatively greater retention of interrupted tasks than of completed tasks. B. Zeigarnik, German psychologist, reported the experiments in 1927. Kurt Lewin attributes the phenomenon to the operation of a *Spannung* (tension) which continues to be active until tasks are completed.

Zeihen, Theodor (1862–): German psychiatrist-philosopher who conducted some experiments in the field of psychiatry.

zoanthropy: delusion that the individual has been transformed into an animal. (Daniel 4 contains an account of Nebuchadnezzar's zoanthropic delusion.)

zoerasty: sexual relations with animals.

Zöllner's illusion: geometrical figure in which parallel lines appear to slant away from one another, the effect being due to alternate angles formed by bisecting short lines.

zone, erogenous: area of the body which, when stimulated, affords sexual pleasure. According to psychoanalysts, the first definite erogenous zone is the mouth; next, the anus; and lastly, the genitalia.

zones, retinal: areas of the retina mapped for sensitivity to chromatic and achromatic stimuli. Clerk Maxwell (1870) was one of the first to map the color zones. According to some theorists, the primitive eye responded only to light-waves for achromatic (grays) vision; next (phylogenetically), for blues and yellows; and finally, for reds and greens. The mapped zones are, in a general way, supportive of the theory; the region of the fovea being most sensitive for reds and greens; the middle zones, for blues and yellows; and the periphery, for grays, white, and black.

zoöphilia: abnormal degree of affection for animals or a particular animal.

zoöphobia: intense fear of animals or a particular species of animal.

z-score: type of standard score in which deviations of raw scores from the mean are expressed in terms of the standard deviation of the distribution.

Zurich school: psychiatrists of Zurich, Switzerland, who, under the leadership of C. G. Jung and E. Bleuler, were among the first to recognize the worth of Freud's contributions.

Zwaardemaker, H.: Danish physiologist who (1895) reported a major classification of olfactory sensations and who perfected the double olfactometer. The Zwaardemaker classification of elementary odors is as follows: ethereal, aromatic, balsamic, amber-musk, alliaceous, empyreumatic, hircine, repulsive, and nauseous.

zygote: fertilized egg resulting from union of two cells to make a single cell.